ARMY @ LOVE
THE HOT ZONE CLUB

RICK VEITCH
Writer and penciller

GARY ERSKINE
Inker

JOSÉ VILLARRUBIA
BRIAN MILLER
Colorists

TRAVIS LANHAM
Letterer

ARMY@LOVE CREATED BY RICK VEITCH

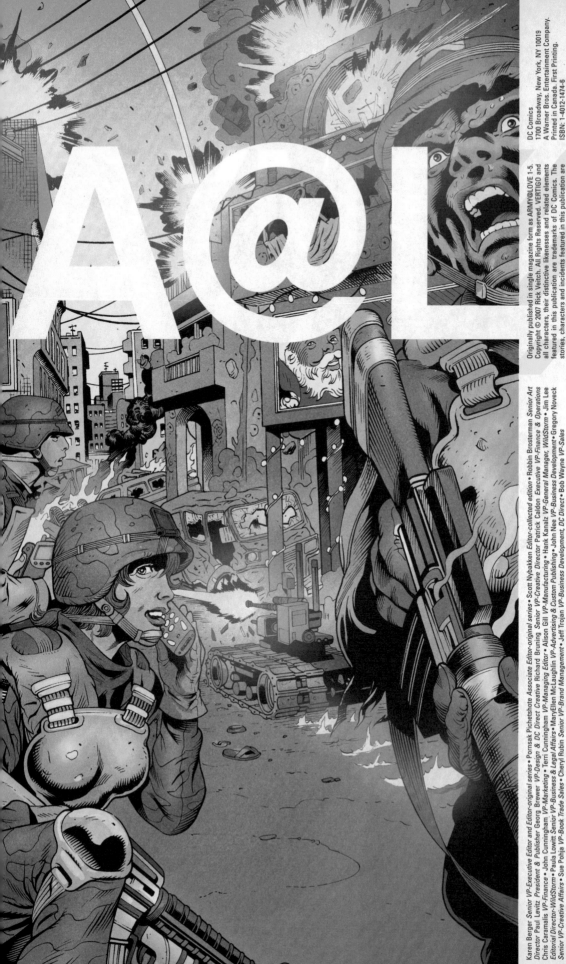

Karen Berger *Senior VP-Executive Editor and Editor-original series* • Scott Nybakken *Editor-collected edition* • Pornsak Pichetshote *Associate Editor-original series* • Robbin Brosterman *Senior Art
Director* Paul Levitz *President & Publisher* Georg Brewer *VP-Design & DC Direct Creative* Richard Bruning *Senior VP-Creative Director* Patrick Caldon *Executive VP-Finance & Operations*
Chris Caramalis *VP-Finance* • John Cunningham *VP-Marketing* • Terri Cunningham *VP-Managing Editor* • Alison Gill *VP-Manufacturing* • Hank Kanalz *VP-General Manager, WildStorm* • Jim Lee
Editorial Director-WildStorm • Paula Lowitt *Senior VP-Business & Legal Affairs* • MaryEllen McLaughlin *VP-Advertising & Custom Publishing* • John Nee *VP-Business Development* Gregory Noveck
Senior VP-Creative Affairs • Sue Pohja *VP-Book Trade Sales* • Cheryl Rubin *Senior VP-Brand Management* • Jeff Trojan *VP-Business Development, DC Direct* • Bob Wayne *VP-Sales*

Cover illustration by Rick Veitch and Gary Erskine. Cover color by Brian Miller. Publication design by Brainchild Studios/NYC.
ARMY@LOVE: THE HOT ZONE CLUB. Published by DC Comics. Cover, introduction and compilation copyright © 2007 DC Comics. All Rights Reserved.

Originally published in single magazine form as ARMY@LOVE 1-5.
Copyright © 2007 Rick Veitch. All Rights Reserved. VERTIGO and
all characters, their distinctive likenesses and related elements
featured in this publication are trademarks of DC Comics. The
stories, characters and incidents featured in this publication are
entirely fictional. DC Comics does not read or accept unsolicited
submissions of ideas, stories or artwork.

DC Comics
1700 Broadway, New York, NY 10019
A Warner Bros. Entertainment Company.
Printed in Canada. First Printing.
ISBN: 1-4012-1474-6
ISBN 13: 978-1-4012-1474-6

ARMY@LOVE V1.0 SPECIFICATIONS

SITUATION REPORT

MY FIRST EXPERIENCE WITH BATTLE WAS DURING A TOUR OF DUTY IN AFBAGHISTAN WITH THE 42ND INFANTRY UNDER THE COMMAND OF COLONEL **RICK "MAD DOG" VEITCH.** IT WAS THERE I LEARNED MY FIRST IMPORTANT TRUTHS ABOUT WAR.

INTRO@WAR
By Peter Kuper

Though the troop's morale and motivation were high, unfortunately so were our hormone levels. With bullets whizzing past my head and bombs exploding all around, I discovered it was hard to concentrate on killing the enemy with a hot female recruit's glistening body flexing next to mine. The second lesson I learned was that the first casualty in war is the truth, and this apparently also applies to introductions.

So, full disclosure, the closest I've ever come to a battlefield was in the bedroom with one of my old girlfriends, in the dining room with family members, and in the back of my brain at all times. Actually, I do battle in my studio on a monthly basis, trying to come up with unexpected ways for a black spy and a white spy to destroy each other, but you'll have to ask Alfred E. Neuman if that counts as going to war.

Still, for my money, I know at least as much about declaring war as the leaders who see fit to send our troops to places with names they can barely spell. I'm a lousy speller too, so I've had to look up lots of things, and while I was at it I stumbled upon the word "quagmire." Here's the definition in case, like me, you couldn't remember it:

quag·mire (kwăg′mīr′) *noun.*

Muddle, mix-up, mess, predicament, can of worms, quandary, tangle, imbroglio, trouble, confusion, difficulty, sticky situation, pickle, stew, dilemma, fix, bind.

Curiously, printed next to that definition was a photo of our president smiling broadly, pointing to a map of Vietnam, or Iraq (he was holding it upside down, so it was hard to tell which).

This brings me to ARMY@LOVE.

No doubt our troops in Afghanistan and Iraq know plenty about feeling like the world is topsy-turvy, but what Rick Veitch has done is hold a recent snapshot of war up to the light. Or to be more accurate, he's aimed his long-range night-vision goggles at a disturbing possible future for our military machine.

Drafting Gary Erskine, José Villarrubia, Brian Miller and Travis Lanham as shock troops on his mission, Veitch has attacked sacred cows and blown them to smithereens.

It's really quite disgraceful.

How dare he suggest that in the future corporate advertising could show up on military vehicles? Whatever would possess him to imply that the army would ever draft "special needs" individuals into battle? What kind of person would conjure up a scenario where recruiters would promote the opportunity to have adrenaline-pumped battlefield intercourse as a perk for joining the army?

This kind of thinking is as cynical as suggesting that the biggest reason America preemptively attacked Iraq was for their oil. Or worst still, that the war was about creating incredible windfall profits for companies like Halliburton. Just because our vice president had been named CEO of that sagging company before taking office is no reason to suggest favoritism. Sure, Halliburton subsequently received vast no-bid war reconstruction contracts that sent their stock through the roof. But it would be unfair to imply this had anything to do with Dick Cheney's relationship to the company. He stepped down as chairman *months* before the Supreme Court handed the election to his administration.

Let's face it, there are going to be some people in this world who just see the worst side to everything. These naysayers will finger-point at success and call it failure. When Exxon posted their highest profits ever recently, some saw the health of one of our global corporations as a sign of national sickness. Sure, gas prices have reached levels we'd only have expected to see in a sci-fi pulp magazine from the 1950s, but that's no cause to attack the foundations of capitalism!

Well, let me tell you, Mr. Veitch, as our former Secretary of Defense Donald Rumsfeld thoughtfully pointed out, "Freedom isn't tidy!"

Comics like ARMY@LOVE are helping neither the morale nor motivation of troops put in harm's way by our leaders.

When you make the shocking discovery that you're setting out for hell in a little speedboat, maybe you'll think twice about the wisdom of combining sex, drugs, rock 'n' roll and war — in a *comic book* no less!

Fine, go ahead and laugh your cynical laugh and hum some catchy tune while strumming on your satanic electric guitar.

I promise, there will be a time of reckoning for your ilk.

There will be no stairway to heaven on the road you've chosen. When true believers like Jerry Falwell and Tammy Faye Bakker look down from Kingdom Come, they'll enjoy watching you burn at your drawing table. They can be confident that you will never be joining their army.

It's probably too late to mend your ways, but your audience can still save themselves by reading no further.

Please, don't join Veitch in this hell. Put ARMY@LOVE back on the shelf — or better yet, send it back from whence it came with a contained nuclear blast.

Then do something thoroughly American like go to the mall, play a video game, or... question authority.

Perhaps it's true that all is fair in love and war, but just maybe the next time our leaders try to send us to hell in a hand basket festooned with corporate logos, we won't get fooled again.

ARMY@LOVE has taught me this much: the story ain't over 'til the fat lady lip-syncs.

Peter Kuper is co-founder of the zine World War 3 Illustrated. *His illustrations and comics appear regularly in* Time, The New York Times *and* MAD MAGAZINE, *where he has illustrated "Spy vs. Spy" every month since 1997. He has written and illustrated a variety books, including* Mind's Eye, Sticks and Stones *and* The System. *He's also adapted many of Franz Kafka's works into comics, including* The Metamorphosis. *His most recent graphic novel,* Stop Forgetting To Remember, *is the autobiography of his alter ego Walter Kurtz.*

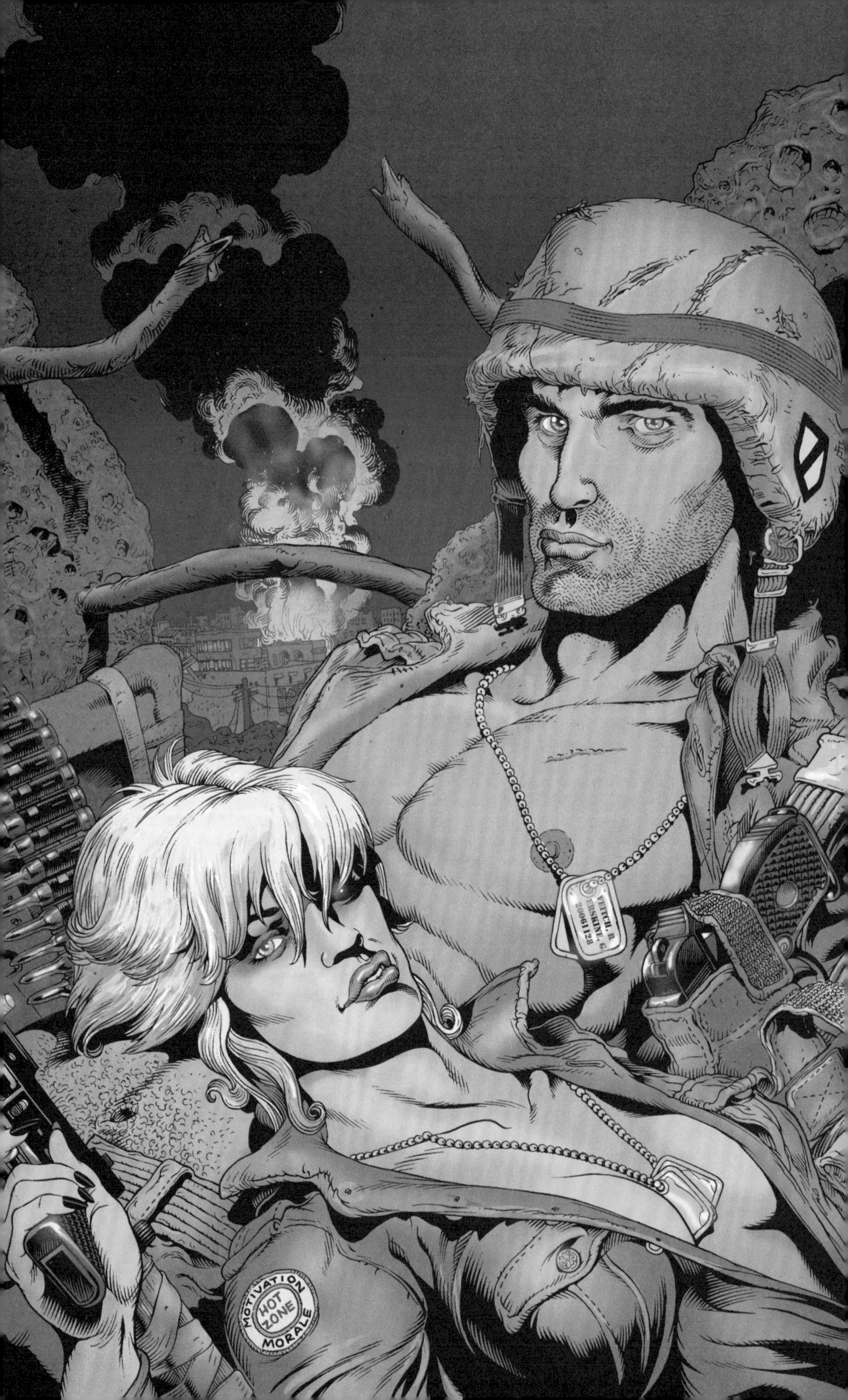
VEITCH, R
ERSKINE, G
20061128
MOTIVATION
HOT ZONE
MORALE

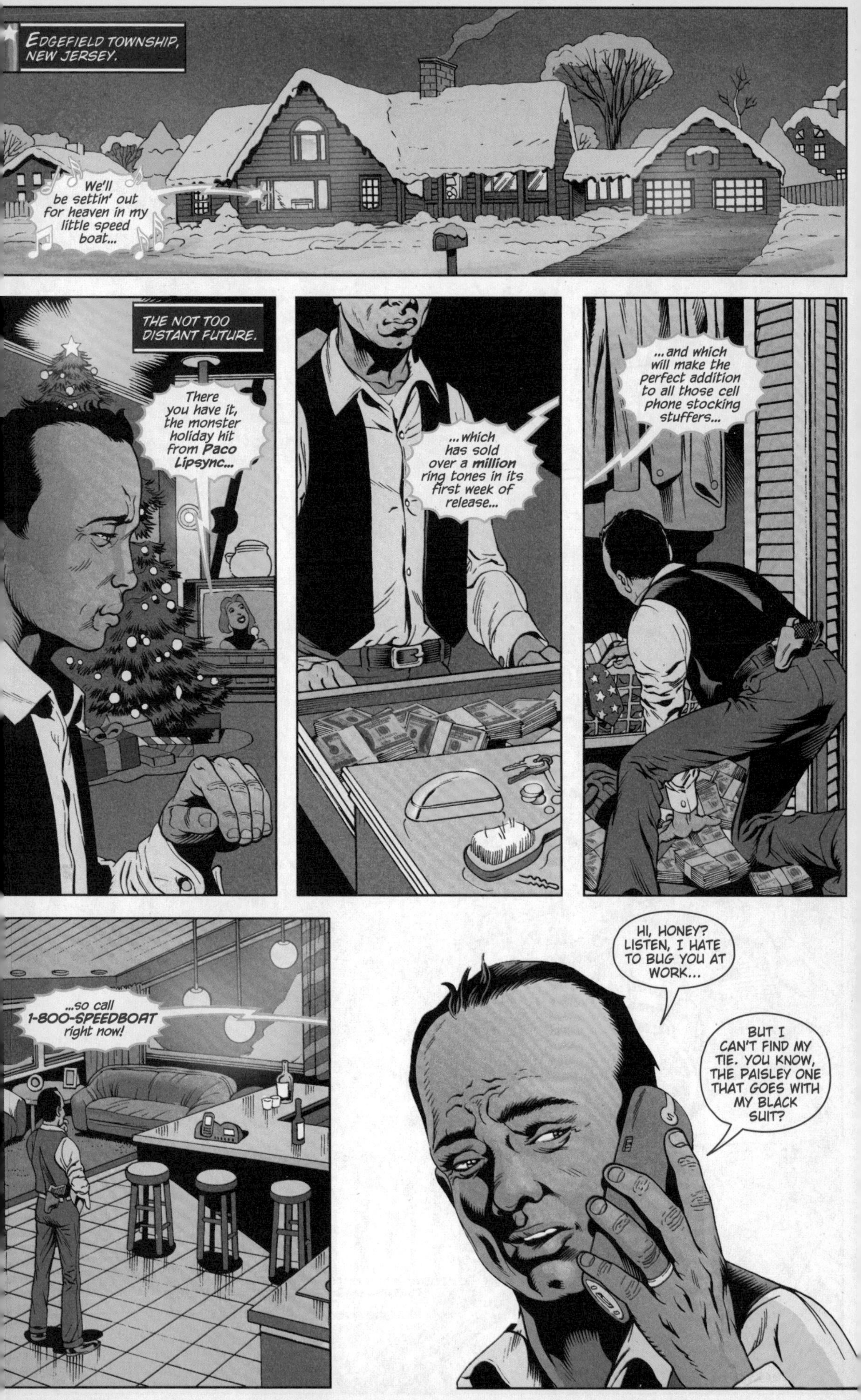
EDGEFIELD TOWNSHIP, NEW JERSEY.
We'll be settin' out for heaven in my little speed boat...
THE NOT TOO DISTANT FUTURE.
There you have it, the monster holiday hit from Paco Lipsync...
...which has sold over a million ring tones in its first week of release...
...and which will make the perfect addition to all those cell phone stocking stuffers...
...so call 1-800-SPEEDBOAT right now!
HI, HONEY? LISTEN, I HATE TO BUG YOU AT WORK...
BUT I CAN'T FIND MY TIE. YOU KNOW, THE PAISLEY ONE THAT GOES WITH MY BLACK SUIT?

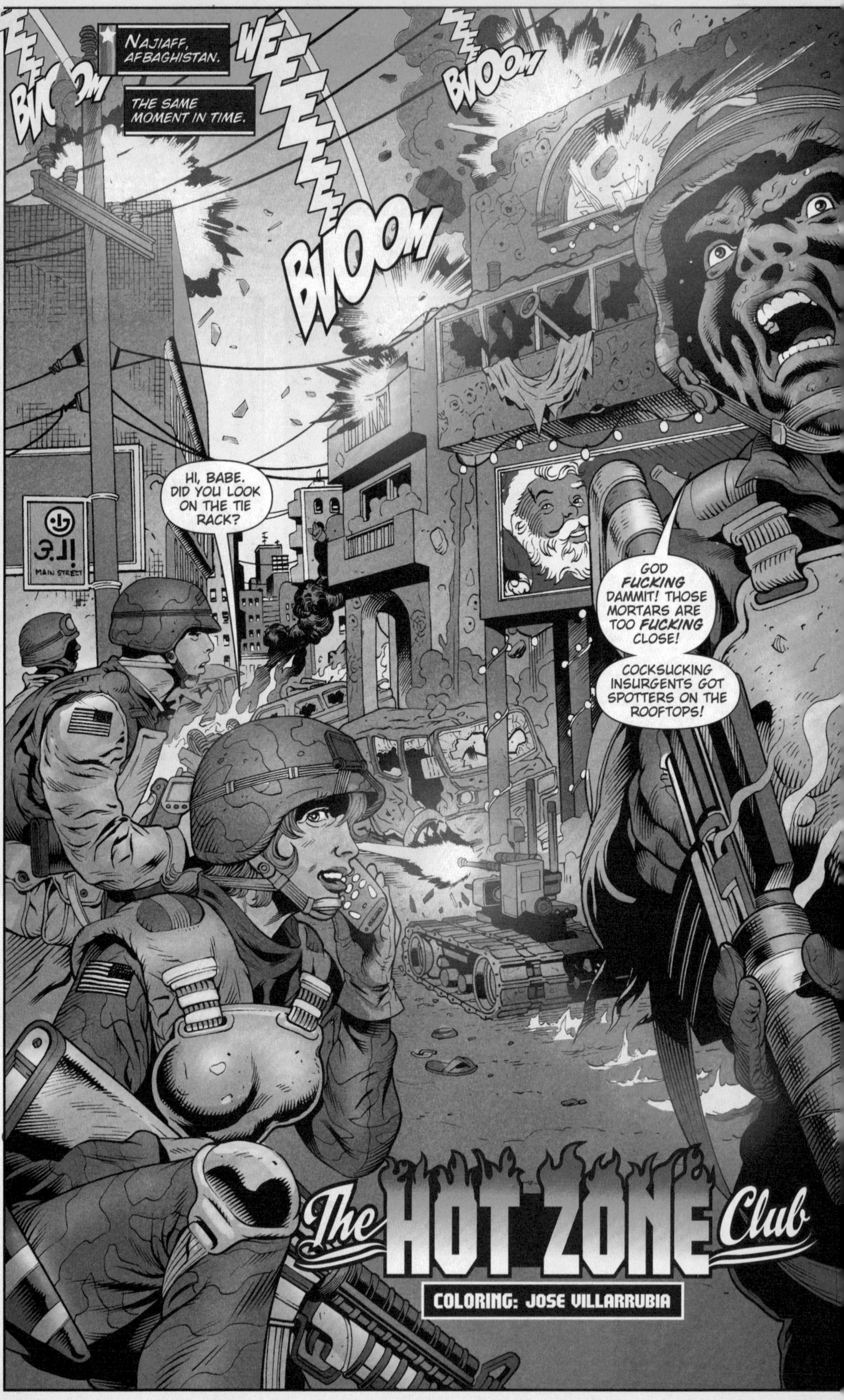
NAJIAFF, AFBAGHISTAN.
THE SAME MOMENT IN TIME.
WEEEEEEEEE
BVOOM
BVOOM
HI, BABE. DID YOU LOOK ON THE TIE RACK?
MAIN STREET
GOD *FUCKING* DAMMIT! THOSE MORTARS ARE TOO *FUCKING* CLOSE!
COCKSUCKING INSURGENTS GOT SPOTTERS ON THE ROOFTOPS!
The HOT ZONE Club
COLORING: JOSE VILLARRUBIA

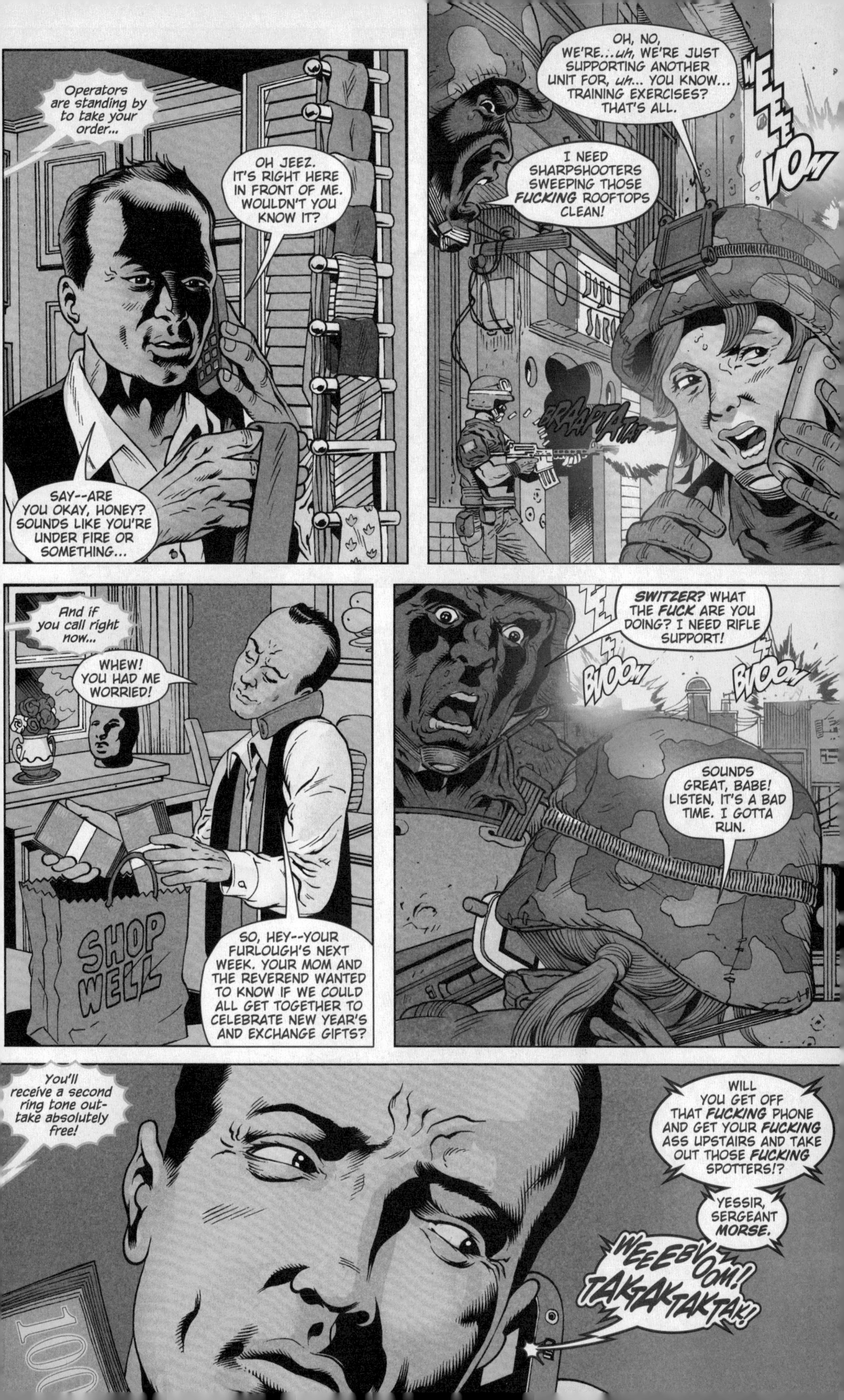
Operators are standing by to take your order...
OH JEEZ. IT'S RIGHT HERE IN FRONT OF ME. WOULDN'T YOU KNOW IT?
SAY--ARE YOU OKAY, HONEY? SOUNDS LIKE YOU'RE UNDER FIRE OR SOMETHING...
OH, NO, WE'RE...*uh*, WE'RE JUST SUPPORTING ANOTHER UNIT FOR, *uh*... YOU KNOW... TRAINING EXERCISES? THAT'S ALL.
WEEEEVOW
I NEED SHARPSHOOTERS SWEEPING THOSE *FUCKING* ROOFTOPS CLEAN!
BRAAPTATAT
And if you call right now...
WHEW! YOU HAD ME WORRIED!
SHOP WELL
SO, HEY--YOUR FURLOUGH'S NEXT WEEK. YOUR MOM AND THE REVEREND WANTED TO KNOW IF WE COULD ALL GET TOGETHER TO CELEBRATE NEW YEAR'S AND EXCHANGE GIFTS?
SWITZER? WHAT THE *FUCK* ARE YOU DOING? I NEED RIFLE SUPPORT!
BVOOM
BVOOM
SOUNDS GREAT, BABE! LISTEN, IT'S A BAD TIME. I GOTTA RUN.
You'll receive a second ring tone out-take absolutely free!
WILL YOU GET OFF THAT *FUCKING* PHONE AND GET YOUR *FUCKING* ASS UPSTAIRS AND TAKE OUT THOSE *FUCKING* SPOTTERS!?
YESSIR, SERGEANT *MORSE.*
WEEEBVOOM! TAKTAKTAKTAK!

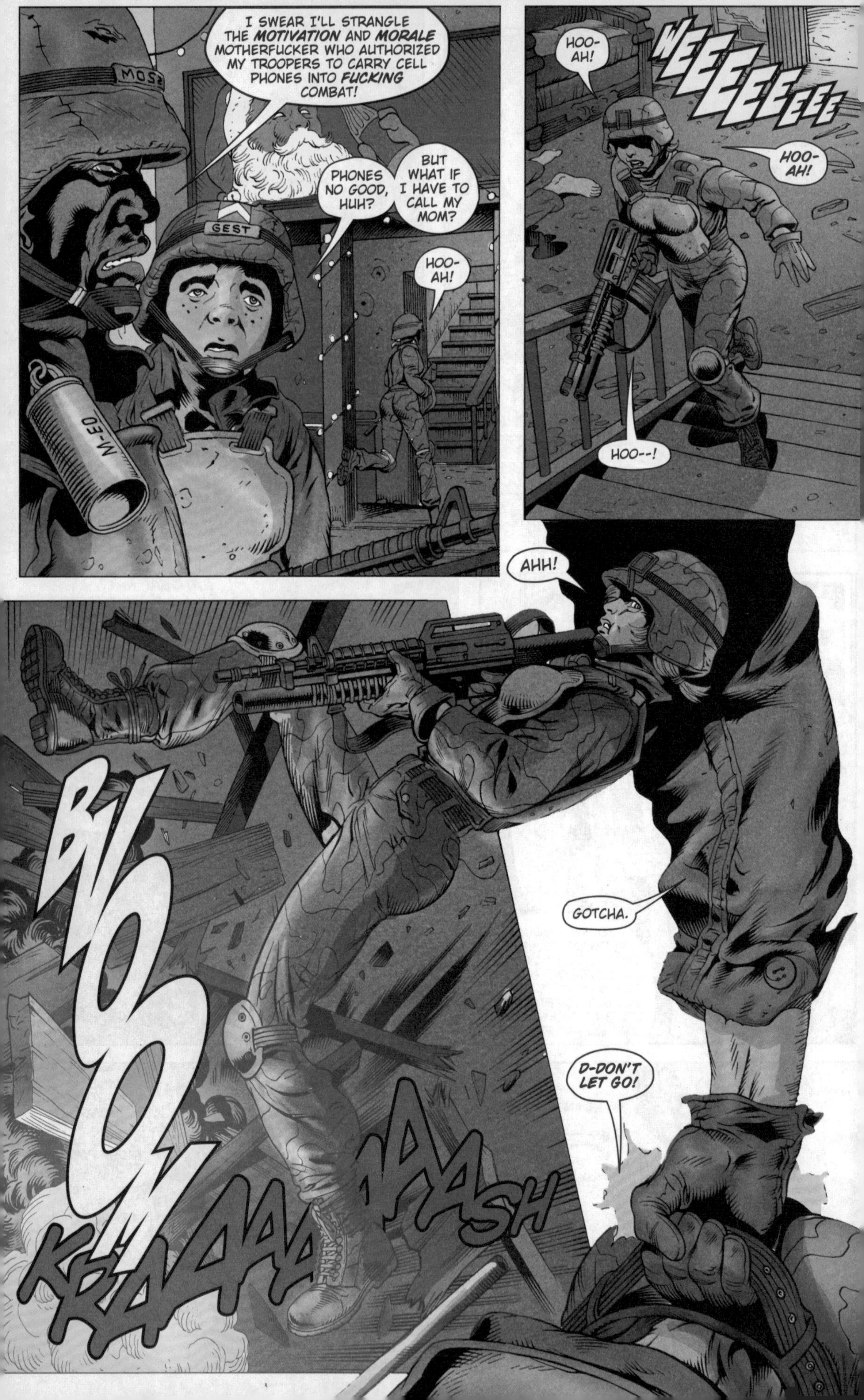
I SWEAR I'LL STRANGLE THE MOTIVATION AND MORALE MOTHERFUCKER WHO AUTHORIZED MY TROOPERS TO CARRY CELL PHONES INTO FUCKING COMBAT!
PHONES NO GOOD, HUH?
BUT WHAT IF I HAVE TO CALL MY MOM?
HOO-AH!
GEST
M-EO
HOO-AH!
WEEEEEEEE
HOO-AH!
HOO--!
AHH!
GOTCHA.
D-DON'T LET GO!
BLOOM
KRAAAAAAASH

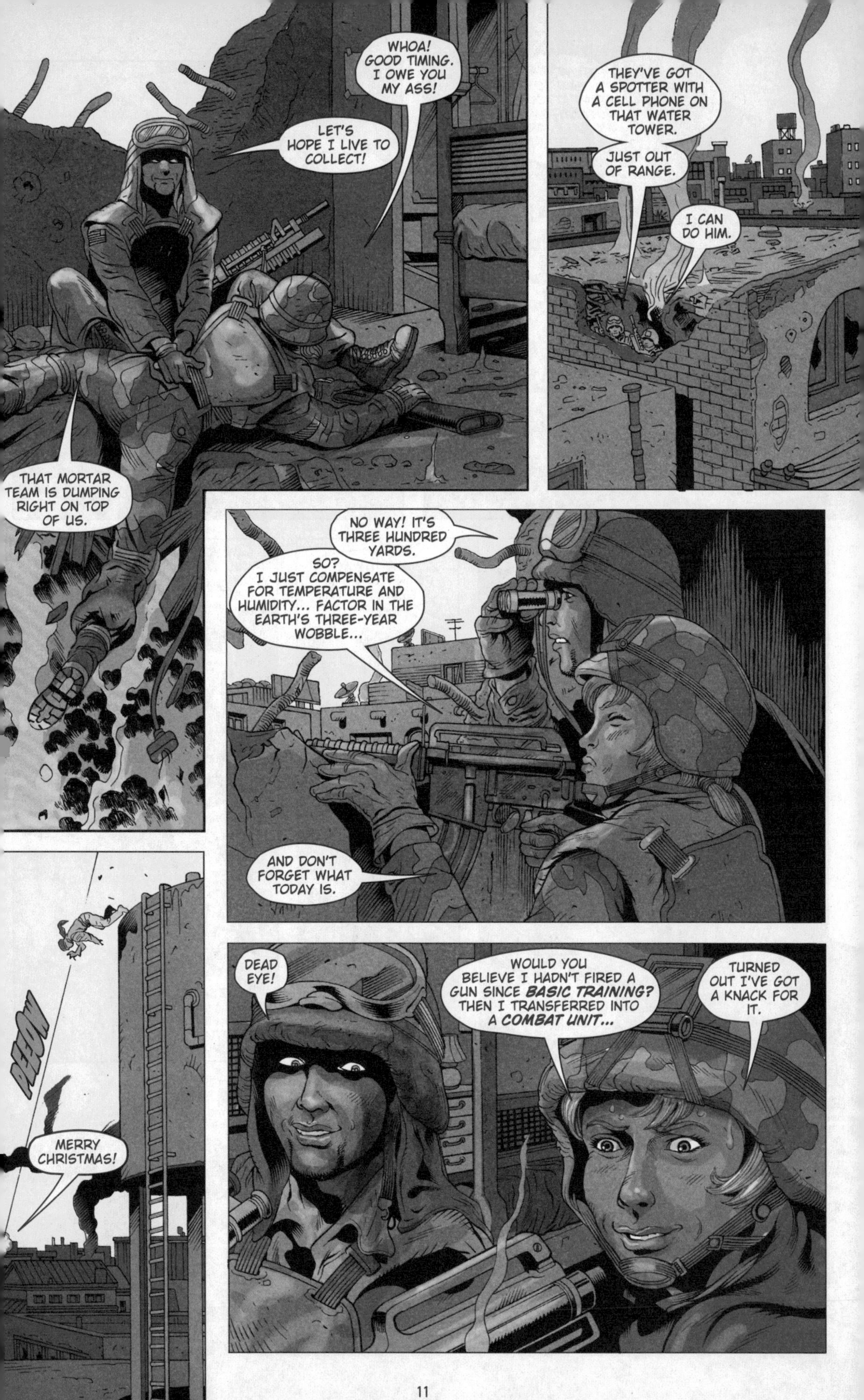
WHOA! GOOD TIMING. I OWE YOU MY ASS!
LET'S HOPE I LIVE TO COLLECT!
THAT MORTAR TEAM IS DUMPING RIGHT ON TOP OF US.
THEY'VE GOT A SPOTTER WITH A CELL PHONE ON THAT WATER TOWER.
JUST OUT OF RANGE.
I CAN DO HIM.
NO WAY! IT'S THREE HUNDRED YARDS.
SO? I JUST COMPENSATE FOR TEMPERATURE AND HUMIDITY... FACTOR IN THE EARTH'S THREE-YEAR WOBBLE...
AND DON'T FORGET WHAT TODAY IS.
PEEOW
MERRY CHRISTMAS!
DEAD EYE!
WOULD YOU BELIEVE I HADN'T FIRED A GUN SINCE *BASIC TRAINING*? THEN I TRANSFERRED INTO A *COMBAT UNIT*...
TURNED OUT I'VE GOT A KNACK FOR IT.

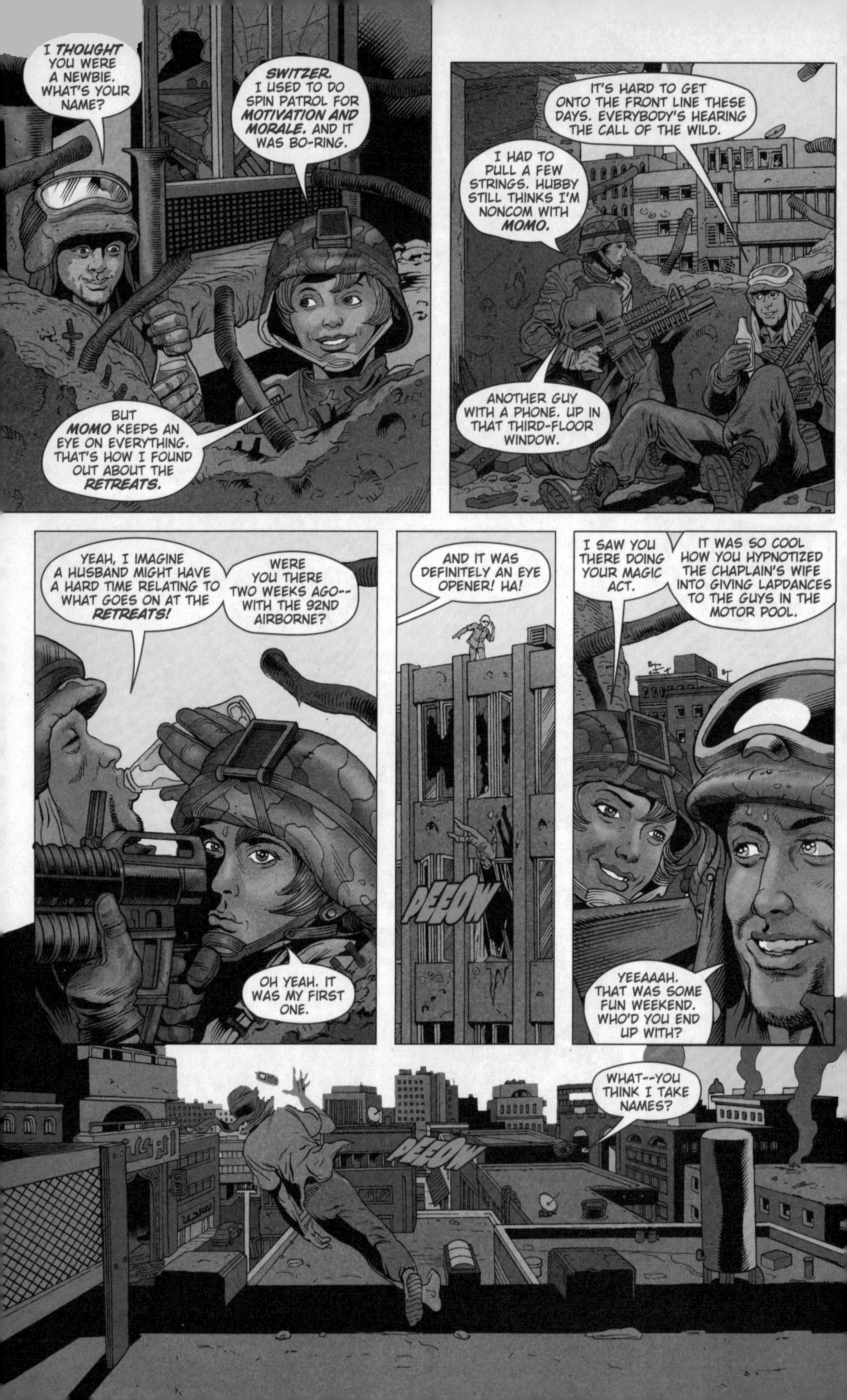
I THOUGHT YOU WERE A NEWBIE. WHAT'S YOUR NAME?
SWITZER. I USED TO DO SPIN PATROL FOR MOTIVATION AND MORALE. AND IT WAS BO-RING.
BUT MOMO KEEPS AN EYE ON EVERYTHING. THAT'S HOW I FOUND OUT ABOUT THE RETREATS.
IT'S HARD TO GET ONTO THE FRONT LINE THESE DAYS. EVERYBODY'S HEARING THE CALL OF THE WILD.
I HAD TO PULL A FEW STRINGS. HUBBY STILL THINKS I'M NONCOM WITH MOMO.
ANOTHER GUY WITH A PHONE. UP IN THAT THIRD-FLOOR WINDOW.
YEAH, I IMAGINE A HUSBAND MIGHT HAVE A HARD TIME RELATING TO WHAT GOES ON AT THE RETREATS!
WERE YOU THERE TWO WEEKS AGO--WITH THE 92ND AIRBORNE?
OH YEAH. IT WAS MY FIRST ONE.
AND IT WAS DEFINITELY AN EYE OPENER! HA!
PEEOW
I SAW YOU THERE DOING YOUR MAGIC ACT.
IT WAS SO COOL HOW YOU HYPNOTIZED THE CHAPLAIN'S WIFE INTO GIVING LAPDANCES TO THE GUYS IN THE MOTOR POOL.
YEEAAAH. THAT WAS SOME FUN WEEKEND. WHO'D YOU END UP WITH?
WHAT--YOU THINK I TAKE NAMES?
PEEOW

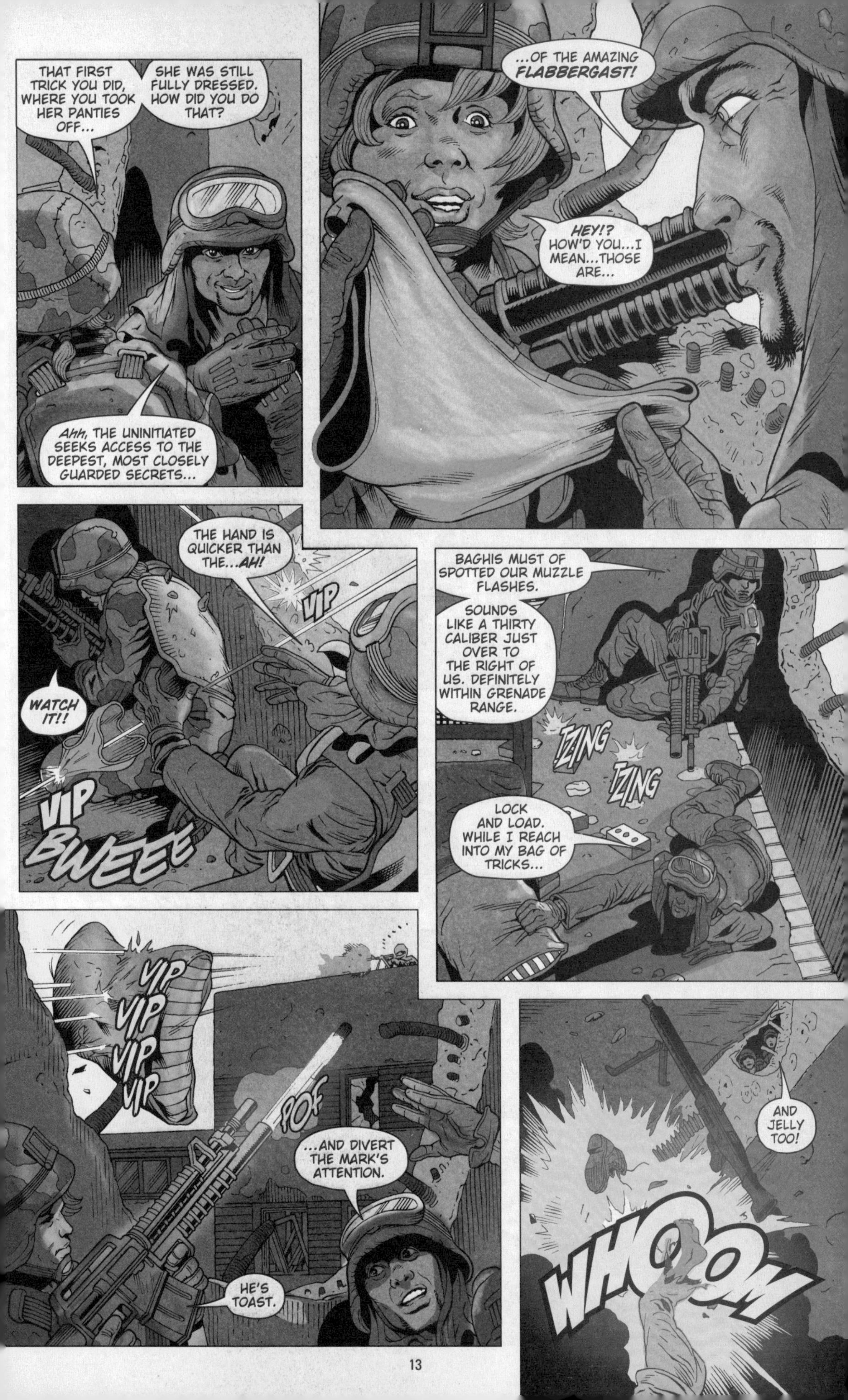
THAT FIRST TRICK YOU DID, WHERE YOU TOOK HER PANTIES OFF...
SHE WAS STILL FULLY DRESSED. HOW DID YOU DO THAT?
Ahh, THE UNINITIATED SEEKS ACCESS TO THE DEEPEST, MOST CLOSELY GUARDED SECRETS...
...OF THE AMAZING FLABBERGAST!
HEY!? HOW'D YOU...I MEAN...THOSE ARE...
THE HAND IS QUICKER THAN THE...AH!
VIP
WATCH IT!!
VIP
BWEEE
BAGHIS MUST OF SPOTTED OUR MUZZLE FLASHES.
SOUNDS LIKE A THIRTY CALIBER JUST OVER TO THE RIGHT OF US. DEFINITELY WITHIN GRENADE RANGE.
TZING
TZING
LOCK AND LOAD. WHILE I REACH INTO MY BAG OF TRICKS...
VIP
VIP
VIP
VIP
POF
...AND DIVERT THE MARK'S ATTENTION.
HE'S TOAST.
AND JELLY TOO!
WHOOM

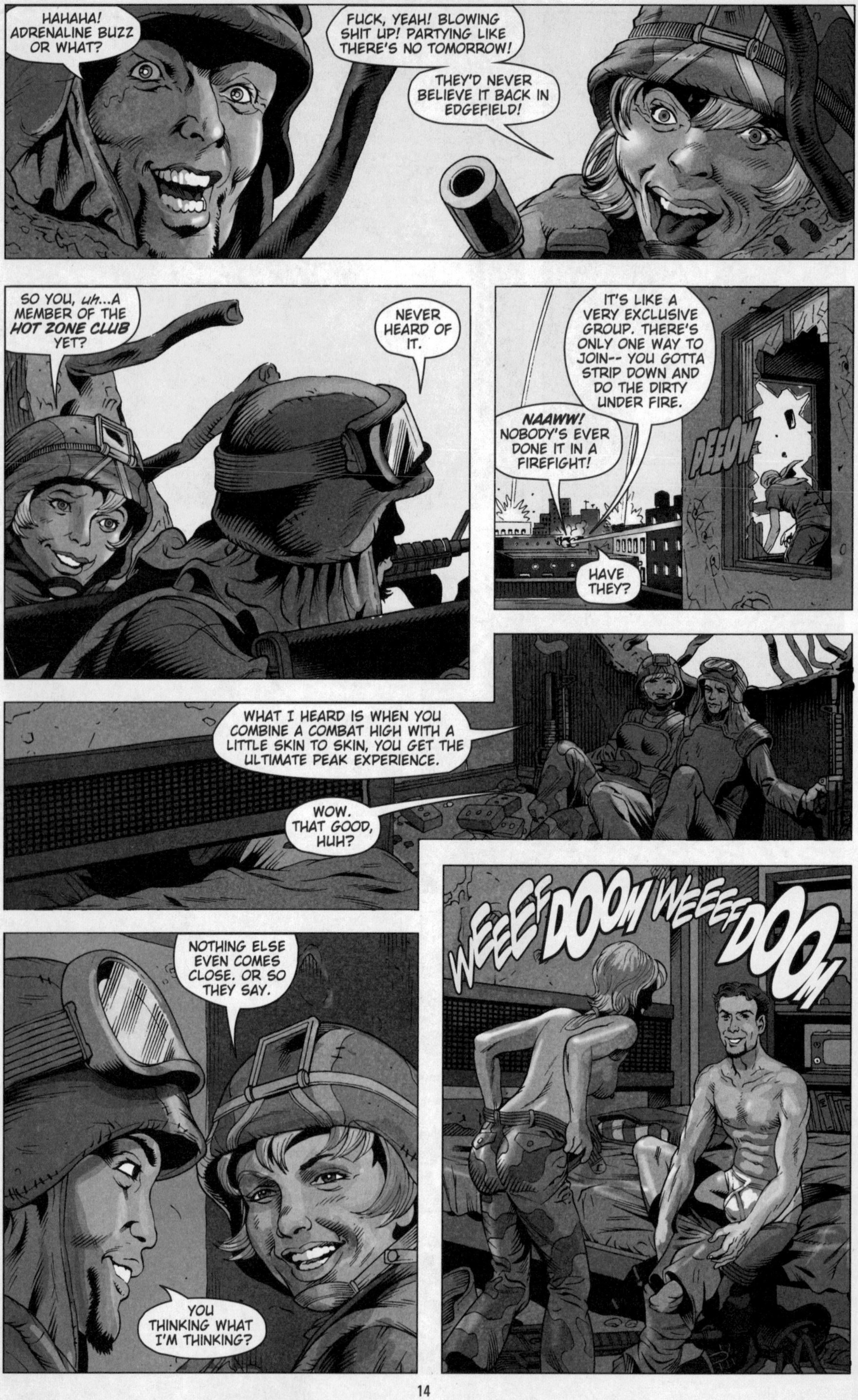
HAHAHA! ADRENALINE BUZZ OR WHAT?
FUCK, YEAH! BLOWING SHIT UP! PARTYING LIKE THERE'S NO TOMORROW!
THEY'D NEVER BELIEVE IT BACK IN EDGEFIELD!
SO YOU, *uh*...A MEMBER OF THE **HOT ZONE CLUB** YET?
NEVER HEARD OF IT.
IT'S LIKE A VERY EXCLUSIVE GROUP. THERE'S ONLY ONE WAY TO JOIN-- YOU GOTTA STRIP DOWN AND DO THE DIRTY UNDER FIRE.
NAAWW! NOBODY'S EVER DONE IT IN A FIREFIGHT!
PEEOW
HAVE THEY?
WHAT I HEARD IS WHEN YOU COMBINE A COMBAT HIGH WITH A LITTLE SKIN TO SKIN, YOU GET THE ULTIMATE PEAK EXPERIENCE.
WOW. THAT GOOD, HUH?
NOTHING ELSE EVEN COMES CLOSE. OR SO THEY SAY.
YOU THINKING WHAT I'M THINKING?
WEEEFDOOM WEEEFDOOM

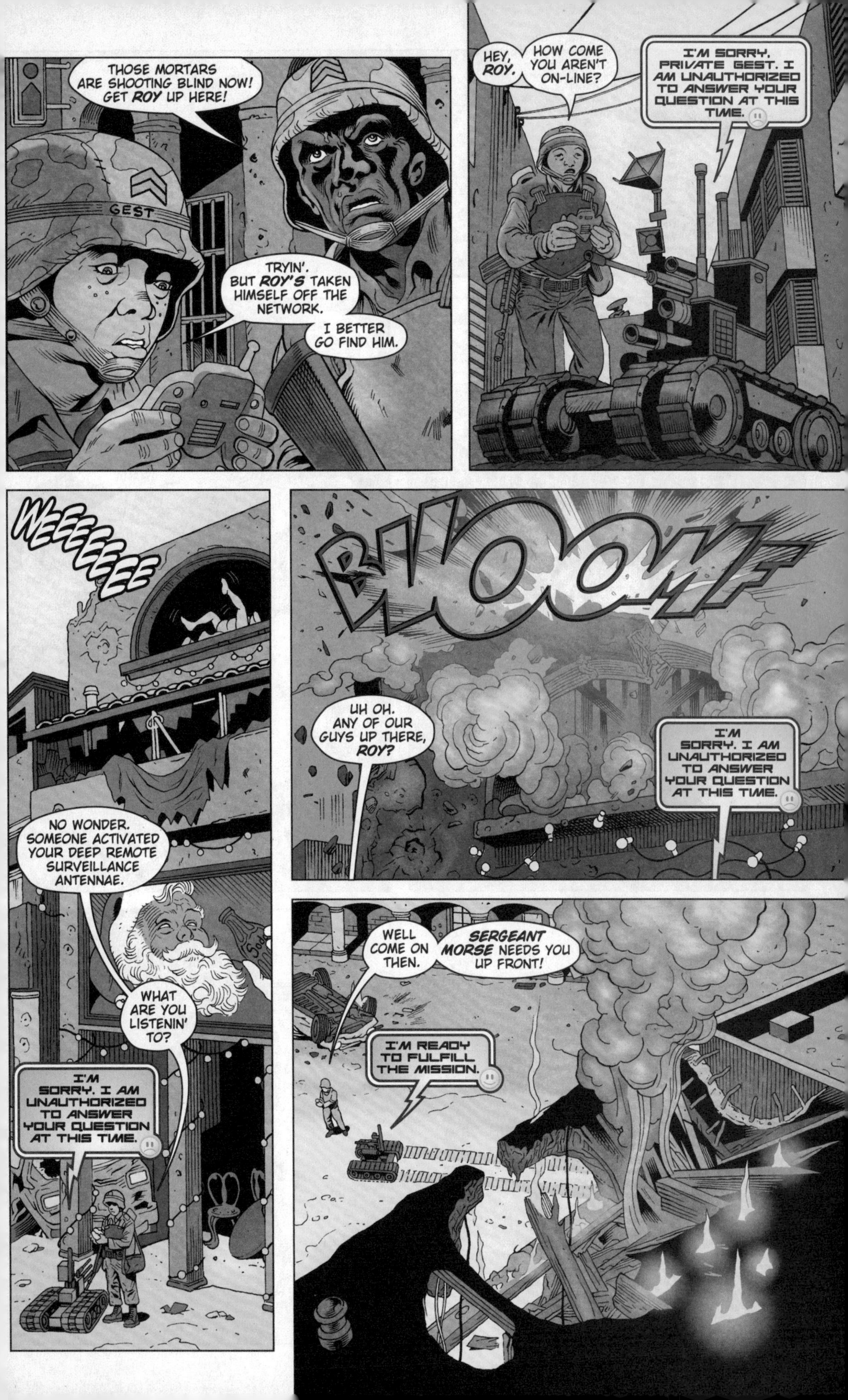
THOSE MORTARS ARE SHOOTING BLIND NOW! GET ROY UP HERE!
GEST
TRYIN'. BUT ROY'S TAKEN HIMSELF OFF THE NETWORK.
I BETTER GO FIND HIM.
HEY, ROY.
HOW COME YOU AREN'T ON-LINE?
I'M SORRY, PRIVATE GEST. I AM UNAUTHORIZED TO ANSWER YOUR QUESTION AT THIS TIME.
WEEEEEEEE
BLOOMF
UH OH. ANY OF OUR GUYS UP THERE, ROY?
I'M SORRY. I AM UNAUTHORIZED TO ANSWER YOUR QUESTION AT THIS TIME.
NO WONDER. SOMEONE ACTIVATED YOUR DEEP REMOTE SURVEILLANCE ANTENNAE.
WHAT ARE YOU LISTENIN' TO?
I'M SORRY. I AM UNAUTHORIZED TO ANSWER YOUR QUESTION AT THIS TIME.
WELL COME ON THEN.
SERGEANT MORSE NEEDS YOU UP FRONT!
I'M READY TO FULFILL THE MISSION.

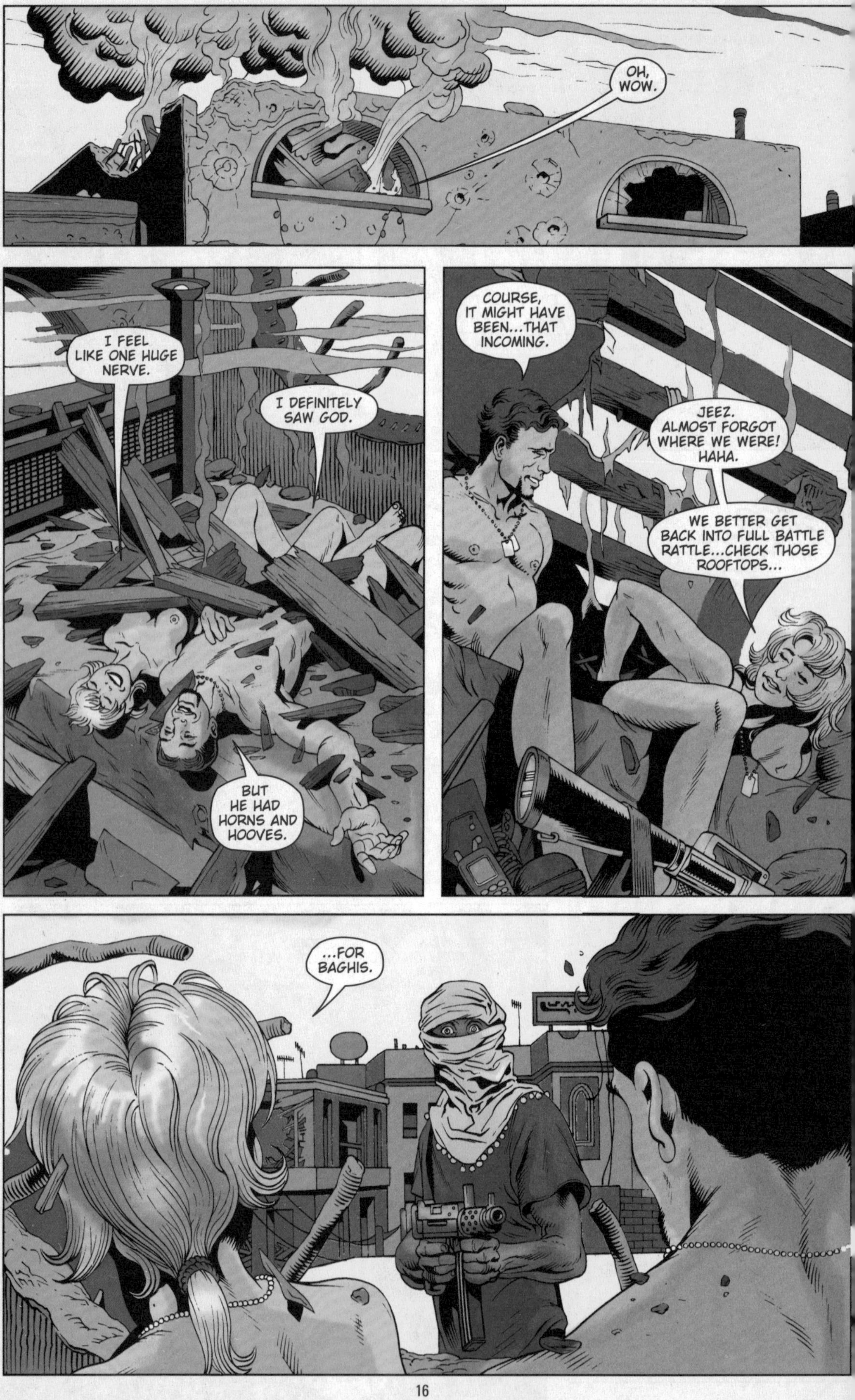
OH, WOW.
I FEEL LIKE ONE HUGE NERVE.
I DEFINITELY SAW GOD.
BUT HE HAD HORNS AND HOOVES.
COURSE, IT MIGHT HAVE BEEN...THAT INCOMING.
JEEZ. ALMOST FORGOT WHERE WE WERE! HAHA.
WE BETTER GET BACK INTO FULL BATTLE RATTLE...CHECK THOSE ROOFTOPS...
...FOR BAGHIS.

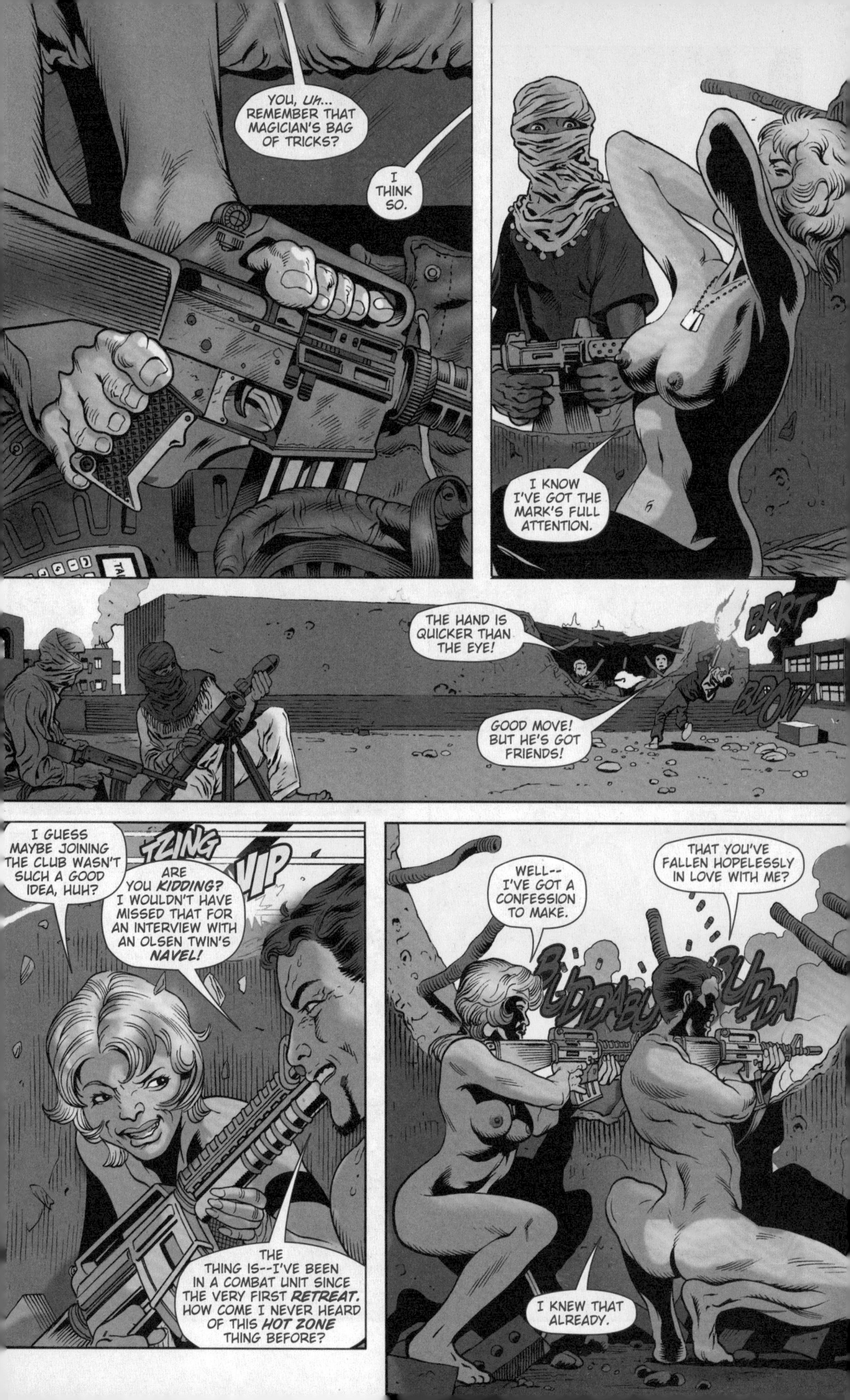
YOU, UH... REMEMBER THAT MAGICIAN'S BAG OF TRICKS?
I THINK SO.
I KNOW I'VE GOT THE MARK'S FULL ATTENTION.
THE HAND IS QUICKER THAN THE EYE!
BRRT
BOOW
GOOD MOVE! BUT HE'S GOT FRIENDS!
I GUESS MAYBE JOINING THE CLUB WASN'T SUCH A GOOD IDEA, HUH?
TZING
VIP
ARE YOU KIDDING? I WOULDN'T HAVE MISSED THAT FOR AN INTERVIEW WITH AN OLSEN TWIN'S NAVEL!
THE THING IS--I'VE BEEN IN A COMBAT UNIT SINCE THE VERY FIRST RETREAT. HOW COME I NEVER HEARD OF THIS HOT ZONE THING BEFORE?
WELL-- I'VE GOT A CONFESSION TO MAKE.
THAT YOU'VE FALLEN HOPELESSLY IN LOVE WITH ME?
BUDDABUDDABUDDA
I KNEW THAT ALREADY.

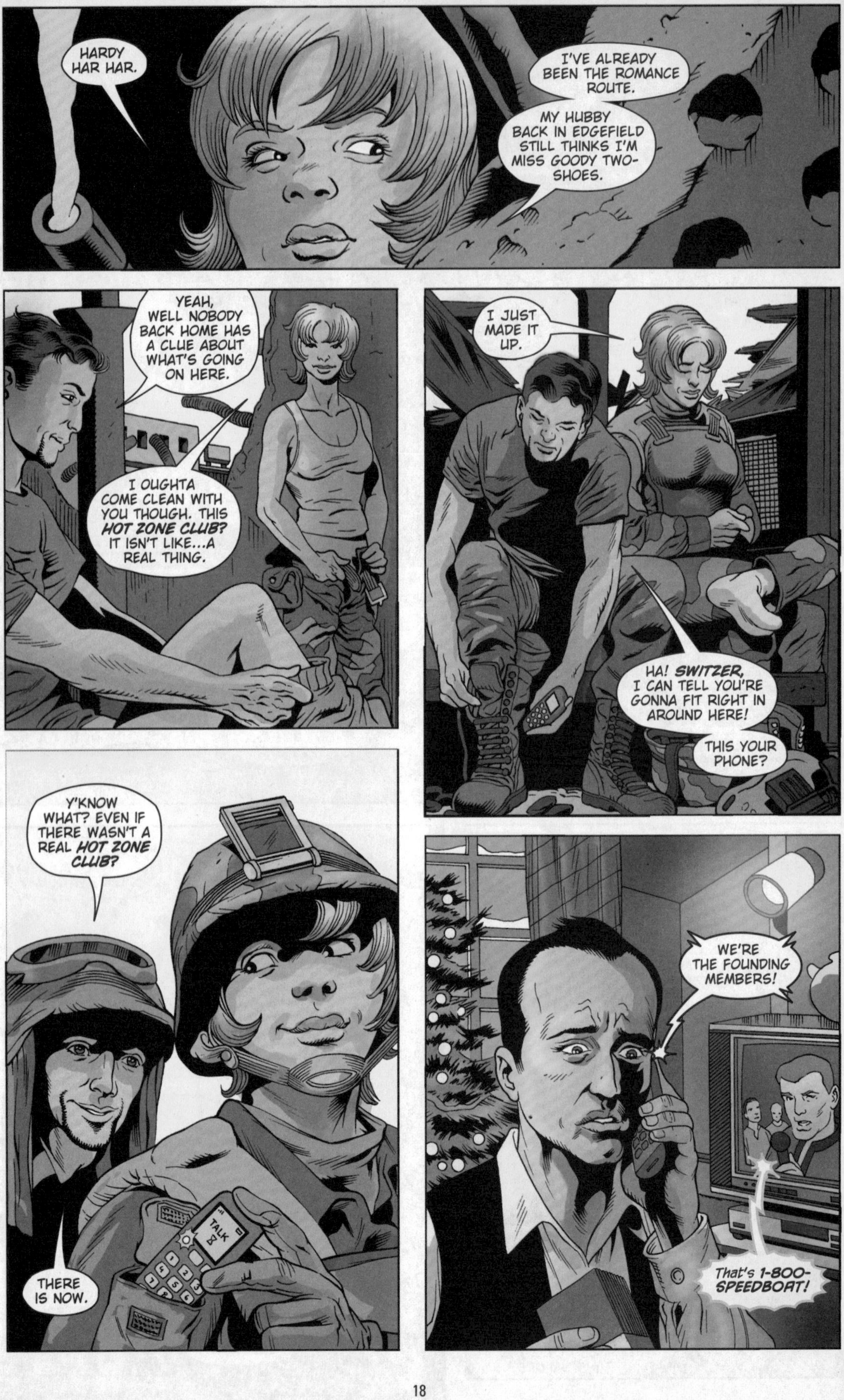
HARDY HAR HAR.
I'VE ALREADY BEEN THE ROMANCE ROUTE.
MY HUBBY BACK IN EDGEFIELD STILL THINKS I'M MISS GOODY TWO-SHOES.
YEAH, WELL NOBODY BACK HOME HAS A CLUE ABOUT WHAT'S GOING ON HERE.
I OUGHTA COME CLEAN WITH YOU THOUGH. THIS HOT ZONE CLUB? IT ISN'T LIKE...A REAL THING.
I JUST MADE IT UP.
HA! SWITZER, I CAN TELL YOU'RE GONNA FIT RIGHT IN AROUND HERE!
THIS YOUR PHONE?
Y'KNOW WHAT? EVEN IF THERE WASN'T A REAL HOT ZONE CLUB?
TALK
THERE IS NOW.
WE'RE THE FOUNDING MEMBERS!
That's 1-800-SPEEDBOAT!

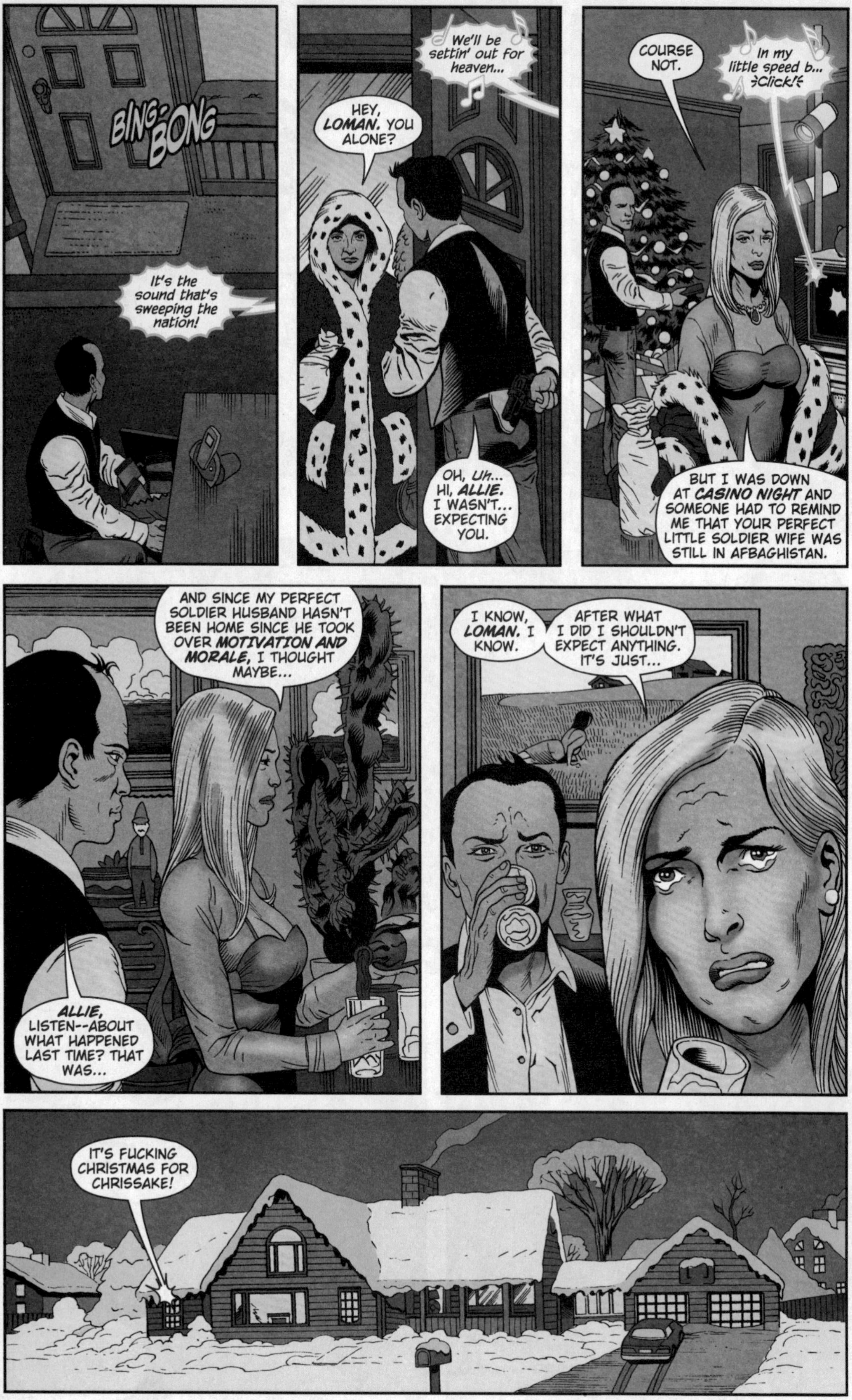
BING-BONG
It's the sound that's sweeping the nation!
We'll be settin' out for heaven...
HEY, LOMAN. YOU ALONE?
OH, Uh... HI, ALLIE. I WASN'T... EXPECTING YOU.
COURSE NOT.
In my little speed b... Click!
BUT I WAS DOWN AT CASINO NIGHT AND SOMEONE HAD TO REMIND ME THAT YOUR PERFECT LITTLE SOLDIER WIFE WAS STILL IN AFBAGHISTAN.
AND SINCE MY PERFECT SOLDIER HUSBAND HASN'T BEEN HOME SINCE HE TOOK OVER MOTIVATION AND MORALE, I THOUGHT MAYBE...
ALLIE, LISTEN--ABOUT WHAT HAPPENED LAST TIME? THAT WAS...
I KNOW, LOMAN. I KNOW.
AFTER WHAT I DID I SHOULDN'T EXPECT ANYTHING. IT'S JUST...
IT'S FUCKING CHRISTMAS FOR CHRISSAKE!

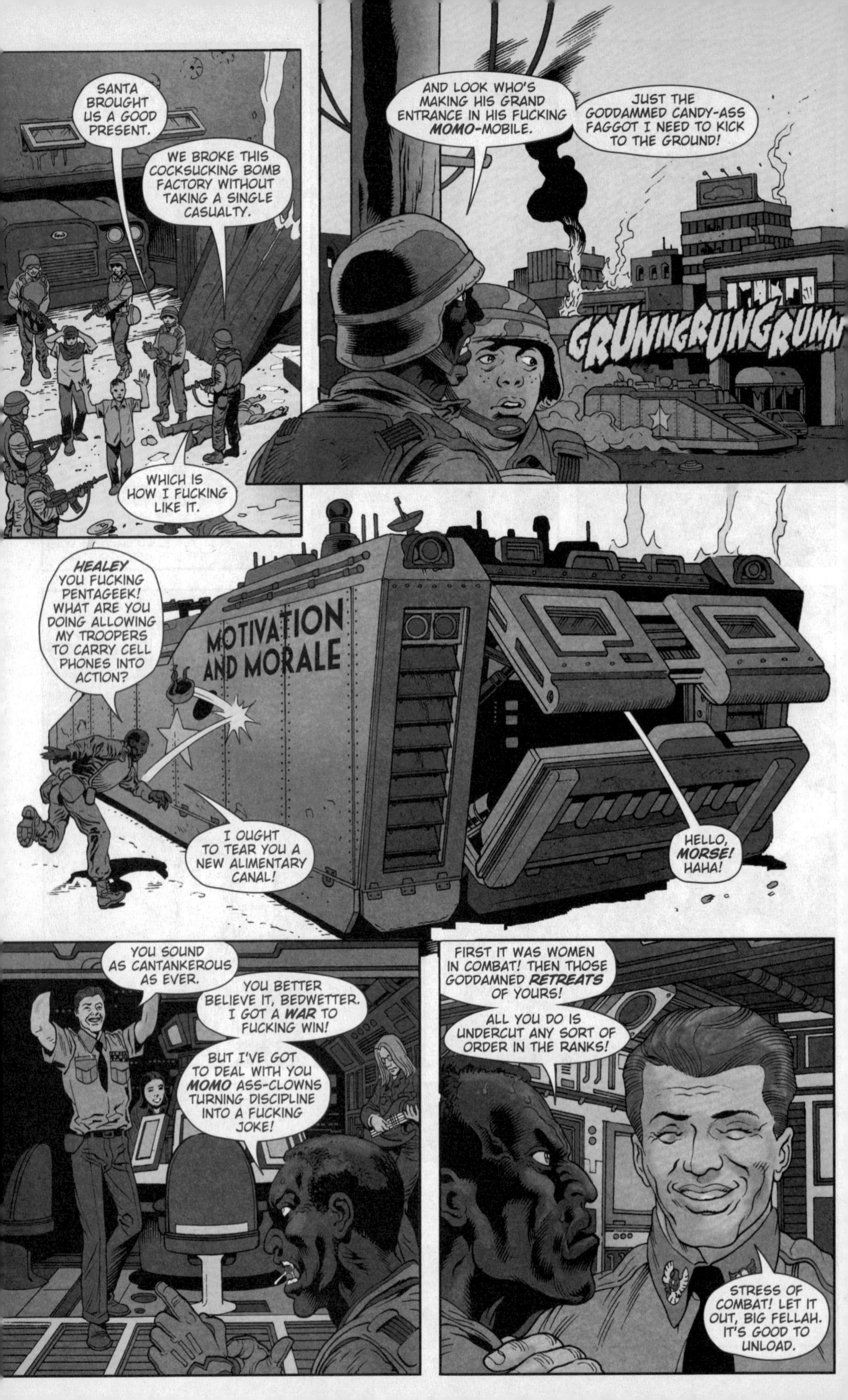
SANTA BROUGHT US A GOOD PRESENT.
WE BROKE THIS COCKSUCKING BOMB FACTORY WITHOUT TAKING A SINGLE CASUALTY.
WHICH IS HOW I FUCKING LIKE IT.
AND LOOK WHO'S MAKING HIS GRAND ENTRANCE IN HIS FUCKING MOMO-MOBILE.
JUST THE GODDAMMED CANDY-ASS FAGGOT I NEED TO KICK TO THE GROUND!
GRUNNGRUNGRUNN
HEALEY YOU FUCKING PENTAGEEK! WHAT ARE YOU DOING ALLOWING MY TROOPERS TO CARRY CELL PHONES INTO ACTION?
MOTIVATION AND MORALE
I OUGHT TO TEAR YOU A NEW ALIMENTARY CANAL!
HELLO, MORSE! HAHA!
YOU SOUND AS CANTANKEROUS AS EVER.
YOU BETTER BELIEVE IT, BEDWETTER. I GOT A WAR TO FUCKING WIN!
BUT I'VE GOT TO DEAL WITH YOU MOMO ASS-CLOWNS TURNING DISCIPLINE INTO A FUCKING JOKE!
FIRST IT WAS WOMEN IN COMBAT! THEN THOSE GODDAMNED RETREATS OF YOURS!
ALL YOU DO IS UNDERCUT ANY SORT OF ORDER IN THE RANKS!
STRESS OF COMBAT! LET IT OUT, BIG FELLAH. IT'S GOOD TO UNLOAD.

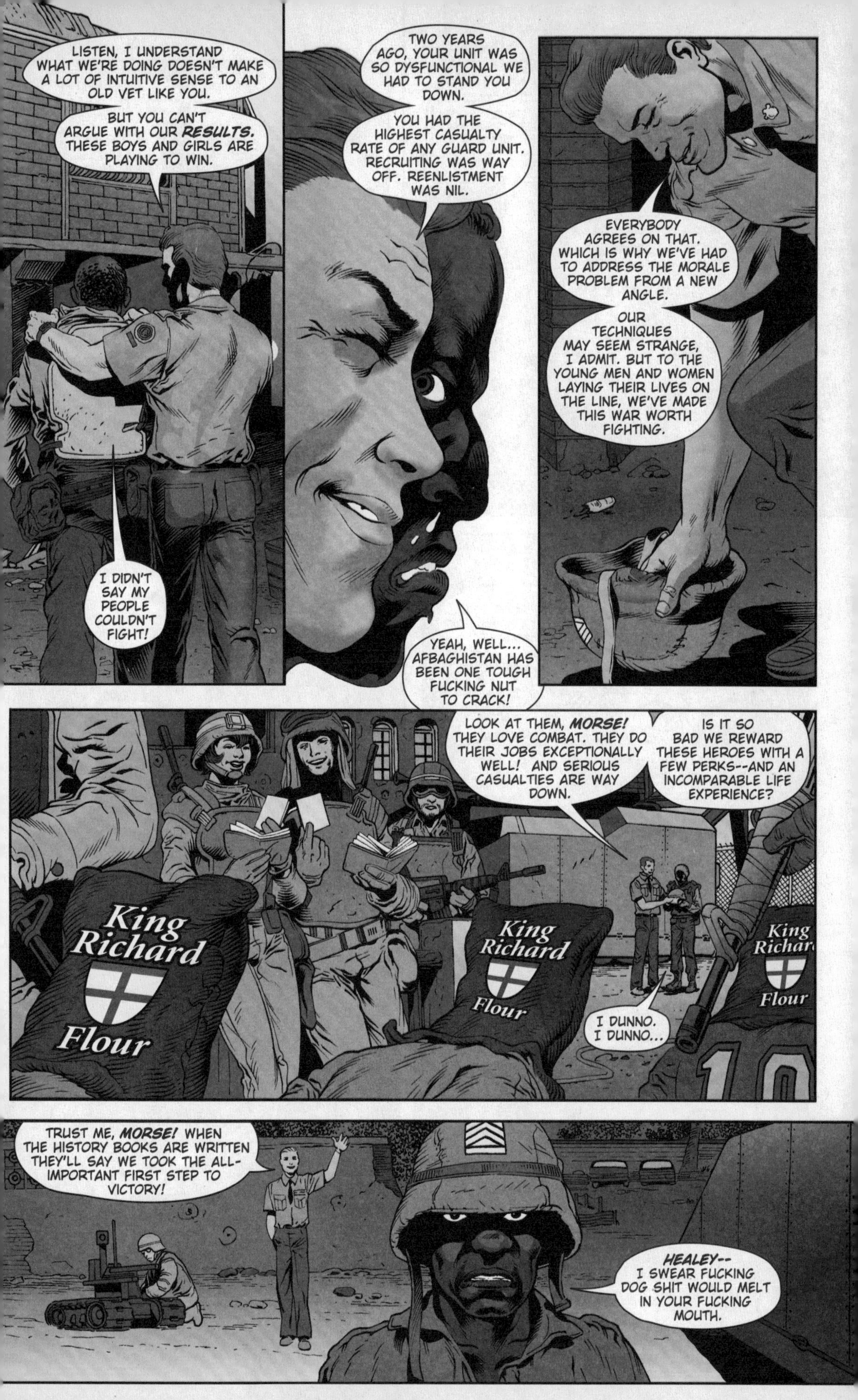
LISTEN, I UNDERSTAND WHAT WE'RE DOING DOESN'T MAKE A LOT OF INTUITIVE SENSE TO AN OLD VET LIKE YOU.
BUT YOU CAN'T ARGUE WITH OUR RESULTS. THESE BOYS AND GIRLS ARE PLAYING TO WIN.
I DIDN'T SAY MY PEOPLE COULDN'T FIGHT!
TWO YEARS AGO, YOUR UNIT WAS SO DYSFUNCTIONAL WE HAD TO STAND YOU DOWN.
YOU HAD THE HIGHEST CASUALTY RATE OF ANY GUARD UNIT. RECRUITING WAS WAY OFF. REENLISTMENT WAS NIL.
YEAH, WELL... AFGHAGHISTAN HAS BEEN ONE TOUGH FUCKING NUT TO CRACK!
EVERYBODY AGREES ON THAT. WHICH IS WHY WE'VE HAD TO ADDRESS THE MORALE PROBLEM FROM A NEW ANGLE.
OUR TECHNIQUES MAY SEEM STRANGE, I ADMIT. BUT TO THE YOUNG MEN AND WOMEN LAYING THEIR LIVES ON THE LINE, WE'VE MADE THIS WAR WORTH FIGHTING.
LOOK AT THEM, MORSE! THEY LOVE COMBAT. THEY DO THEIR JOBS EXCEPTIONALLY WELL! AND SERIOUS CASUALTIES ARE WAY DOWN.
IS IT SO BAD WE REWARD THESE HEROES WITH A FEW PERKS--AND AN INCOMPARABLE LIFE EXPERIENCE?
King Richard Flour
King Richard Flour
I DUNNO. I DUNNO...
TRUST ME, MORSE! WHEN THE HISTORY BOOKS ARE WRITTEN THEY'LL SAY WE TOOK THE ALL-IMPORTANT FIRST STEP TO VICTORY!
HEALEY-- I SWEAR FUCKING DOG SHIT WOULD MELT IN YOUR FUCKING MOUTH.

HELLO, *BEAU!* YOU BEEN TAKING GOOD CARE OF *ROY,* HERE?

UH-HUH. TELL HIM, *ROY.*

PRIVATE GEST HAS BEEN PERFORMING MY MAINTENANCE REGULARLY, COLONEL HEALEY.

I FIGURED YOU WERE GETTING ALONG SPLENDIDLY, *BEAU.*

I HADN'T HEARD FROM YOUR *MOM* SINCE YESTERDAY!

WHAT YOU DOING TO *ROY,* COLONEL?

OH, I'M JUST, *Uh*...CHECKING HIS SOFTWARE, *BEAU.*

LOOKS LIKE HE, *Uh,* MISSED ONE OF HIS RECENT UPDATES.

NOPE. NOPE. *ROY'S* ALL CAUGHT UP. HE SAID SO HIMSELF!

WELL, I'M SURE HE NEEDS SOMETHING. MAYBE A GREASE JOB AND OIL CHANGE?

NO! YOU HEARD *ROY!*

HE SAID I DO A *VERY GOOD* JOB TAKING CARE OF HIM! *ALWAYS!*

AT EASE, SOLDIER.

YES, SIR. BUT...

SAY HI TO YOUR MOTHER FOR ME.

YES, SIR.

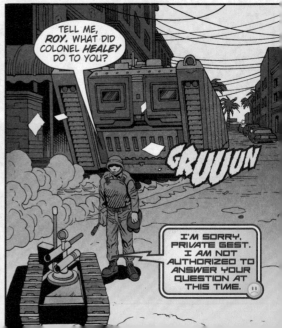

TELL ME, *ROY.* WHAT DID COLONEL *HEALEY* DO TO YOU?

GRUUUN

I'M SORRY, PRIVATE GEST. I AM NOT AUTHORIZED TO ANSWER YOUR QUESTION AT THIS TIME.

MOTIVATION AND MORALE

GRUNN GRUN GRUUNN

O-KAY. *ROY'S* DEEP REMOTE SURVEILLANCE PICKED UP A POTENTIAL PROBLEM.

WOYNER? PULL UP THE SEXUAL ACTIVITY FILES FOR OUR OLD FRIEND *SWITZER* AND SPECIALIST CLASS TWO *FLABBERGAST?*

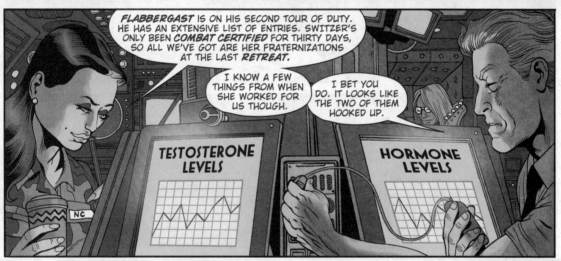

FLABBERGAST IS ON HIS SECOND TOUR OF DUTY. HE HAS AN EXTENSIVE LIST OF ENTRIES. SWITZER'S ONLY BEEN *COMBAT CERTIFIED* FOR THIRTY DAYS, SO ALL WE'VE GOT ARE HER FRATERNIZATIONS AT THE LAST *RETREAT.*

I KNOW A FEW THINGS FROM WHEN SHE WORKED FOR US THOUGH.

I BET YOU DO. IT LOOKS LIKE THE TWO OF THEM HOOKED UP.

TESTOSTERONE LEVELS

HORMONE LEVELS

"SO, *UH...* YOU A MEMBER OF THE *HOT ZONE CLUB* YET?"

"NEVER HEARD OF IT. WHAT IS IT?"

"IT'S LIKE A VERY EXCLUSIVE GROUP. THERE'S ONLY ONE WAY TO JOIN--YOU GOTTA STRIP DOWN AND DO THE DIRTY UNDER FIRE."

HORMONE LEVELS

HOT ZONE CLUB!? I LIKE THAT. IT'S CATCHY!

"WHAT I HEARD IS WHEN YOU COMBINE A COMBAT HIGH WITH A LITTLE SKIN TO SKIN, YOU GET THE ULTIMATE PEAK EXPERIENCE."

"WOW. THAT GOOD, HUH?"

"NOTHING ELSE EVEN COMES CLOSE. OR SO THEY SAY."

"YOU THINKING WHAT I'M THINKING?"

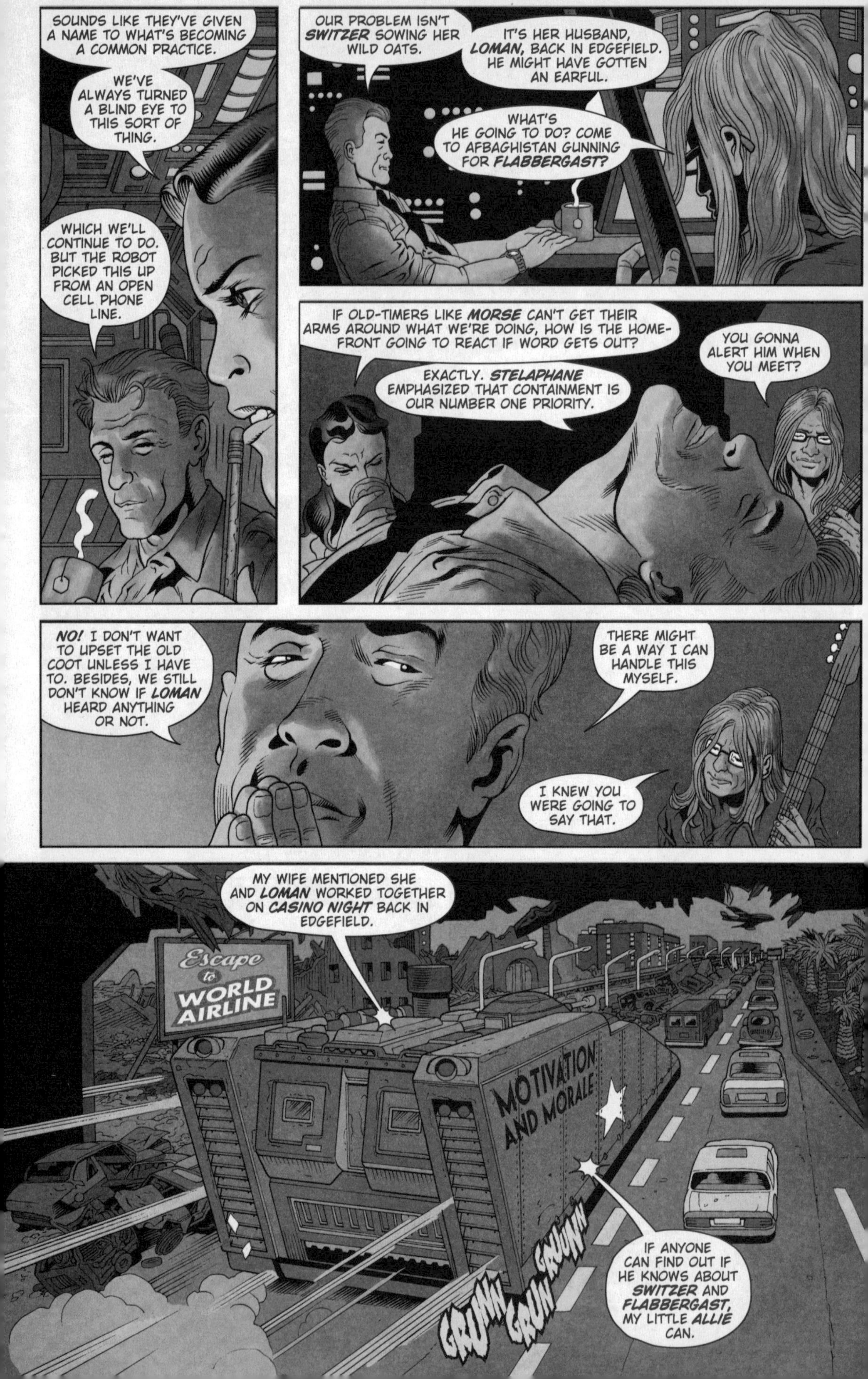
SOUNDS LIKE THEY'VE GIVEN A NAME TO WHAT'S BECOMING A COMMON PRACTICE.
WE'VE ALWAYS TURNED A BLIND EYE TO THIS SORT OF THING.
WHICH WE'LL CONTINUE TO DO. BUT THE ROBOT PICKED THIS UP FROM AN OPEN CELL PHONE LINE.
OUR PROBLEM ISN'T SWITZER SOWING HER WILD OATS.
IT'S HER HUSBAND, LOMAN, BACK IN EDGEFIELD. HE MIGHT HAVE GOTTEN AN EARFUL.
WHAT'S HE GOING TO DO? COME TO AFBAGHISTAN GUNNING FOR FLABBERGAST?
IF OLD-TIMERS LIKE MORSE CAN'T GET THEIR ARMS AROUND WHAT WE'RE DOING, HOW IS THE HOME-FRONT GOING TO REACT IF WORD GETS OUT?
EXACTLY. STELAPHANE EMPHASIZED THAT CONTAINMENT IS OUR NUMBER ONE PRIORITY.
YOU GONNA ALERT HIM WHEN YOU MEET?
NO! I DON'T WANT TO UPSET THE OLD COOT UNLESS I HAVE TO. BESIDES, WE STILL DON'T KNOW IF LOMAN HEARD ANYTHING OR NOT.
THERE MIGHT BE A WAY I CAN HANDLE THIS MYSELF.
I KNEW YOU WERE GOING TO SAY THAT.
MY WIFE MENTIONED SHE AND LOMAN WORKED TOGETHER ON CASINO NIGHT BACK IN EDGEFIELD.
Escape to WORLD AIRLINE
MOTIVATION AND MORALE
IF ANYONE CAN FIND OUT IF HE KNOWS ABOUT SWITZER AND FLABBERGAST, MY LITTLE ALLIE CAN.
GRUNN GRUN GRUNN

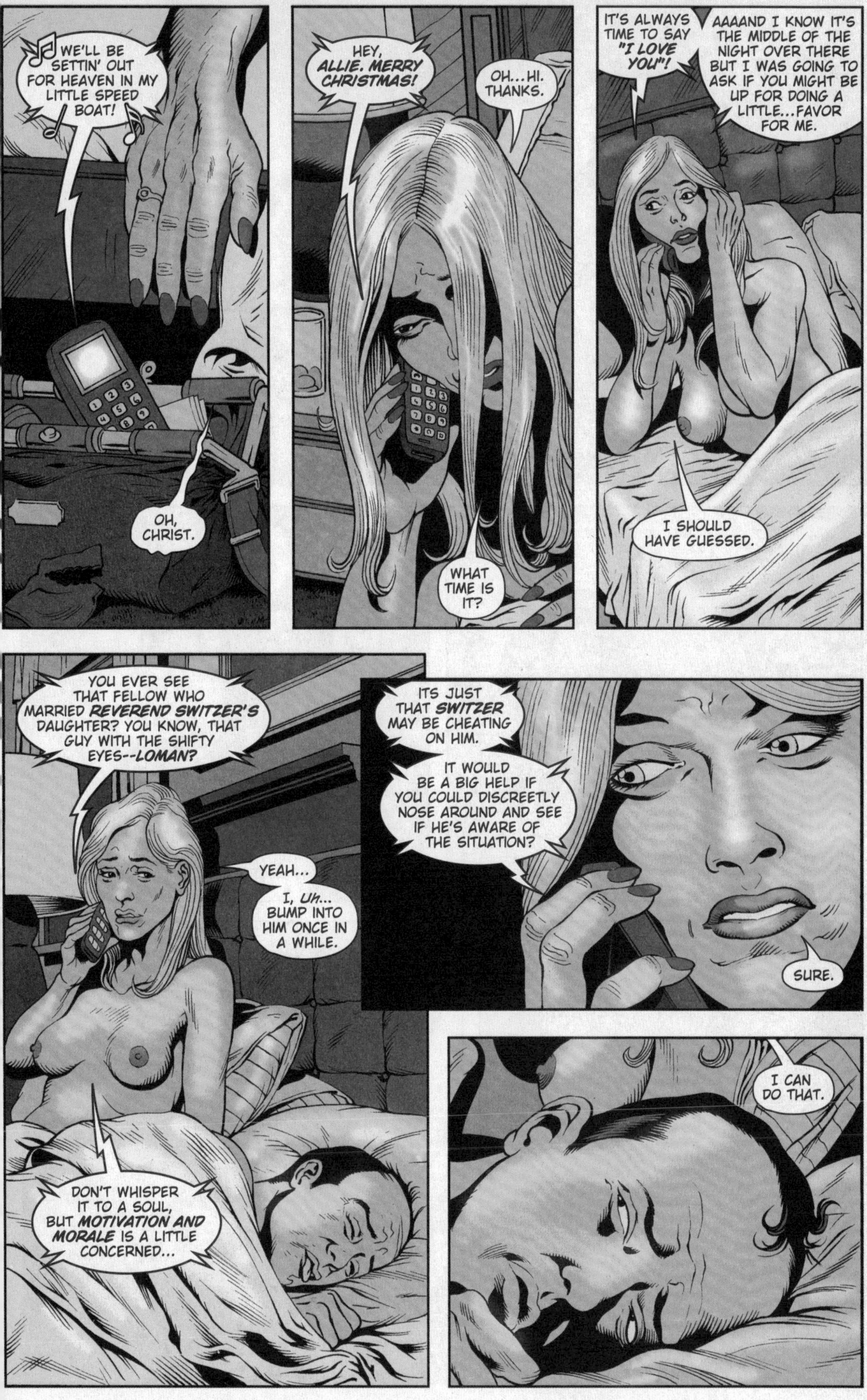
WE'LL BE SETTIN' OUT FOR HEAVEN IN MY LITTLE SPEED BOAT!
OH, CHRIST.
HEY, ALLIE. MERRY CHRISTMAS!
OH...HI. THANKS.
WHAT TIME IS IT?
IT'S ALWAYS TIME TO SAY "I LOVE YOU"!
AAAAND I KNOW IT'S THE MIDDLE OF THE NIGHT OVER THERE BUT I WAS GOING TO ASK IF YOU MIGHT BE UP FOR DOING A LITTLE...FAVOR FOR ME.
I SHOULD HAVE GUESSED.
YOU EVER SEE THAT FELLOW WHO MARRIED REVEREND SWITZER'S DAUGHTER? YOU KNOW, THAT GUY WITH THE SHIFTY EYES--LOMAN?
YEAH...
I, UH... BUMP INTO HIM ONCE IN A WHILE.
DON'T WHISPER IT TO A SOUL, BUT MOTIVATION AND MORALE IS A LITTLE CONCERNED...
ITS JUST THAT SWITZER MAY BE CHEATING ON HIM.
IT WOULD BE A BIG HELP IF YOU COULD DISCREETLY NOSE AROUND AND SEE IF HE'S AWARE OF THE SITUATION?
SURE.
I CAN DO THAT.

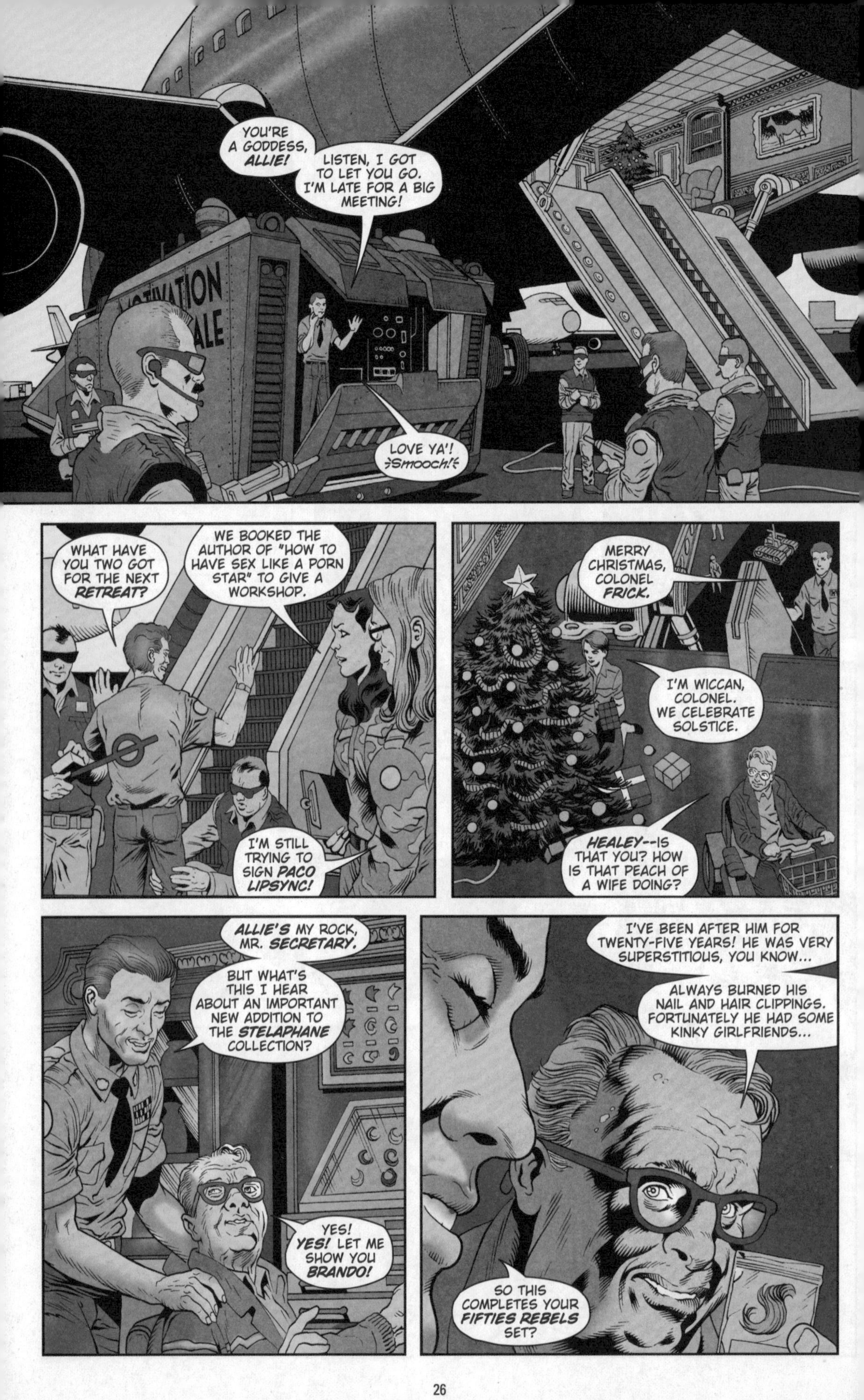

YOU'RE A GODDESS, ALLIE!
LISTEN, I GOT TO LET YOU GO. I'M LATE FOR A BIG MEETING!
LOVE YA'! Smooch!
WHAT HAVE YOU TWO GOT FOR THE NEXT RETREAT?
WE BOOKED THE AUTHOR OF "HOW TO HAVE SEX LIKE A PORN STAR" TO GIVE A WORKSHOP.
I'M STILL TRYING TO SIGN PACO LIPSYNC!
MERRY CHRISTMAS, COLONEL FRICK.
I'M WICCAN, COLONEL. WE CELEBRATE SOLSTICE.
HEALEY--IS THAT YOU? HOW IS THAT PEACH OF A WIFE DOING?
ALLIE'S MY ROCK, MR. SECRETARY.
BUT WHAT'S THIS I HEAR ABOUT AN IMPORTANT NEW ADDITION TO THE STELAPHANE COLLECTION?
YES! YES! LET ME SHOW YOU BRANDO!
I'VE BEEN AFTER HIM FOR TWENTY-FIVE YEARS! HE WAS VERY SUPERSTITIOUS, YOU KNOW...
ALWAYS BURNED HIS NAIL AND HAIR CLIPPINGS. FORTUNATELY HE HAD SOME KINKY GIRLFRIENDS...
SO THIS COMPLETES YOUR FIFTIES REBELS SET?

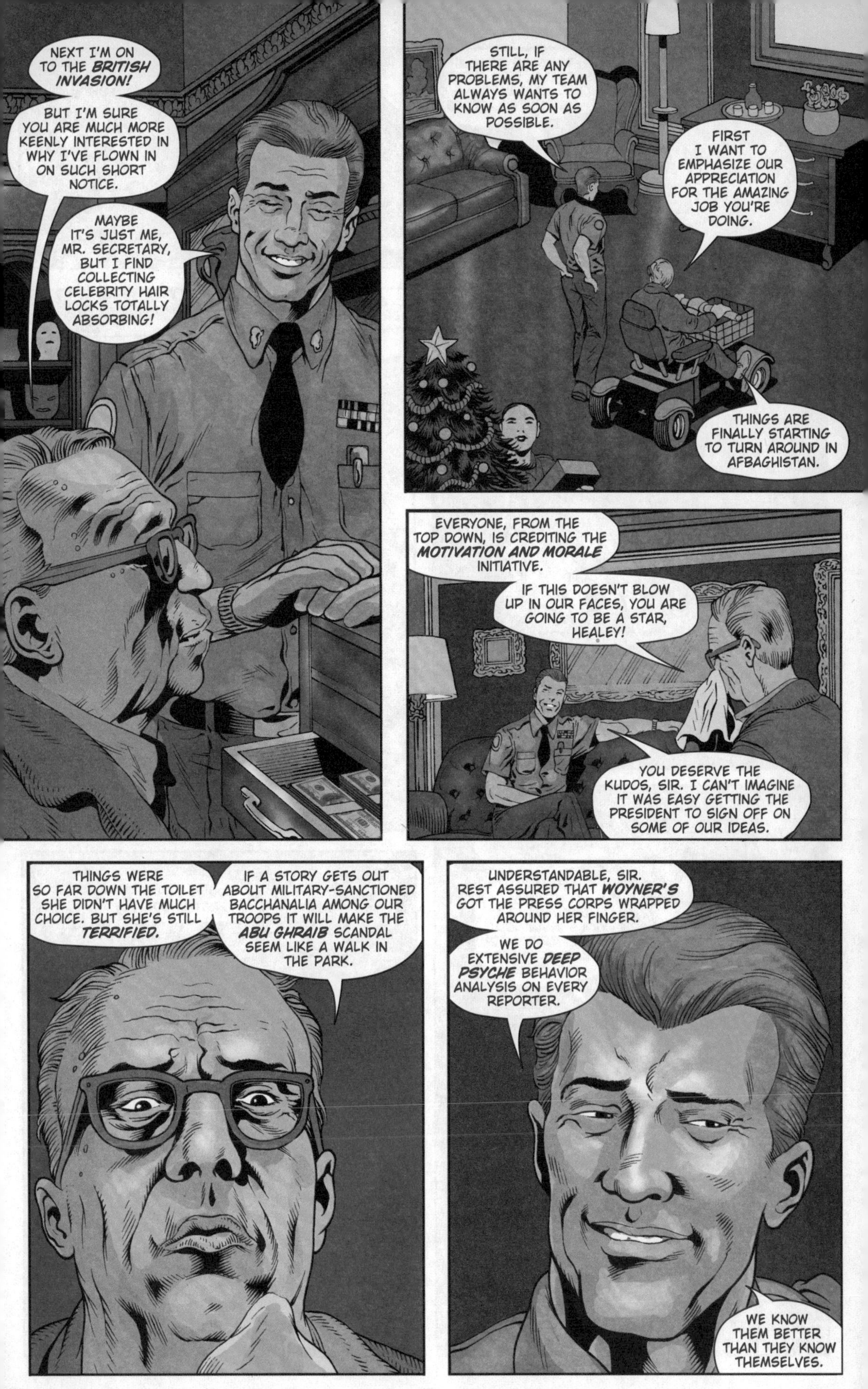
NEXT I'M ON TO THE BRITISH INVASION!
BUT I'M SURE YOU ARE MUCH MORE KEENLY INTERESTED IN WHY I'VE FLOWN IN ON SUCH SHORT NOTICE.
MAYBE IT'S JUST ME, MR. SECRETARY, BUT I FIND COLLECTING CELEBRITY HAIR LOCKS TOTALLY ABSORBING!
STILL, IF THERE ARE ANY PROBLEMS, MY TEAM ALWAYS WANTS TO KNOW AS SOON AS POSSIBLE.
FIRST I WANT TO EMPHASIZE OUR APPRECIATION FOR THE AMAZING JOB YOU'RE DOING.
THINGS ARE FINALLY STARTING TO TURN AROUND IN AFBAGHISTAN.
EVERYONE, FROM THE TOP DOWN, IS CREDITING THE MOTIVATION AND MORALE INITIATIVE.
IF THIS DOESN'T BLOW UP IN OUR FACES, YOU ARE GOING TO BE A STAR, HEALEY!
YOU DESERVE THE KUDOS, SIR. I CAN'T IMAGINE IT WAS EASY GETTING THE PRESIDENT TO SIGN OFF ON SOME OF OUR IDEAS.
THINGS WERE SO FAR DOWN THE TOILET SHE DIDN'T HAVE MUCH CHOICE. BUT SHE'S STILL TERRIFIED.
IF A STORY GETS OUT ABOUT MILITARY-SANCTIONED BACCHANALIA AMONG OUR TROOPS IT WILL MAKE THE ABU GHRAIB SCANDAL SEEM LIKE A WALK IN THE PARK.
UNDERSTANDABLE, SIR. REST ASSURED THAT WOYNER'S GOT THE PRESS CORPS WRAPPED AROUND HER FINGER.
WE DO EXTENSIVE DEEP PSYCHE BEHAVIOR ANALYSIS ON EVERY REPORTER.
WE KNOW THEM BETTER THAN THEY KNOW THEMSELVES.

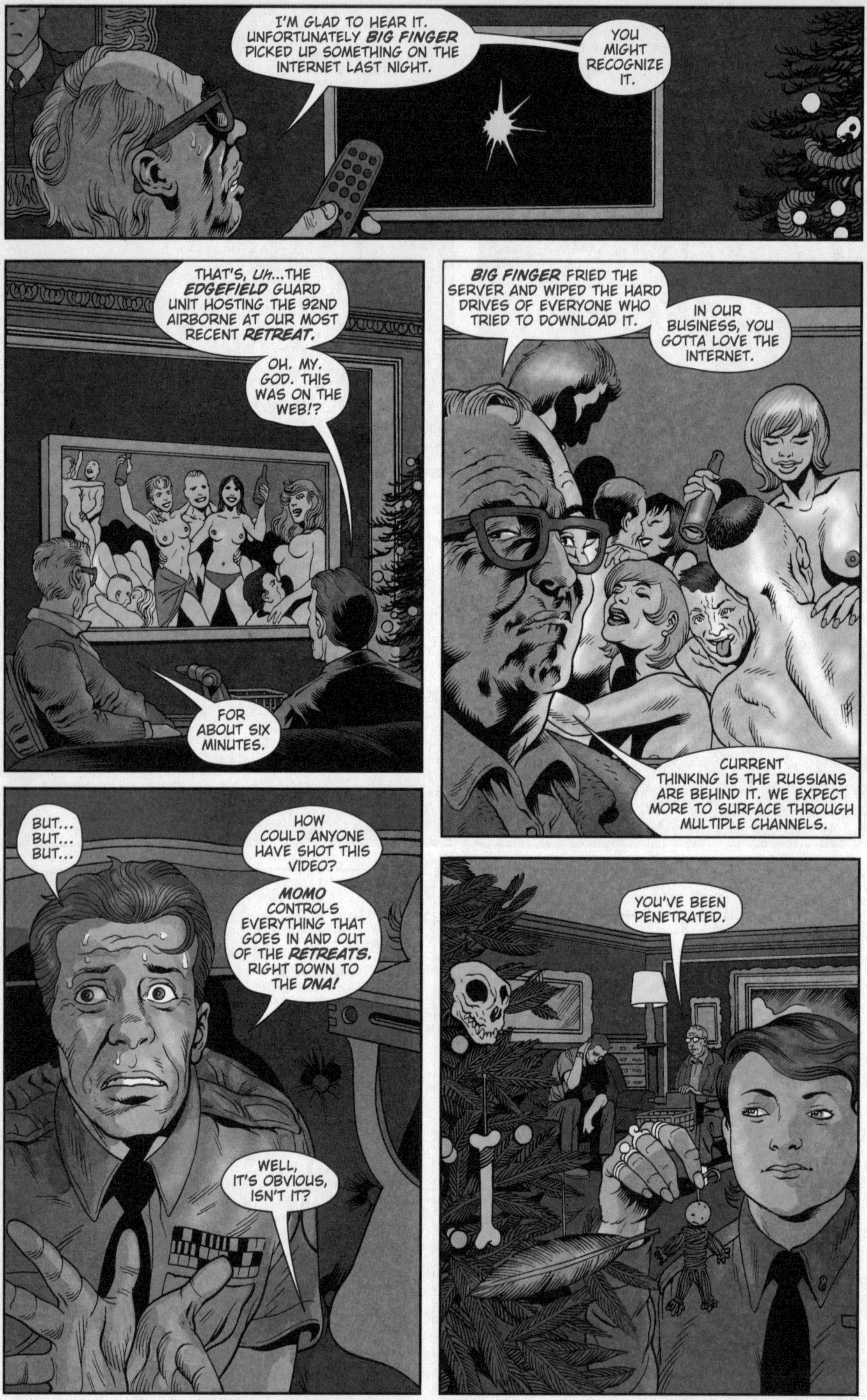
I'M GLAD TO HEAR IT. UNFORTUNATELY BIG FINGER PICKED UP SOMETHING ON THE INTERNET LAST NIGHT.
YOU MIGHT RECOGNIZE IT.
THAT'S, Uh...THE EDGEFIELD GUARD UNIT HOSTING THE 92ND AIRBORNE AT OUR MOST RECENT RETREAT.
OH. MY. GOD. THIS WAS ON THE WEB!?
FOR ABOUT SIX MINUTES.
BIG FINGER FRIED THE SERVER AND WIPED THE HARD DRIVES OF EVERYONE WHO TRIED TO DOWNLOAD IT.
IN OUR BUSINESS, YOU GOTTA LOVE THE INTERNET.
CURRENT THINKING IS THE RUSSIANS ARE BEHIND IT. WE EXPECT MORE TO SURFACE THROUGH MULTIPLE CHANNELS.
BUT... BUT... BUT...
HOW COULD ANYONE HAVE SHOT THIS VIDEO?
MOMO CONTROLS EVERYTHING THAT GOES IN AND OUT OF THE RETREATS. RIGHT DOWN TO THE DNA!
WELL, IT'S OBVIOUS, ISN'T IT?
YOU'VE BEEN PENETRATED.

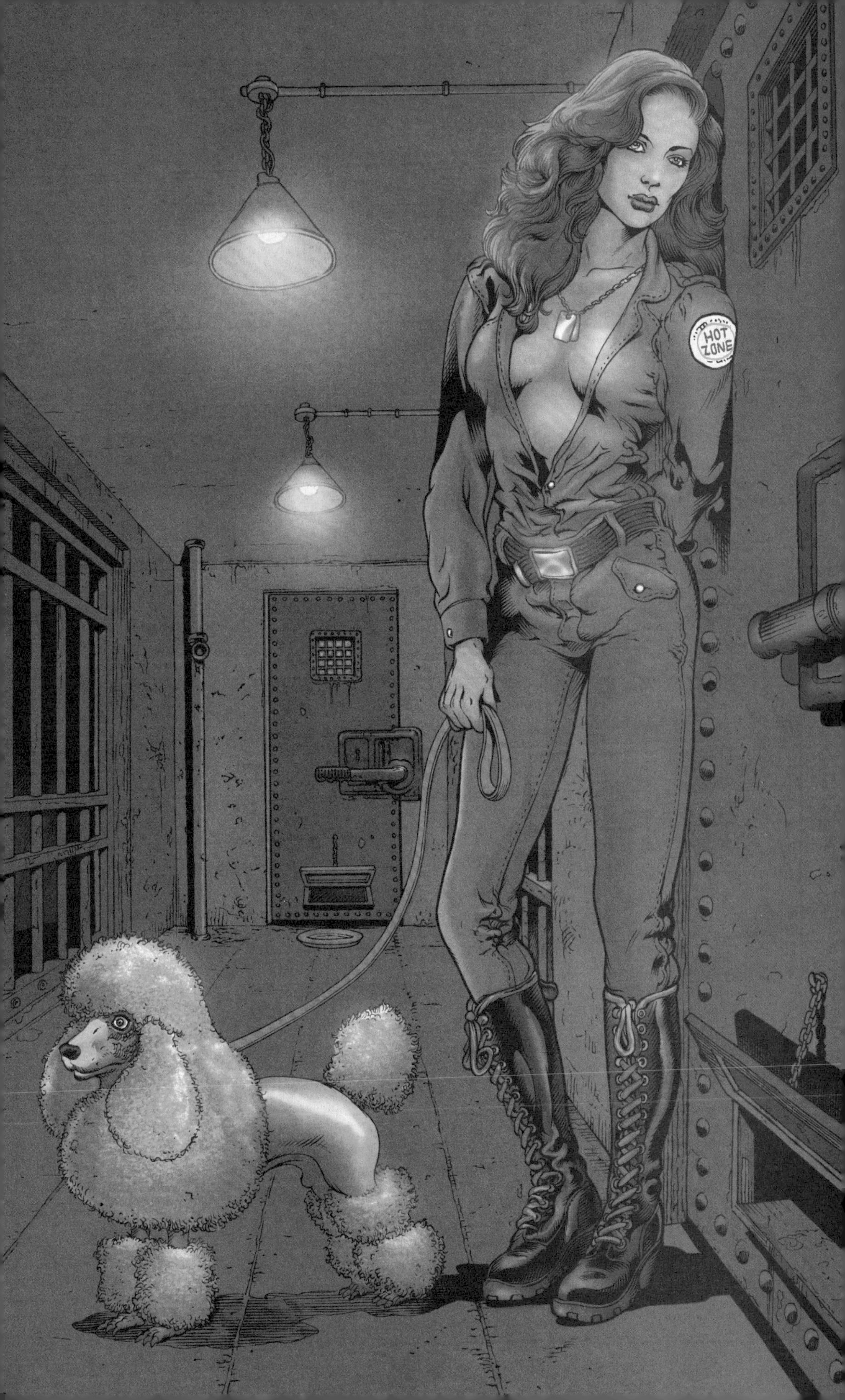
HOT ZONE

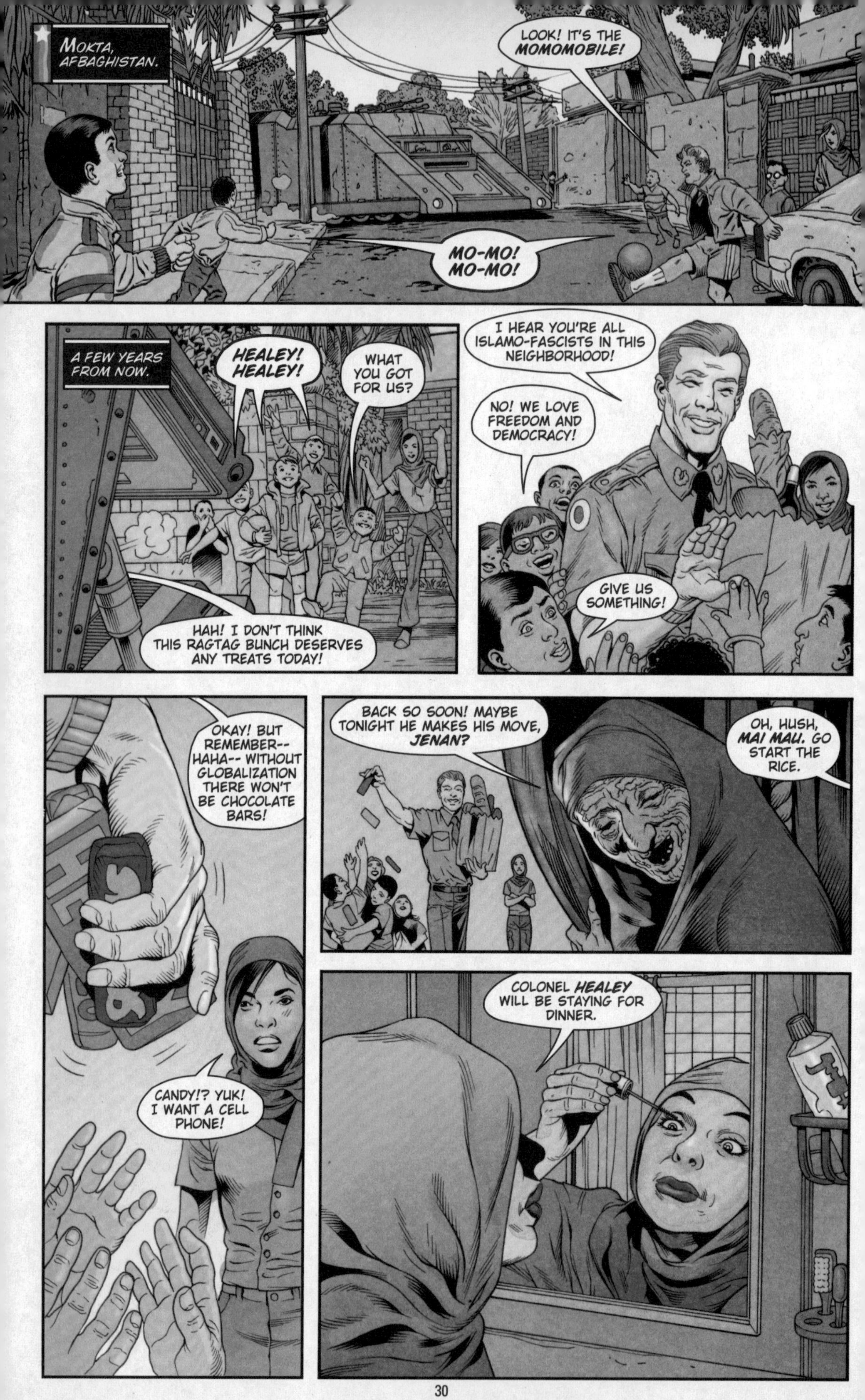
MOKTA, AFBAGHISTAN.
LOOK! IT'S THE MOMOMOBILE!
MO-MO! MO-MO!
A FEW YEARS FROM NOW.
HEALEY! HEALEY!
WHAT YOU GOT FOR US?
HAH! I DON'T THINK THIS RAGTAG BUNCH DESERVES ANY TREATS TODAY!
I HEAR YOU'RE ALL ISLAMO-FASCISTS IN THIS NEIGHBORHOOD!
NO! WE LOVE FREEDOM AND DEMOCRACY!
GIVE US SOMETHING!
OKAY! BUT REMEMBER-- HAHA-- WITHOUT GLOBALIZATION THERE WON'T BE CHOCOLATE BARS!
CANDY!? YUK! I WANT A CELL PHONE!
BACK SO SOON! MAYBE TONIGHT HE MAKES HIS MOVE, JENAN?
OH, HUSH, MAI MAU. GO START THE RICE.
COLONEL HEALEY WILL BE STAYING FOR DINNER.

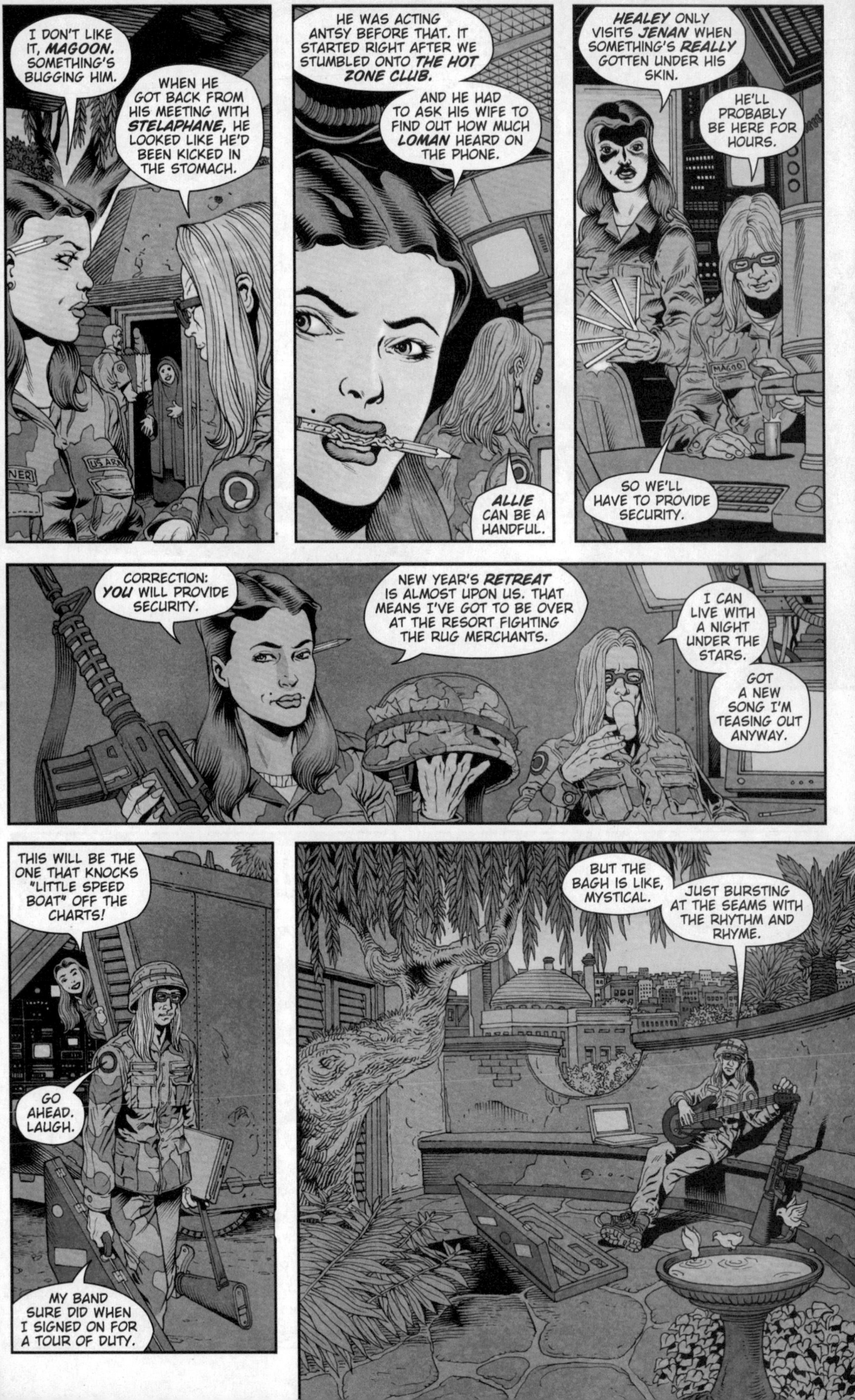

I DON'T LIKE IT, MAGOON. SOMETHING'S BUGGING HIM.
WHEN HE GOT BACK FROM HIS MEETING WITH STELAPHANE, HE LOOKED LIKE HE'D BEEN KICKED IN THE STOMACH.
HE WAS ACTING ANTSY BEFORE THAT. IT STARTED RIGHT AFTER WE STUMBLED ONTO THE HOT ZONE CLUB.
AND HE HAD TO ASK HIS WIFE TO FIND OUT HOW MUCH LOMAN HEARD ON THE PHONE.
ALLIE CAN BE A HANDFUL.
HEALEY ONLY VISITS JENAN WHEN SOMETHING'S REALLY GOTTEN UNDER HIS SKIN.
HE'LL PROBABLY BE HERE FOR HOURS.
SO WE'LL HAVE TO PROVIDE SECURITY.
CORRECTION: YOU WILL PROVIDE SECURITY.
NEW YEAR'S RETREAT IS ALMOST UPON US. THAT MEANS I'VE GOT TO BE OVER AT THE RESORT FIGHTING THE RUG MERCHANTS.
I CAN LIVE WITH A NIGHT UNDER THE STARS.
GOT A NEW SONG I'M TEASING OUT ANYWAY.
THIS WILL BE THE ONE THAT KNOCKS "LITTLE SPEED BOAT" OFF THE CHARTS!
GO AHEAD. LAUGH.
MY BAND SURE DID WHEN I SIGNED ON FOR A TOUR OF DUTY.
BUT THE BAGH IS LIKE, MYSTICAL.
JUST BURSTING AT THE SEAMS WITH THE RHYTHM AND RHYME.

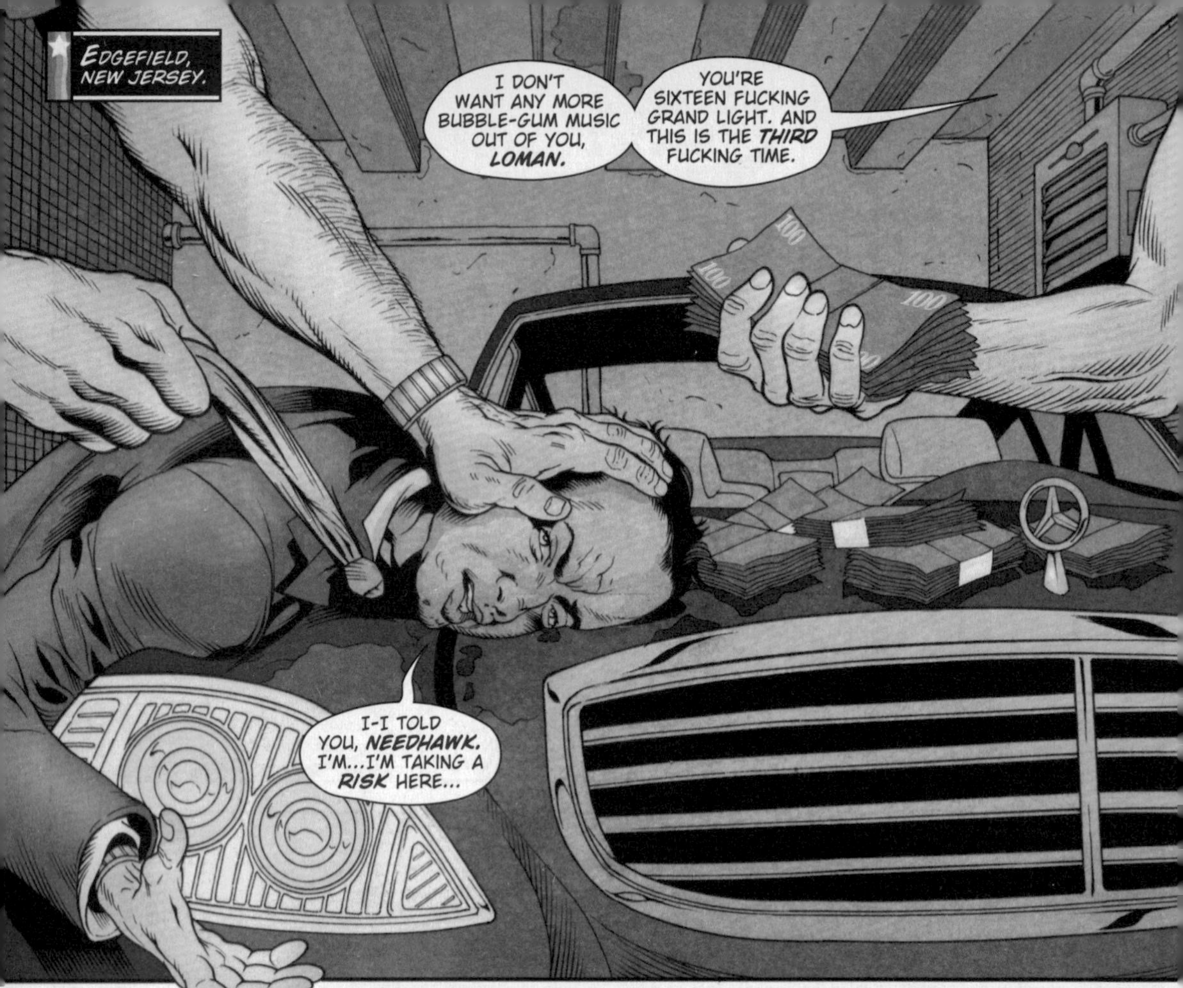
EDGEFIELD, NEW JERSEY.
I DON'T WANT ANY MORE BUBBLE-GUM MUSIC OUT OF YOU, LOMAN.
YOU'RE SIXTEEN FUCKING GRAND LIGHT. AND THIS IS THE THIRD FUCKING TIME.
I-I TOLD YOU, NEEDHAWK. I'M...I'M TAKING A RISK HERE...

WHY WE FIGHT

COLORIST: JOSE VILLARRUBIA

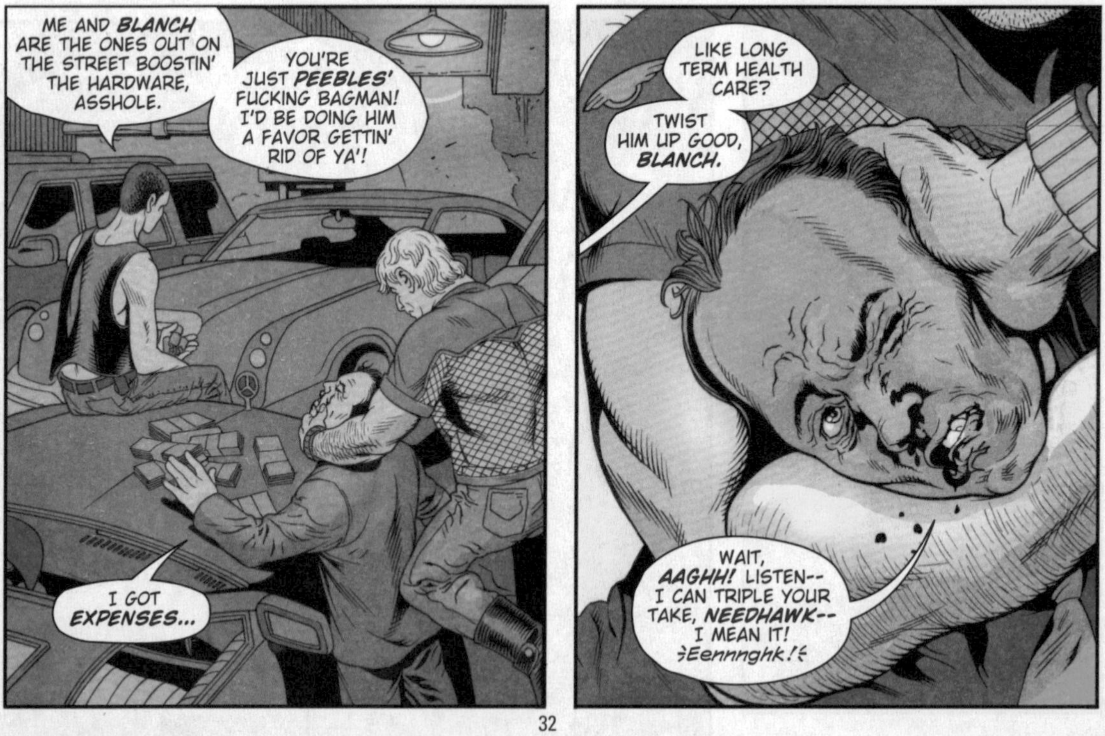
ME AND BLANCH ARE THE ONES OUT ON THE STREET BOOSTIN' THE HARDWARE, ASSHOLE.
YOU'RE JUST PEEBLES' FUCKING BAGMAN! I'D BE DOING HIM A FAVOR GETTIN' RID OF YA'!
I GOT EXPENSES...
LIKE LONG TERM HEALTH CARE?
TWIST HIM UP GOOD, BLANCH.
WAIT, AAGHH! LISTEN-- I CAN TRIPLE YOUR TAKE, NEEDHAWK-- I MEAN IT!
Eennnghk!

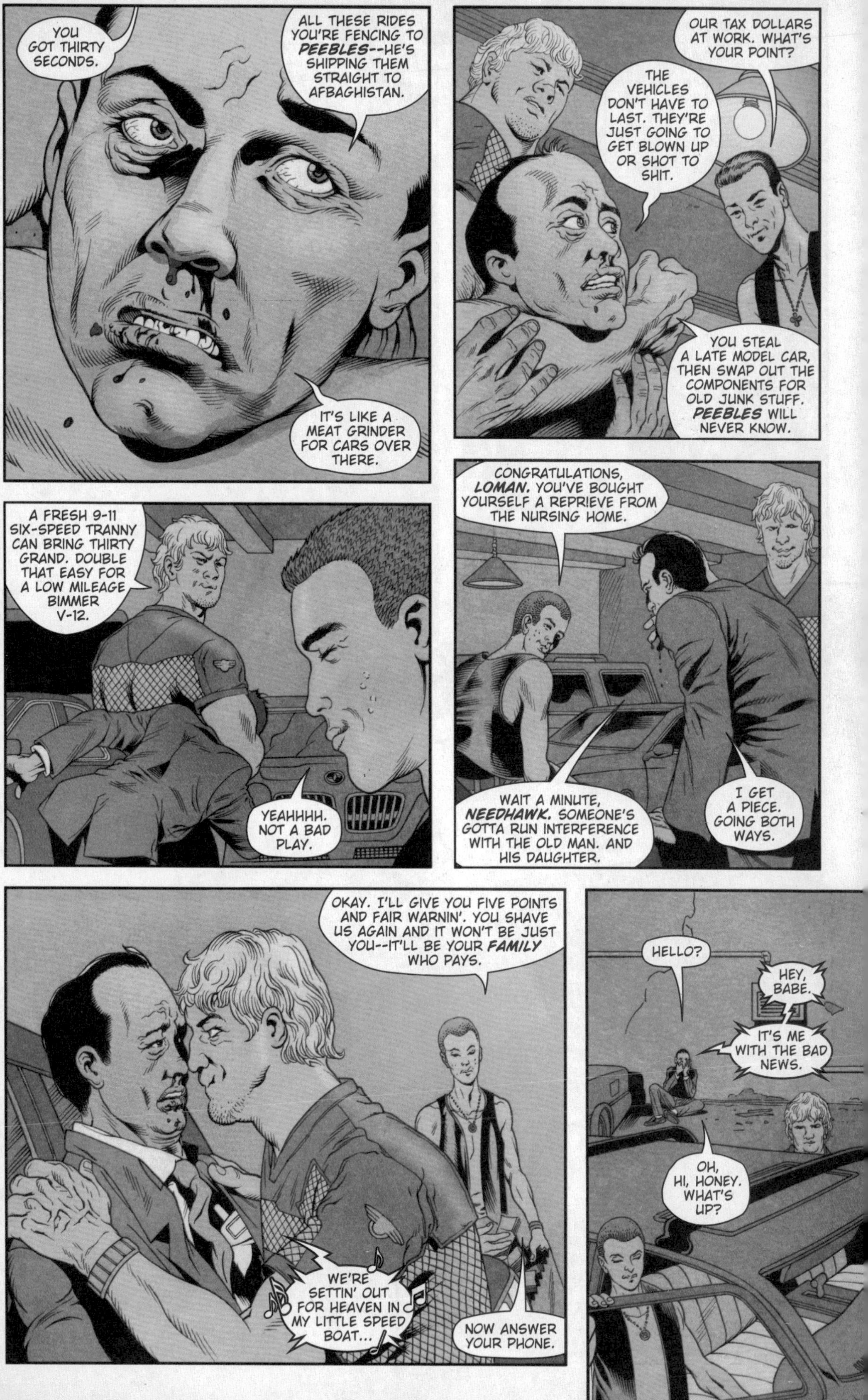
YOU GOT THIRTY SECONDS.
ALL THESE RIDES YOU'RE FENCING TO PEEBLES--HE'S SHIPPING THEM STRAIGHT TO AFBAGHISTAN.
IT'S LIKE A MEAT GRINDER FOR CARS OVER THERE.
OUR TAX DOLLARS AT WORK. WHAT'S YOUR POINT?
THE VEHICLES DON'T HAVE TO LAST. THEY'RE JUST GOING TO GET BLOWN UP OR SHOT TO SHIT.
YOU STEAL A LATE MODEL CAR, THEN SWAP OUT THE COMPONENTS FOR OLD JUNK STUFF. PEEBLES WILL NEVER KNOW.
A FRESH 9-11 SIX-SPEED TRANNY CAN BRING THIRTY GRAND. DOUBLE THAT EASY FOR A LOW MILEAGE BIMMER V-12.
YEAHHHH. NOT A BAD PLAY.
CONGRATULATIONS, LOMAN. YOU'VE BOUGHT YOURSELF A REPRIEVE FROM THE NURSING HOME.
WAIT A MINUTE, NEEDHAWK. SOMEONE'S GOTTA RUN INTERFERENCE WITH THE OLD MAN. AND HIS DAUGHTER.
I GET A PIECE. GOING BOTH WAYS.
OKAY. I'LL GIVE YOU FIVE POINTS AND FAIR WARNIN'. YOU SHAVE US AGAIN AND IT WON'T BE JUST YOU--IT'LL BE YOUR FAMILY WHO PAYS.
WE'RE SETTIN' OUT FOR HEAVEN IN MY LITTLE SPEED BOAT...
NOW ANSWER YOUR PHONE.
HELLO?
HEY, BABE.
IT'S ME WITH THE BAD NEWS.
OH, HI, HONEY. WHAT'S UP?

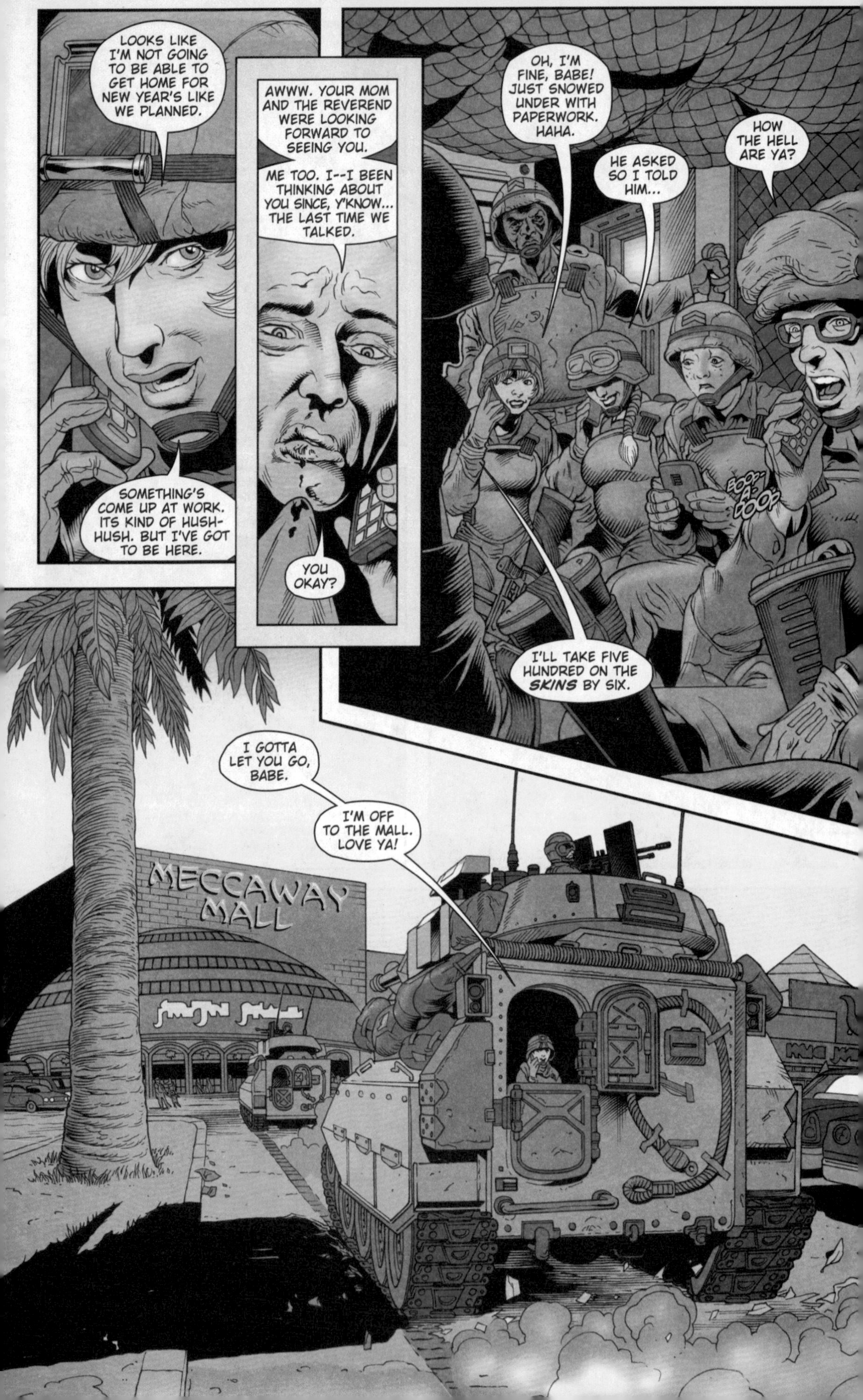
LOOKS LIKE I'M NOT GOING TO BE ABLE TO GET HOME FOR NEW YEAR'S LIKE WE PLANNED.
SOMETHING'S COME UP AT WORK. ITS KIND OF HUSH-HUSH. BUT I'VE GOT TO BE HERE.
AWWW. YOUR MOM AND THE REVEREND WERE LOOKING FORWARD TO SEEING YOU.
ME TOO. I--I BEEN THINKING ABOUT YOU SINCE, Y'KNOW... THE LAST TIME WE TALKED.
YOU OKAY?
OH, I'M FINE, BABE! JUST SNOWED UNDER WITH PAPERWORK. HAHA.
HE ASKED SO I TOLD HIM...
HOW THE HELL ARE YA?
BOOP-A-DOOP
I'LL TAKE FIVE HUNDRED ON THE *SKINS* BY SIX.
I GOTTA LET YOU GO, BABE.
I'M OFF TO THE MALL. LOVE YA!
MECCAWAY MALL

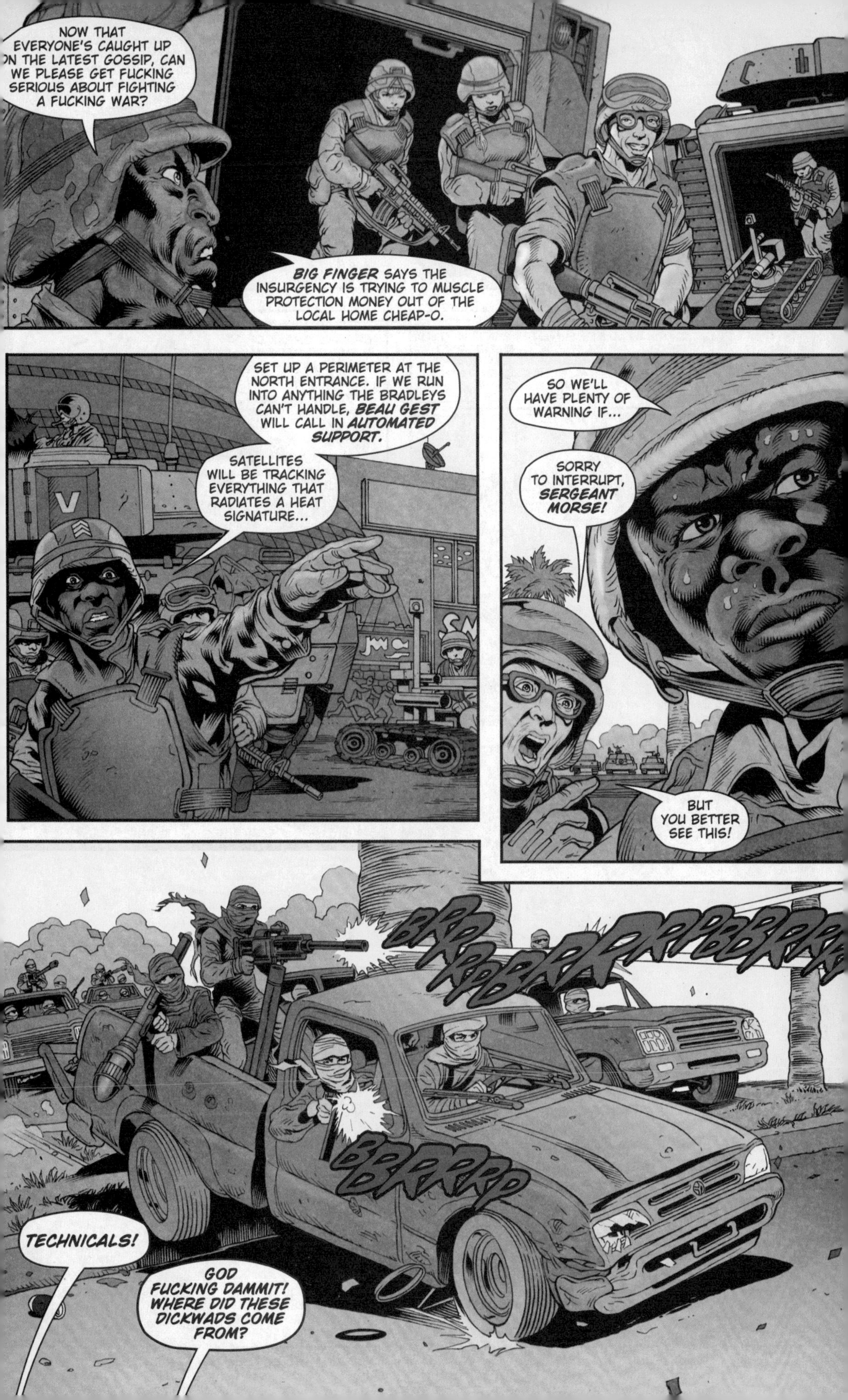
NOW THAT EVERYONE'S CAUGHT UP ON THE LATEST GOSSIP, CAN WE PLEASE GET FUCKING SERIOUS ABOUT FIGHTING A FUCKING WAR?
BIG FINGER SAYS THE INSURGENCY IS TRYING TO MUSCLE PROTECTION MONEY OUT OF THE LOCAL HOME CHEAP-O.
SET UP A PERIMETER AT THE NORTH ENTRANCE. IF WE RUN INTO ANYTHING THE BRADLEYS CAN'T HANDLE, BEAU GEST WILL CALL IN AUTOMATED SUPPORT.
SATELLITES WILL BE TRACKING EVERYTHING THAT RADIATES A HEAT SIGNATURE...
SO WE'LL HAVE PLENTY OF WARNING IF...
SORRY TO INTERRUPT, SERGEANT MORSE!
BUT YOU BETTER SEE THIS!
BRRRRBBRRRRRRRBBRRRR
BRRRRRP
TECHNICALS!
GOD FUCKING DAMMIT! WHERE DID THESE DICKWADS COME FROM?

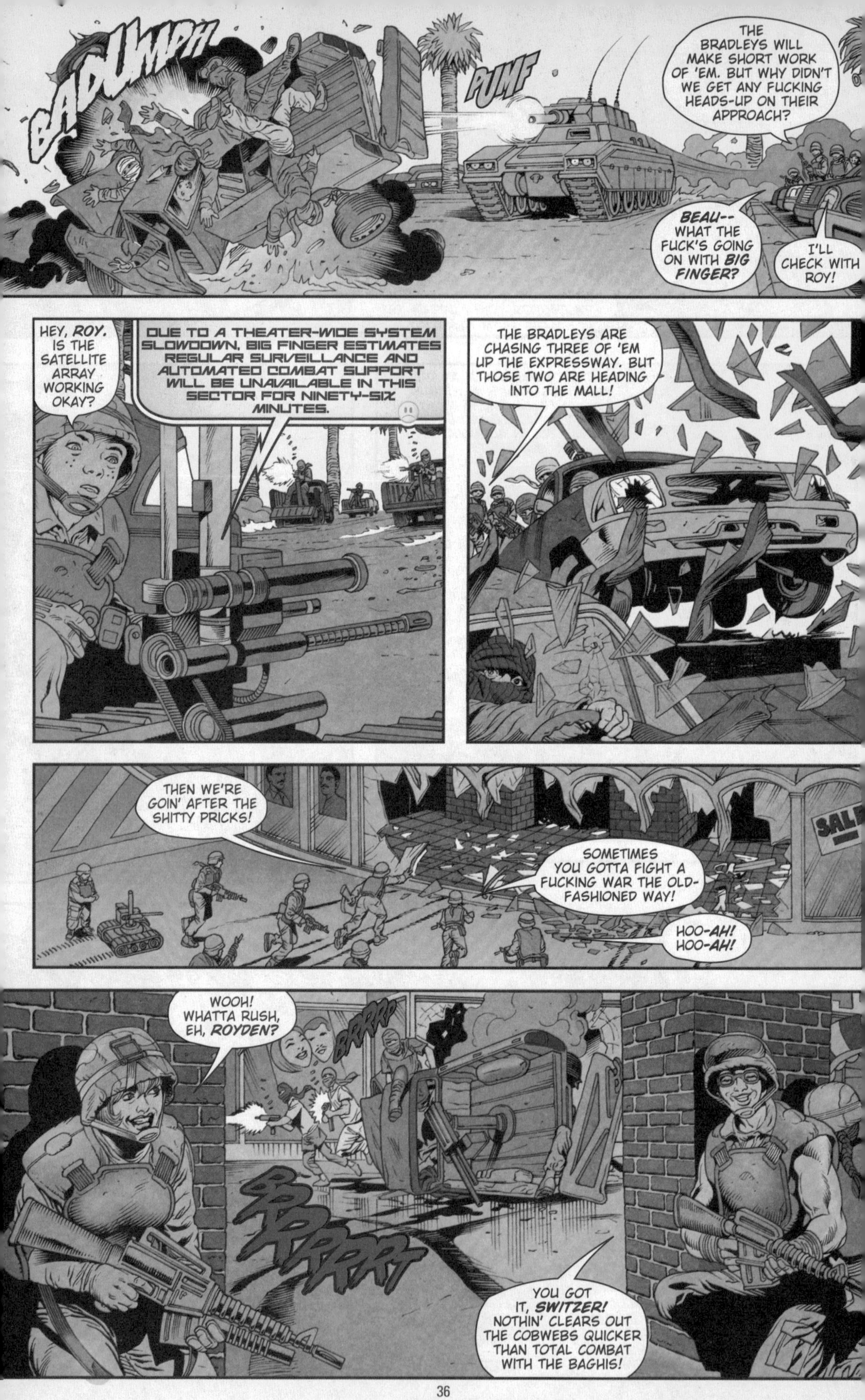
BADUMPH
PUMF
THE BRADLEYS WILL MAKE SHORT WORK OF 'EM. BUT WHY DIDN'T WE GET ANY FUCKING HEADS-UP ON THEIR APPROACH?
BEAU-- WHAT THE FUCK'S GOING ON WITH BIG FINGER?
I'LL CHECK WITH ROY!
HEY, ROY. IS THE SATELLITE ARRAY WORKING OKAY?
DUE TO A THEATER-WIDE SYSTEM SLOWDOWN, BIG FINGER ESTIMATES REGULAR SURVEILLANCE AND AUTOMATED COMBAT SUPPORT WILL BE UNAVAILABLE IN THIS SECTOR FOR NINETY-SIX MINUTES.
THE BRADLEYS ARE CHASING THREE OF 'EM UP THE EXPRESSWAY. BUT THOSE TWO ARE HEADING INTO THE MALL!
THEN WE'RE GOIN' AFTER THE SHITTY PRICKS!
SOMETIMES YOU GOTTA FIGHT A FUCKING WAR THE OLD-FASHIONED WAY!
HOO-AH! HOO-AH!
WOOH! WHATTA RUSH, EH, ROYDEN?
BRRRP
BRRRRRT
YOU GOT IT, SWITZER! NOTHIN' CLEARS OUT THE COBWEBS QUICKER THAN TOTAL COMBAT WITH THE BAGHIS!

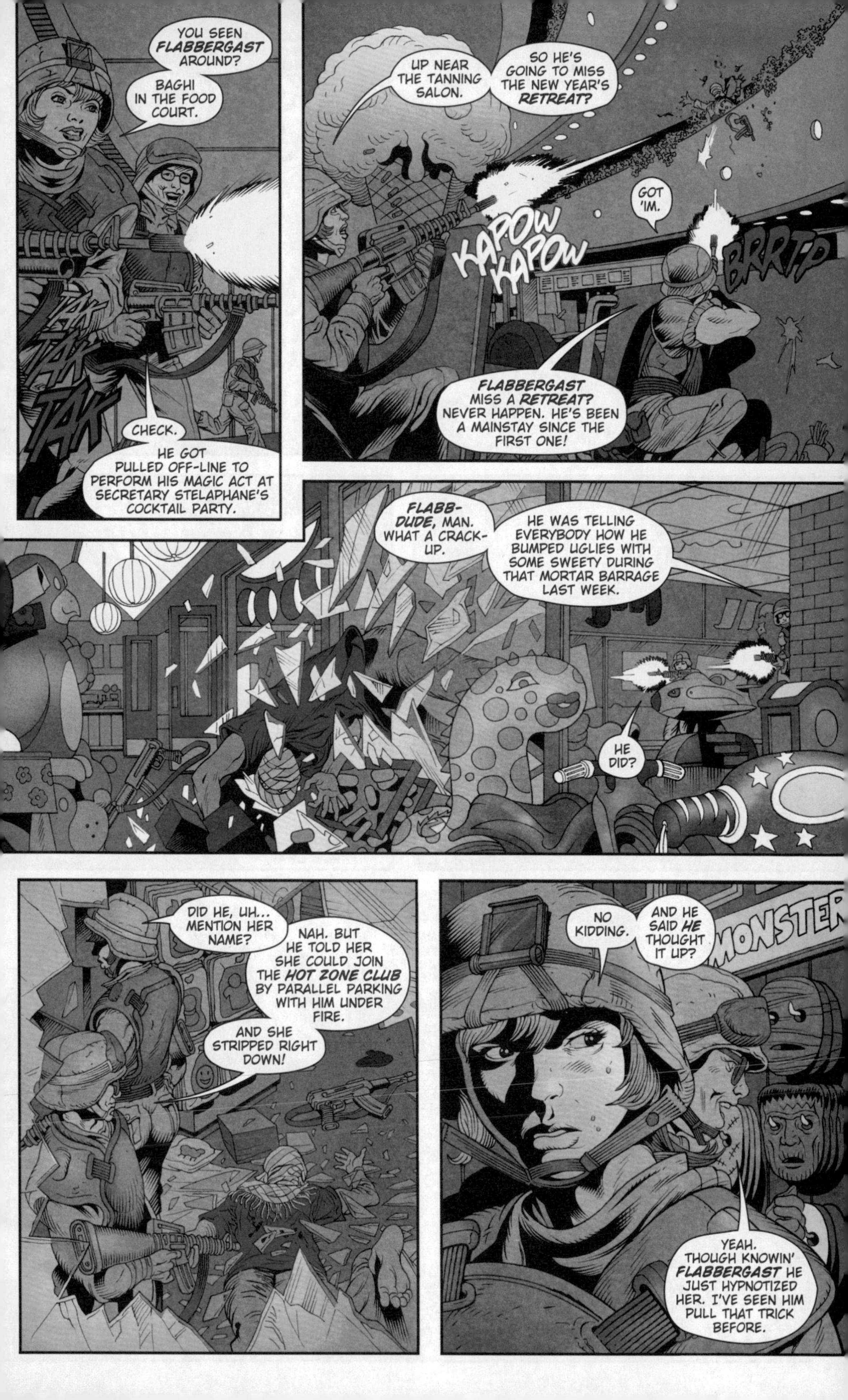
YOU SEEN FLABBERGAST AROUND?
BAGHI IN THE FOOD COURT.
TAK TAK TAK
CHECK.
HE GOT PULLED OFF-LINE TO PERFORM HIS MAGIC ACT AT SECRETARY STELAPHANE'S COCKTAIL PARTY.
UP NEAR THE TANNING SALON.
SO HE'S GOING TO MISS THE NEW YEAR'S RETREAT?
GOT 'IM.
KAPOW KAPOW
BRRTP
FLABBERGAST MISS A RETREAT? NEVER HAPPEN. HE'S BEEN A MAINSTAY SINCE THE FIRST ONE!
FLABB-DUDE, MAN. WHAT A CRACK-UP.
HE WAS TELLING EVERYBODY HOW HE BUMPED UGLIES WITH SOME SWEETY DURING THAT MORTAR BARRAGE LAST WEEK.
HE DID?
DID HE, UH... MENTION HER NAME?
NAH. BUT HE TOLD HER SHE COULD JOIN THE HOT ZONE CLUB BY PARALLEL PARKING WITH HIM UNDER FIRE.
AND SHE STRIPPED RIGHT DOWN!
NO KIDDING.
AND HE SAID HE THOUGHT IT UP?
MONSTER
YEAH. THOUGH KNOWIN' FLABBERGAST HE JUST HYPNOTIZED HER. I'VE SEEN HIM PULL THAT TRICK BEFORE.

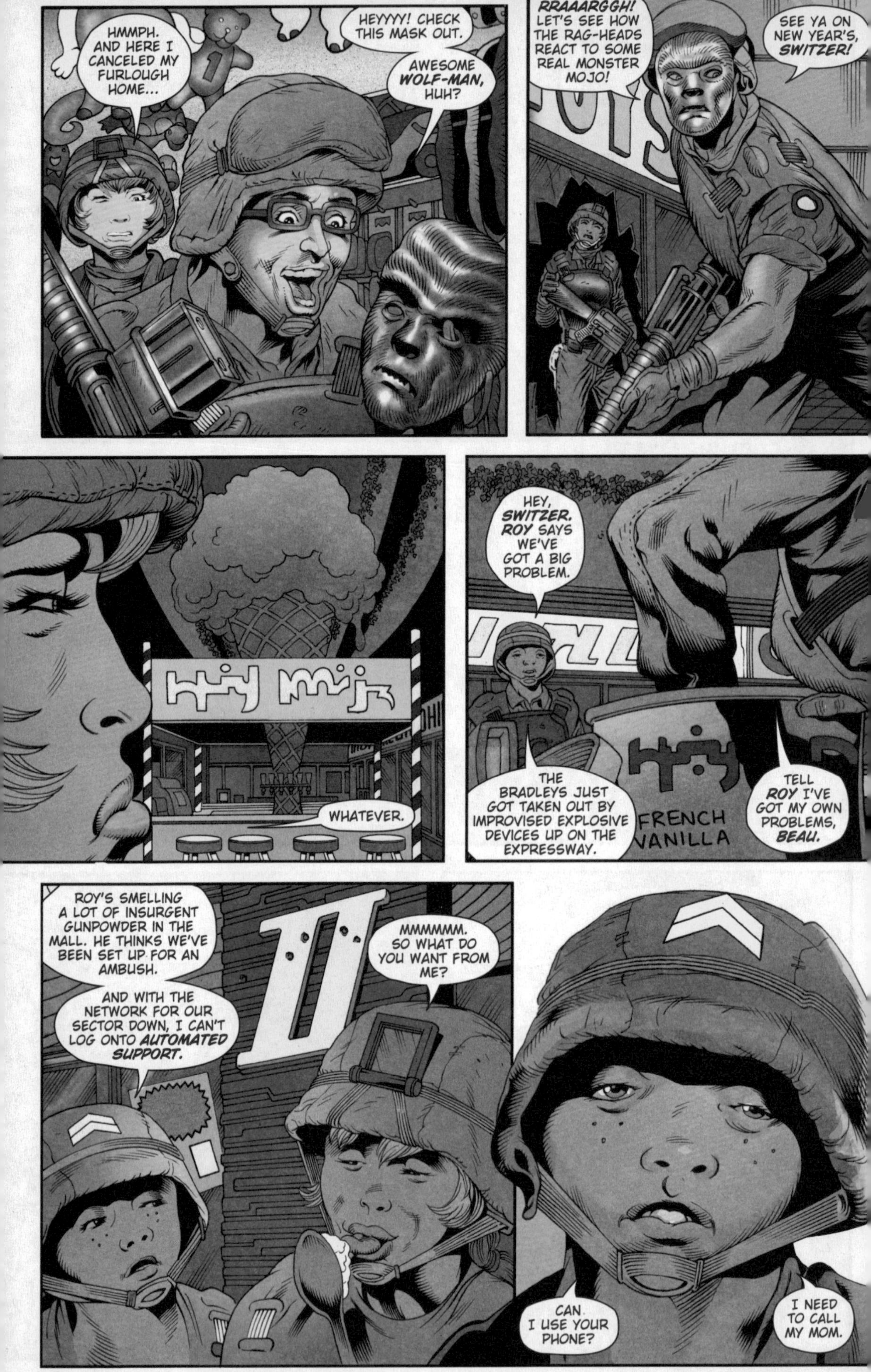

HMMPH. AND HERE I CANCELED MY FURLOUGH HOME...
HEYYYY! CHECK THIS MASK OUT.
AWESOME WOLF-MAN, HUH?
RRAAARGGH! LET'S SEE HOW THE RAG-HEADS REACT TO SOME REAL MONSTER MOJO!
SEE YA ON NEW YEAR'S, SWITZER!
WHATEVER.
HEY, SWITZER. ROY SAYS WE'VE GOT A BIG PROBLEM.
THE BRADLEYS JUST GOT TAKEN OUT BY IMPROVISED EXPLOSIVE DEVICES UP ON THE EXPRESSWAY.
FRENCH VANILLA
TELL ROY I'VE GOT MY OWN PROBLEMS, BEAU.
ROY'S SMELLING A LOT OF INSURGENT GUNPOWDER IN THE MALL. HE THINKS WE'VE BEEN SET UP FOR AN AMBUSH.
AND WITH THE NETWORK FOR OUR SECTOR DOWN, I CAN'T LOG ONTO AUTOMATED SUPPORT.
MMMMMM. SO WHAT DO YOU WANT FROM ME?
CAN I USE YOUR PHONE?
I NEED TO CALL MY MOM.

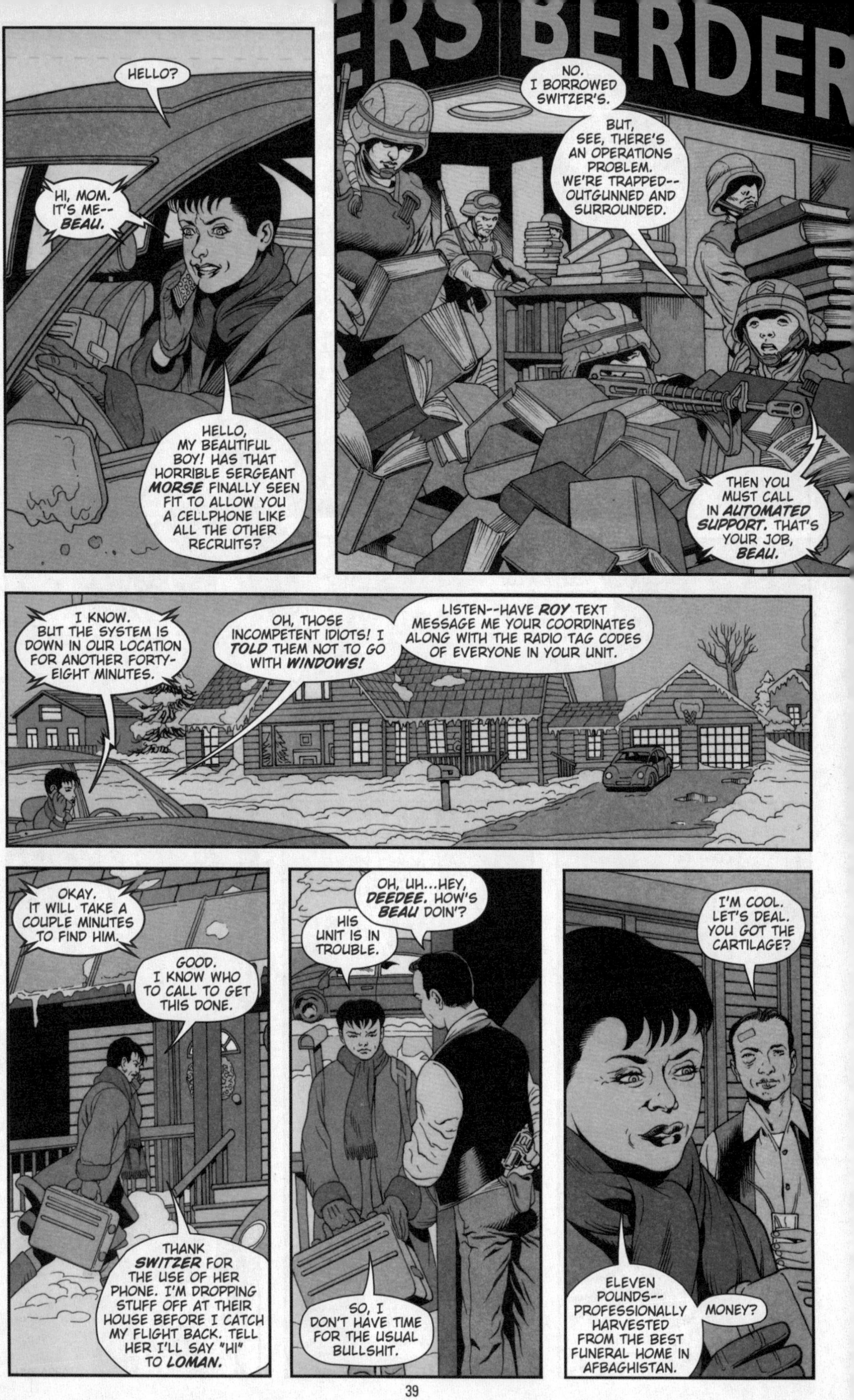
ERS BERDER
HELLO?
HI, MOM. IT'S ME--BEAU.
HELLO, MY BEAUTIFUL BOY! HAS THAT HORRIBLE SERGEANT MORSE FINALLY SEEN FIT TO ALLOW YOU A CELLPHONE LIKE ALL THE OTHER RECRUITS?
NO. I BORROWED SWITZER'S.
BUT, SEE, THERE'S AN OPERATIONS PROBLEM. WE'RE TRAPPED--OUTGUNNED AND SURROUNDED.
THEN YOU MUST CALL IN AUTOMATED SUPPORT. THAT'S YOUR JOB, BEAU.
I KNOW. BUT THE SYSTEM IS DOWN IN OUR LOCATION FOR ANOTHER FORTY-EIGHT MINUTES.
OH, THOSE INCOMPETENT IDIOTS! I TOLD THEM NOT TO GO WITH WINDOWS!
LISTEN--HAVE ROY TEXT MESSAGE ME YOUR COORDINATES ALONG WITH THE RADIO TAG CODES OF EVERYONE IN YOUR UNIT.
OKAY. IT WILL TAKE A COUPLE MINUTES TO FIND HIM.
GOOD. I KNOW WHO TO CALL TO GET THIS DONE.
THANK SWITZER FOR THE USE OF HER PHONE. I'M DROPPING STUFF OFF AT THEIR HOUSE BEFORE I CATCH MY FLIGHT BACK. TELL HER I'LL SAY "HI" TO LOMAN.
OH, UH...HEY, DEEDEE. HOW'S BEAU DOIN'?
HIS UNIT IS IN TROUBLE.
SO, I DON'T HAVE TIME FOR THE USUAL BULLSHIT.
I'M COOL. LET'S DEAL. YOU GOT THE CARTILAGE?
ELEVEN POUNDS--PROFESSIONALLY HARVESTED FROM THE BEST FUNERAL HOME IN AFBAGHISTAN.
MONEY?

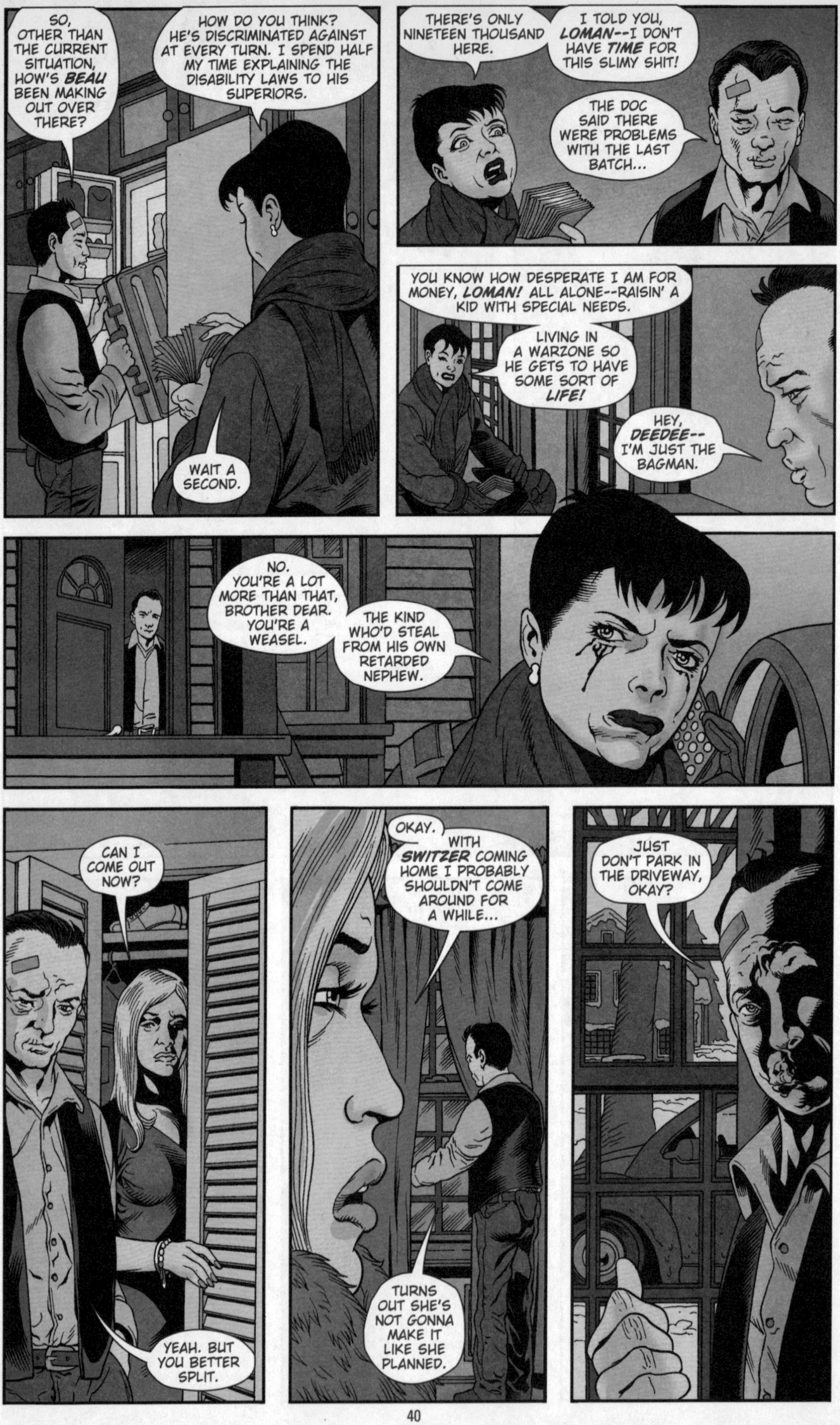
SO, OTHER THAN THE CURRENT SITUATION, HOW'S BEAU BEEN MAKING OUT OVER THERE?
HOW DO YOU THINK? HE'S DISCRIMINATED AGAINST AT EVERY TURN. I SPEND HALF MY TIME EXPLAINING THE DISABILITY LAWS TO HIS SUPERIORS.
WAIT A SECOND.
THERE'S ONLY NINETEEN THOUSAND HERE.
I TOLD YOU, LOMAN--I DON'T HAVE TIME FOR THIS SLIMY SHIT!
THE DOC SAID THERE WERE PROBLEMS WITH THE LAST BATCH...
YOU KNOW HOW DESPERATE I AM FOR MONEY, LOMAN! ALL ALONE--RAISIN' A KID WITH SPECIAL NEEDS.
LIVING IN A WARZONE SO HE GETS TO HAVE SOME SORT OF LIFE!
HEY, DEEDEE-- I'M JUST THE BAGMAN.
NO. YOU'RE A LOT MORE THAN THAT, BROTHER DEAR. YOU'RE A WEASEL.
THE KIND WHO'D STEAL FROM HIS OWN RETARDED NEPHEW.
CAN I COME OUT NOW?
YEAH. BUT YOU BETTER SPLIT.
OKAY.
WITH SWITZER COMING HOME I PROBABLY SHOULDN'T COME AROUND FOR A WHILE...
TURNS OUT SHE'S NOT GONNA MAKE IT LIKE SHE PLANNED.
JUST DON'T PARK IN THE DRIVEWAY, OKAY?

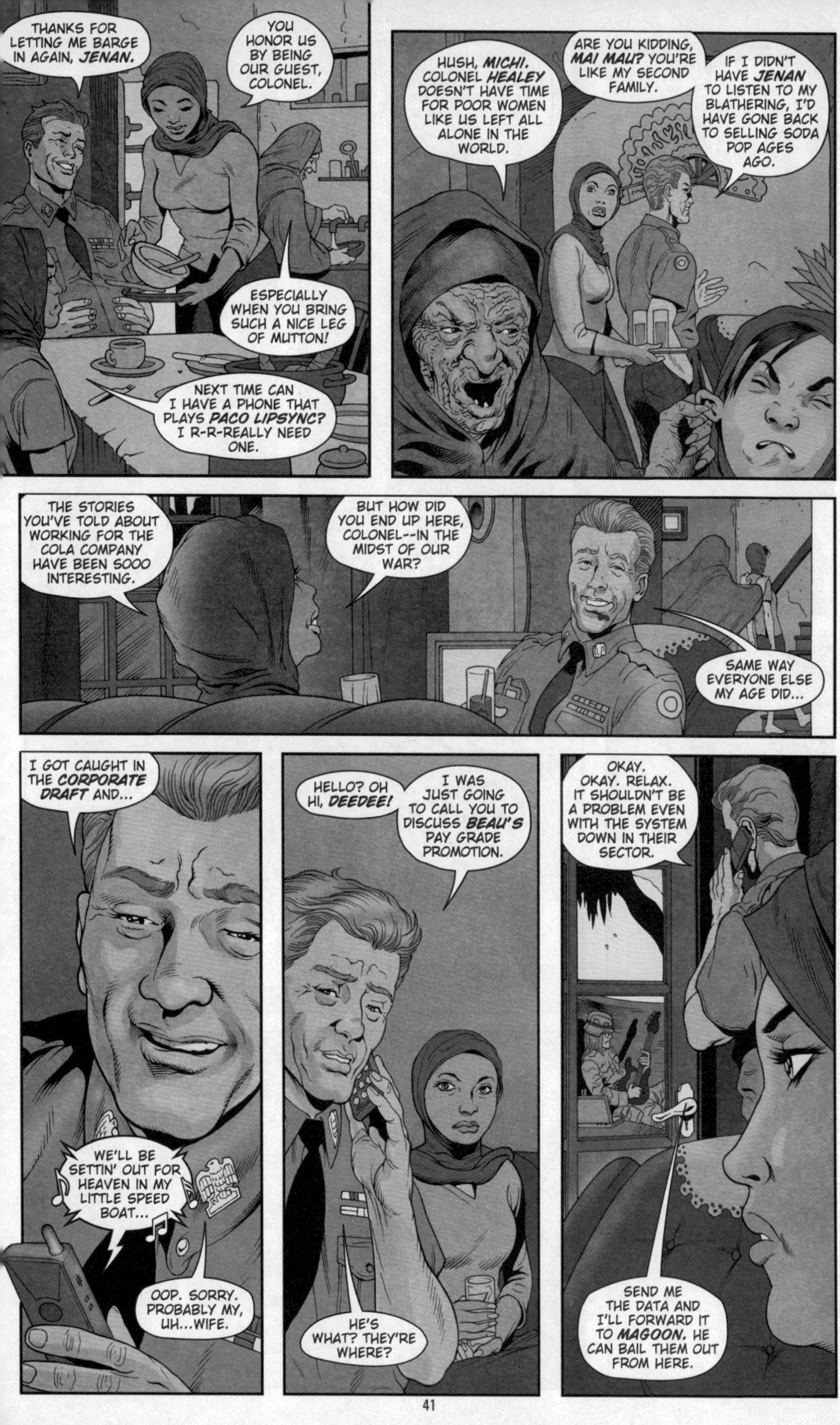
THANKS FOR LETTING ME BARGE IN AGAIN, JENAN.
YOU HONOR US BY BEING OUR GUEST, COLONEL.
ESPECIALLY WHEN YOU BRING SUCH A NICE LEG OF MUTTON!
NEXT TIME CAN I HAVE A PHONE THAT PLAYS PACO LIPSYNC? I R-R-REALLY NEED ONE.
HUSH, MICHI. COLONEL HEALEY DOESN'T HAVE TIME FOR POOR WOMEN LIKE US LEFT ALL ALONE IN THE WORLD.
ARE YOU KIDDING, MAI MAU? YOU'RE LIKE MY SECOND FAMILY.
IF I DIDN'T HAVE JENAN TO LISTEN TO MY BLATHERING, I'D HAVE GONE BACK TO SELLING SODA POP AGES AGO.
THE STORIES YOU'VE TOLD ABOUT WORKING FOR THE COLA COMPANY HAVE BEEN SOOO INTERESTING.
BUT HOW DID YOU END UP HERE, COLONEL--IN THE MIDST OF OUR WAR?
SAME WAY EVERYONE ELSE MY AGE DID...
I GOT CAUGHT IN THE CORPORATE DRAFT AND...
WE'LL BE SETTIN' OUT FOR HEAVEN IN MY LITTLE SPEED BOAT...
OOP. SORRY. PROBABLY MY, UH...WIFE.
HELLO? OH HI, DEEDEE!
I WAS JUST GOING TO CALL YOU TO DISCUSS BEAU'S PAY GRADE PROMOTION.
HE'S WHAT? THEY'RE WHERE?
OKAY. OKAY. RELAX. IT SHOULDN'T BE A PROBLEM EVEN WITH THE SYSTEM DOWN IN THEIR SECTOR.
SEND ME THE DATA AND I'LL FORWARD IT TO MAGOON. HE CAN BAIL THEM OUT FROM HERE.

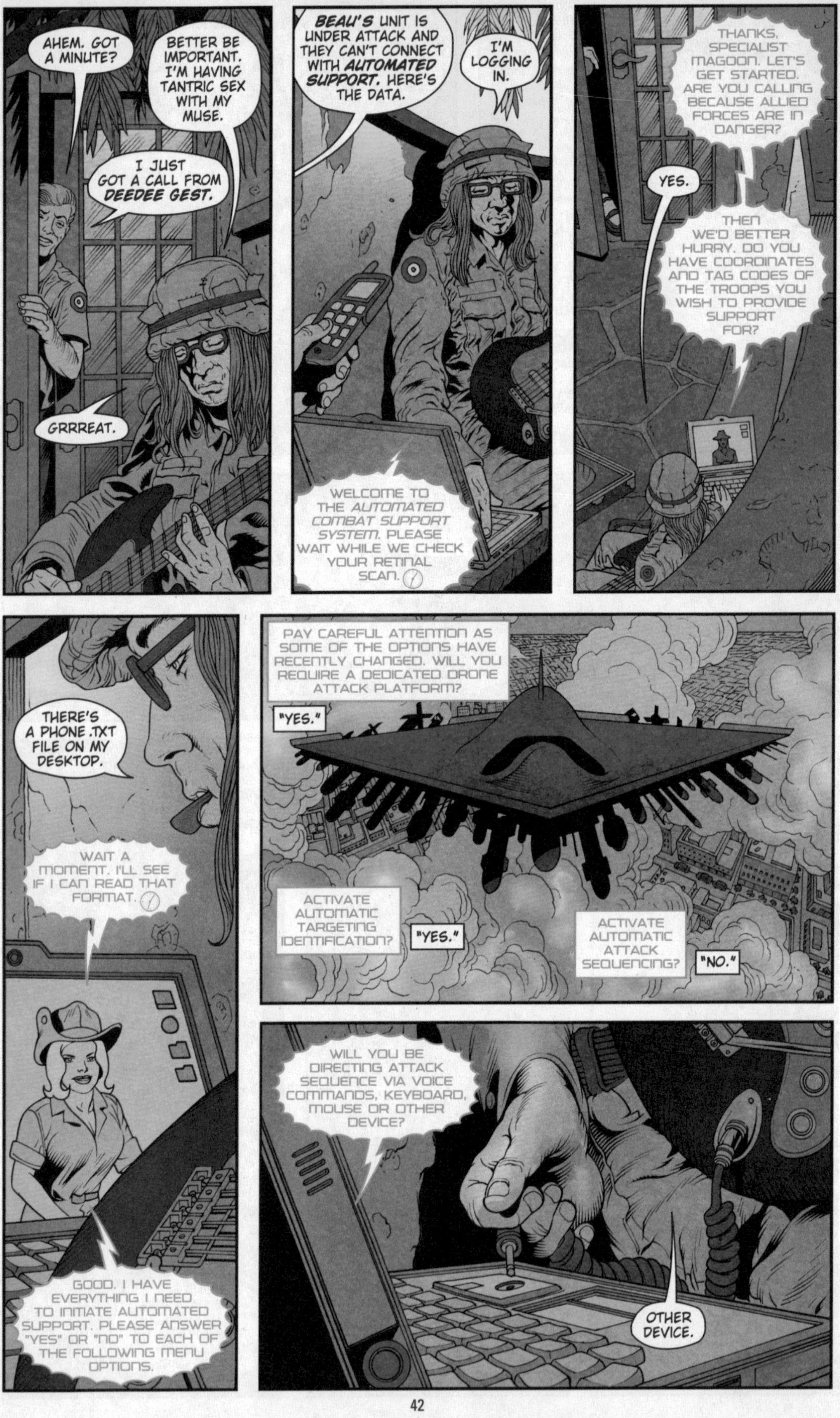
AHEM. GOT A MINUTE?
BETTER BE IMPORTANT. I'M HAVING TANTRIC SEX WITH MY MUSE.
I JUST GOT A CALL FROM DEEDEE GEST.
GRRREAT.
BEAU'S UNIT IS UNDER ATTACK AND THEY CAN'T CONNECT WITH AUTOMATED SUPPORT. HERE'S THE DATA.
I'M LOGGING IN.
WELCOME TO THE AUTOMATED COMBAT SUPPORT SYSTEM. PLEASE WAIT WHILE WE CHECK YOUR RETINAL SCAN.
THANKS, SPECIALIST MAGOON. LET'S GET STARTED. ARE YOU CALLING BECAUSE ALLIED FORCES ARE IN DANGER?
YES.
THEN WE'D BETTER HURRY. DO YOU HAVE COORDINATES AND TAG CODES OF THE TROOPS YOU WISH TO PROVIDE SUPPORT FOR?
THERE'S A PHONE .TXT FILE ON MY DESKTOP.
WAIT A MOMENT. I'LL SEE IF I CAN READ THAT FORMAT.
GOOD. I HAVE EVERYTHING I NEED. TO INITIATE AUTOMATED SUPPORT. PLEASE ANSWER "YES" OR "NO" TO EACH OF THE FOLLOWING MENU OPTIONS.
PAY CAREFUL ATTENTION AS SOME OF THE OPTIONS HAVE RECENTLY CHANGED. WILL YOU REQUIRE A DEDICATED DRONE ATTACK PLATFORM?
"YES."
ACTIVATE AUTOMATIC TARGETING IDENTIFICATION?
"YES."
ACTIVATE AUTOMATIC ATTACK SEQUENCING?
"NO."
WILL YOU BE DIRECTING ATTACK SEQUENCE VIA VOICE COMMANDS, KEYBOARD, MOUSE OR OTHER DEVICE?
OTHER DEVICE.

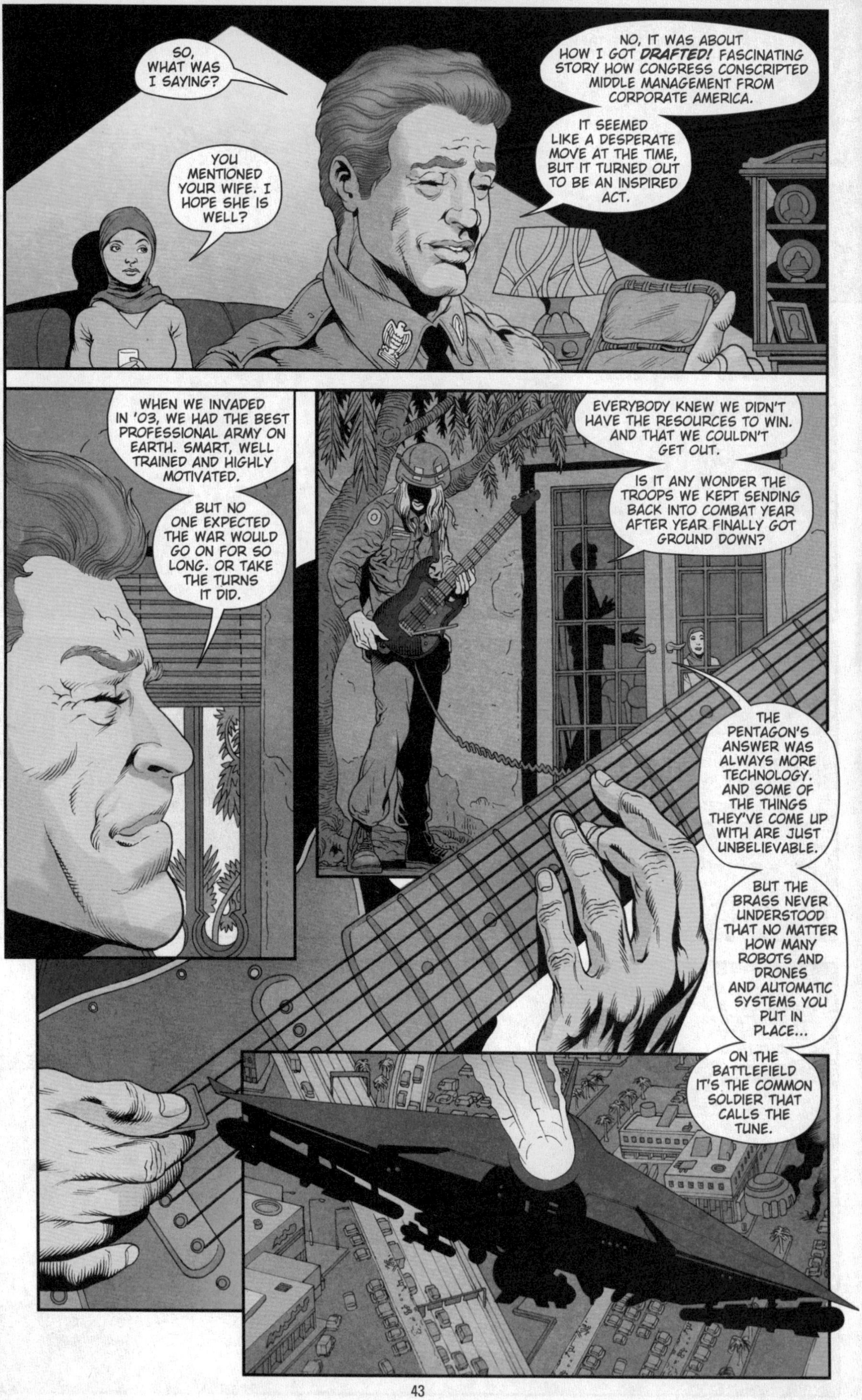
SO, WHAT WAS I SAYING?
YOU MENTIONED YOUR WIFE. I HOPE SHE IS WELL?
NO, IT WAS ABOUT HOW I GOT DRAFTED! FASCINATING STORY HOW CONGRESS CONSCRIPTED MIDDLE MANAGEMENT FROM CORPORATE AMERICA.
IT SEEMED LIKE A DESPERATE MOVE AT THE TIME, BUT IT TURNED OUT TO BE AN INSPIRED ACT.
WHEN WE INVADED IN '03, WE HAD THE BEST PROFESSIONAL ARMY ON EARTH. SMART, WELL TRAINED AND HIGHLY MOTIVATED.
BUT NO ONE EXPECTED THE WAR WOULD GO ON FOR SO LONG. OR TAKE THE TURNS IT DID.
EVERYBODY KNEW WE DIDN'T HAVE THE RESOURCES TO WIN. AND THAT WE COULDN'T GET OUT.
IS IT ANY WONDER THE TROOPS WE KEPT SENDING BACK INTO COMBAT YEAR AFTER YEAR FINALLY GOT GROUND DOWN?
THE PENTAGON'S ANSWER WAS ALWAYS MORE TECHNOLOGY. AND SOME OF THE THINGS THEY'VE COME UP WITH ARE JUST UNBELIEVABLE.
BUT THE BRASS NEVER UNDERSTOOD THAT NO MATTER HOW MANY ROBOTS AND DRONES AND AUTOMATIC SYSTEMS YOU PUT IN PLACE...
ON THE BATTLEFIELD IT'S THE COMMON SOLDIER THAT CALLS THE TUNE.

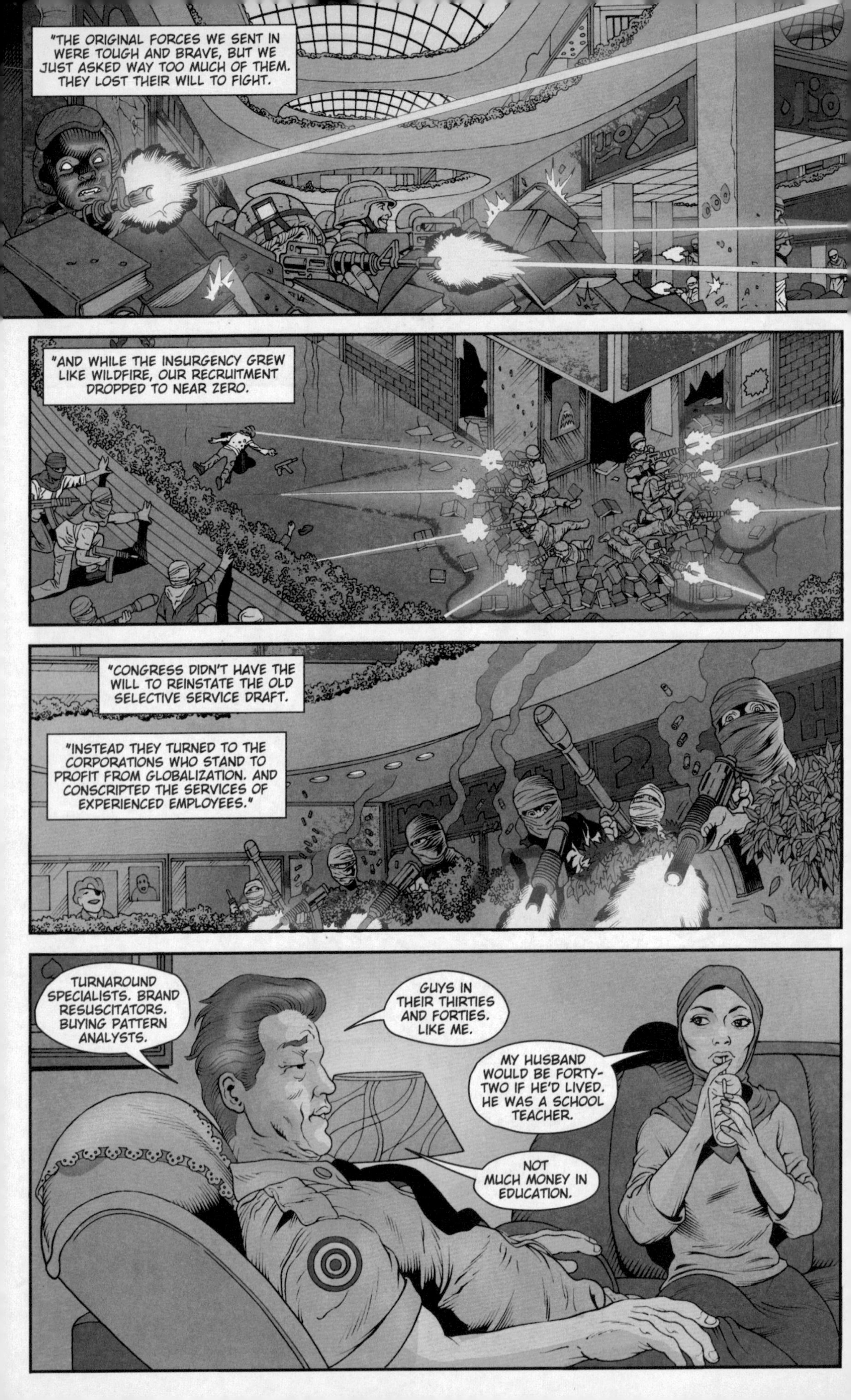
"THE ORIGINAL FORCES WE SENT IN WERE TOUGH AND BRAVE, BUT WE JUST ASKED WAY TOO MUCH OF THEM. THEY LOST THEIR WILL TO FIGHT.
"AND WHILE THE INSURGENCY GREW LIKE WILDFIRE, OUR RECRUITMENT DROPPED TO NEAR ZERO.
"CONGRESS DIDN'T HAVE THE WILL TO REINSTATE THE OLD SELECTIVE SERVICE DRAFT.
"INSTEAD THEY TURNED TO THE CORPORATIONS WHO STAND TO PROFIT FROM GLOBALIZATION. AND CONSCRIPTED THE SERVICES OF EXPERIENCED EMPLOYEES."
TURNAROUND SPECIALISTS. BRAND RESUSCITATORS. BUYING PATTERN ANALYSTS.
GUYS IN THEIR THIRTIES AND FORTIES. LIKE ME.
MY HUSBAND WOULD BE FORTY-TWO IF HE'D LIVED. HE WAS A SCHOOL TEACHER.
NOT MUCH MONEY IN EDUCATION.

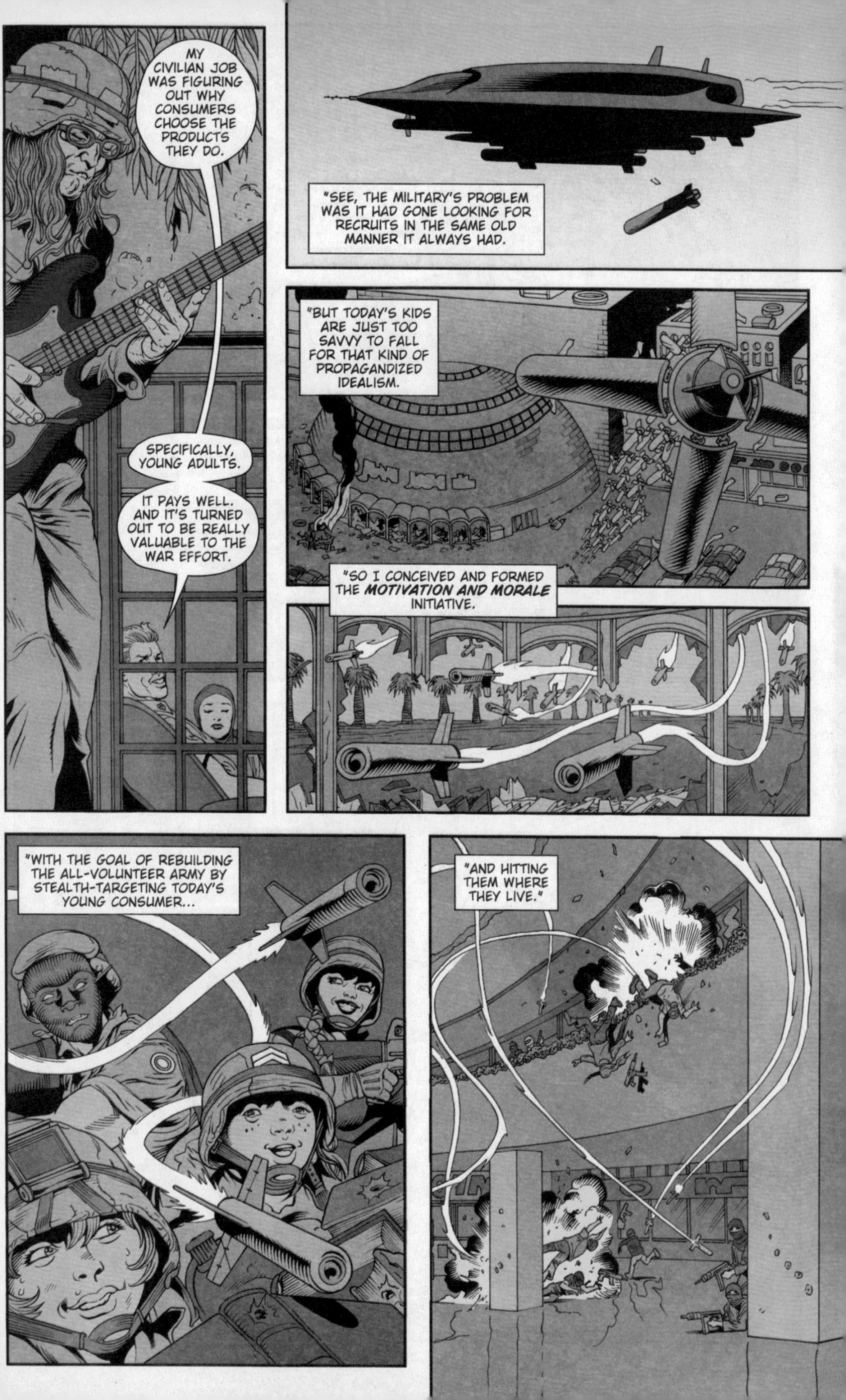

MY CIVILIAN JOB WAS FIGURING OUT WHY CONSUMERS CHOOSE THE PRODUCTS THEY DO.
SPECIFICALLY, YOUNG ADULTS.
IT PAYS WELL. AND IT'S TURNED OUT TO BE REALLY VALUABLE TO THE WAR EFFORT.
"SEE, THE MILITARY'S PROBLEM WAS IT HAD GONE LOOKING FOR RECRUITS IN THE SAME OLD MANNER IT ALWAYS HAD.
"BUT TODAY'S KIDS ARE JUST TOO SAVVY TO FALL FOR THAT KIND OF PROPAGANDIZED IDEALISM.
"SO I CONCEIVED AND FORMED THE MOTIVATION AND MORALE INITIATIVE.
"WITH THE GOAL OF REBUILDING THE ALL-VOLUNTEER ARMY BY STEALTH-TARGETING TODAY'S YOUNG CONSUMER...
"AND HITTING THEM WHERE THEY LIVE."

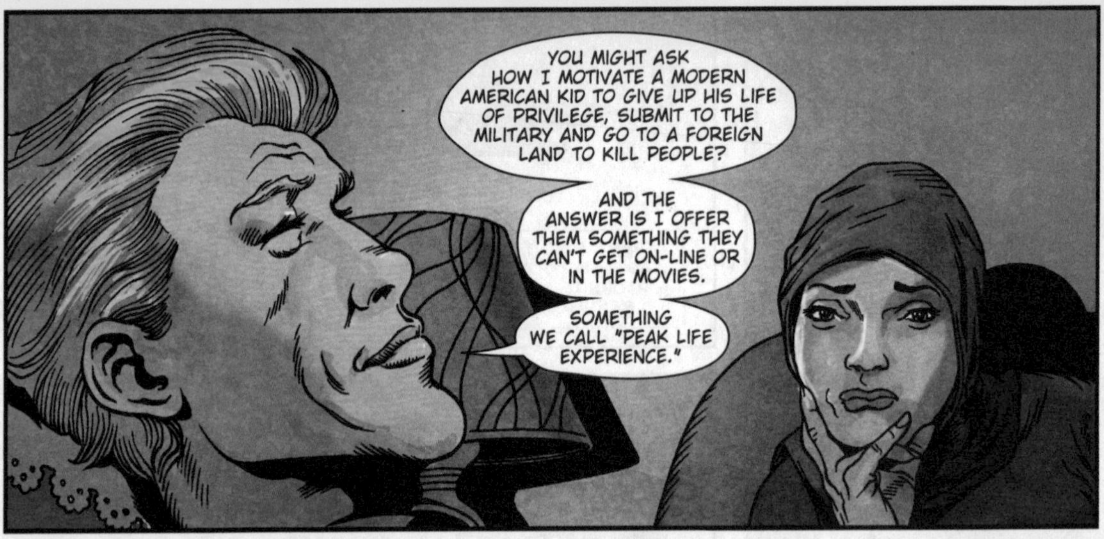
YOU MIGHT ASK HOW I MOTIVATE A MODERN AMERICAN KID TO GIVE UP HIS LIFE OF PRIVILEGE, SUBMIT TO THE MILITARY AND GO TO A FOREIGN LAND TO KILL PEOPLE?
AND THE ANSWER IS I OFFER THEM SOMETHING THEY CAN'T GET ON-LINE OR IN THE MOVIES.
SOMETHING WE CALL "PEAK LIFE EXPERIENCE."

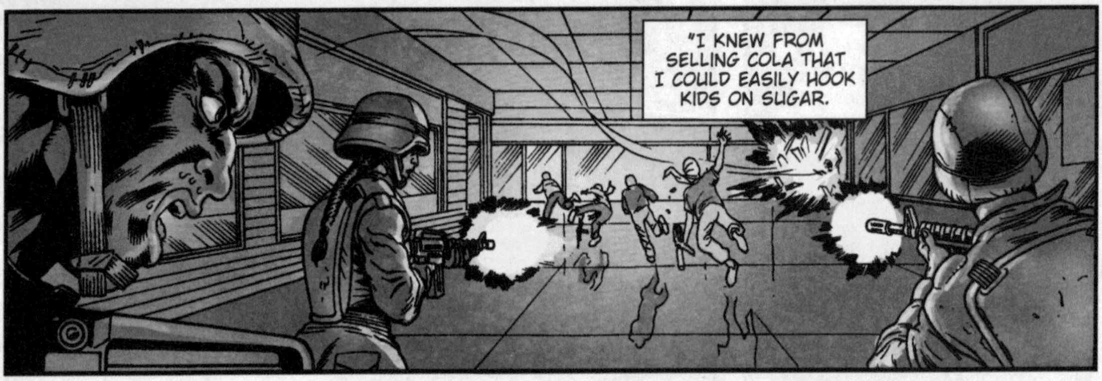
"I KNEW FROM SELLING COLA THAT I COULD EASILY HOOK KIDS ON SUGAR.

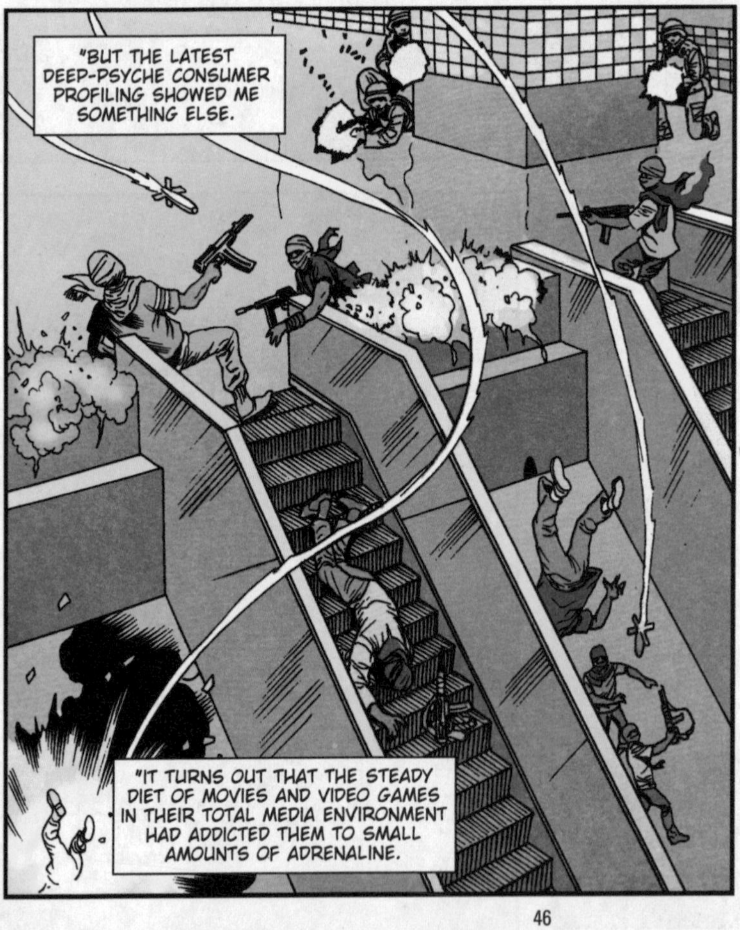
"BUT THE LATEST DEEP-PSYCHE CONSUMER PROFILING SHOWED ME SOMETHING ELSE.
"IT TURNS OUT THAT THE STEADY DIET OF MOVIES AND VIDEO GAMES IN THEIR TOTAL MEDIA ENVIRONMENT HAD ADDICTED THEM TO SMALL AMOUNTS OF ADRENALINE.

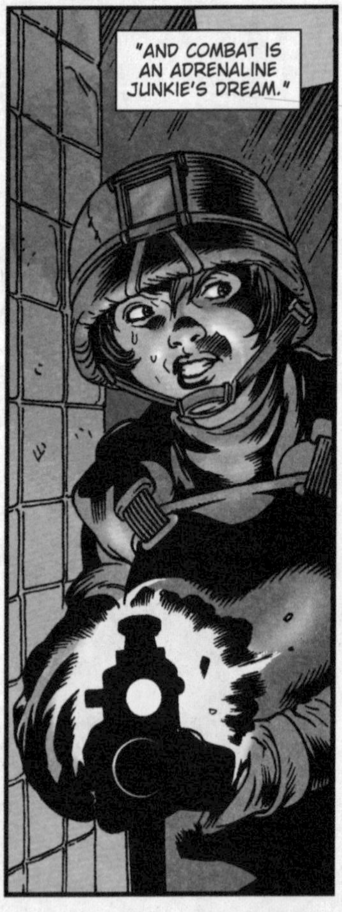
"AND COMBAT IS AN ADRENALINE JUNKIE'S DREAM."

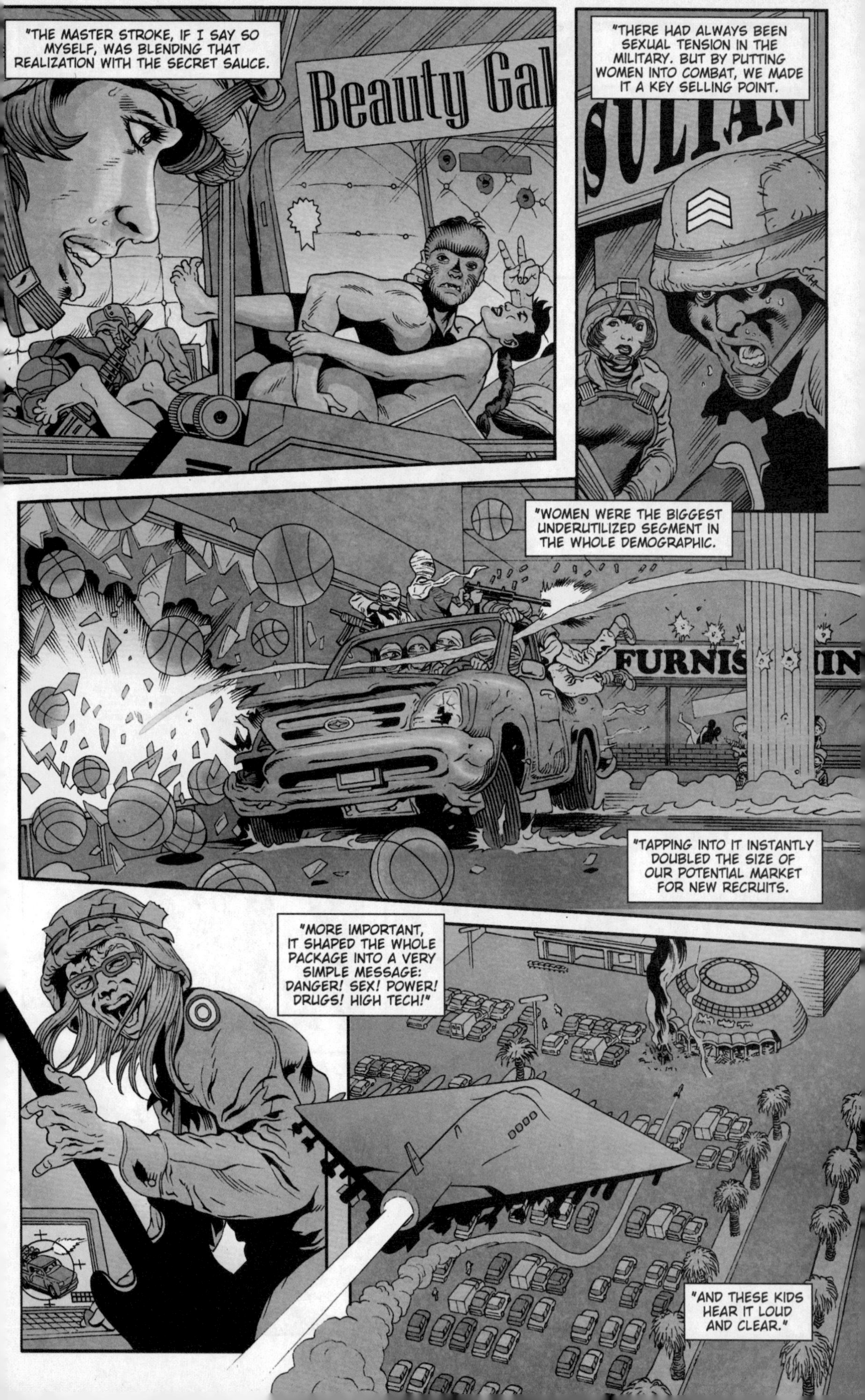
"THE MASTER STROKE, IF I SAY SO MYSELF, WAS BLENDING THAT REALIZATION WITH THE SECRET SAUCE.
Beauty Gal
"THERE HAD ALWAYS BEEN SEXUAL TENSION IN THE MILITARY. BUT BY PUTTING WOMEN INTO COMBAT, WE MADE IT A KEY SELLING POINT.
SULTAN
"WOMEN WERE THE BIGGEST UNDERUTILIZED SEGMENT IN THE WHOLE DEMOGRAPHIC.
FURNIS
"TAPPING INTO IT INSTANTLY DOUBLED THE SIZE OF OUR POTENTIAL MARKET FOR NEW RECRUITS.
"MORE IMPORTANT, IT SHAPED THE WHOLE PACKAGE INTO A VERY SIMPLE MESSAGE: DANGER! SEX! POWER! DRUGS! HIGH TECH!"
"AND THESE KIDS HEAR IT LOUD AND CLEAR."

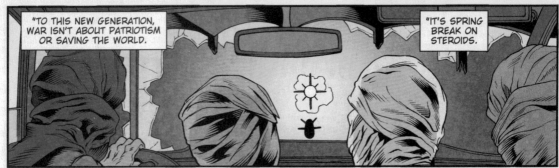

"TO THIS NEW GENERATION, WAR ISN'T ABOUT PATRIOTISM OR SAVING THE WORLD.

"IT'S SPRING BREAK ON STEROIDS.

"AND THE CAMPAIGN HAS WORKED. RECRUITMENT FOR COMBAT UNITS IS WAY UP.

"WE HAVE MOMENTUM ON THE BATTLEFIELD.

"THE TROOPS FEEL IT.

I FEEL IT TOO. MY SUPERIORS ARE ALREADY GROOMING ME FOR THE FAST TRACK. HELL, AFTER THIS IS OVER, I MIGHT EVEN END UP RUNNING FOR CONGRESS.

I LOVE MY WORK. I'M VERY SUCCESSFUL. I SHOULD BE HAPPY. BUT...

I WOULDN'T TELL THIS TO ANYONE ELSE, *JENAN*, BUT SOMEONE IS TRYING TO DESTROY EVERYTHING I'VE ACCOMPLISHED.

AND WHAT'S WORSE IS THAT THIS PERSON MIGHT BE VERY...

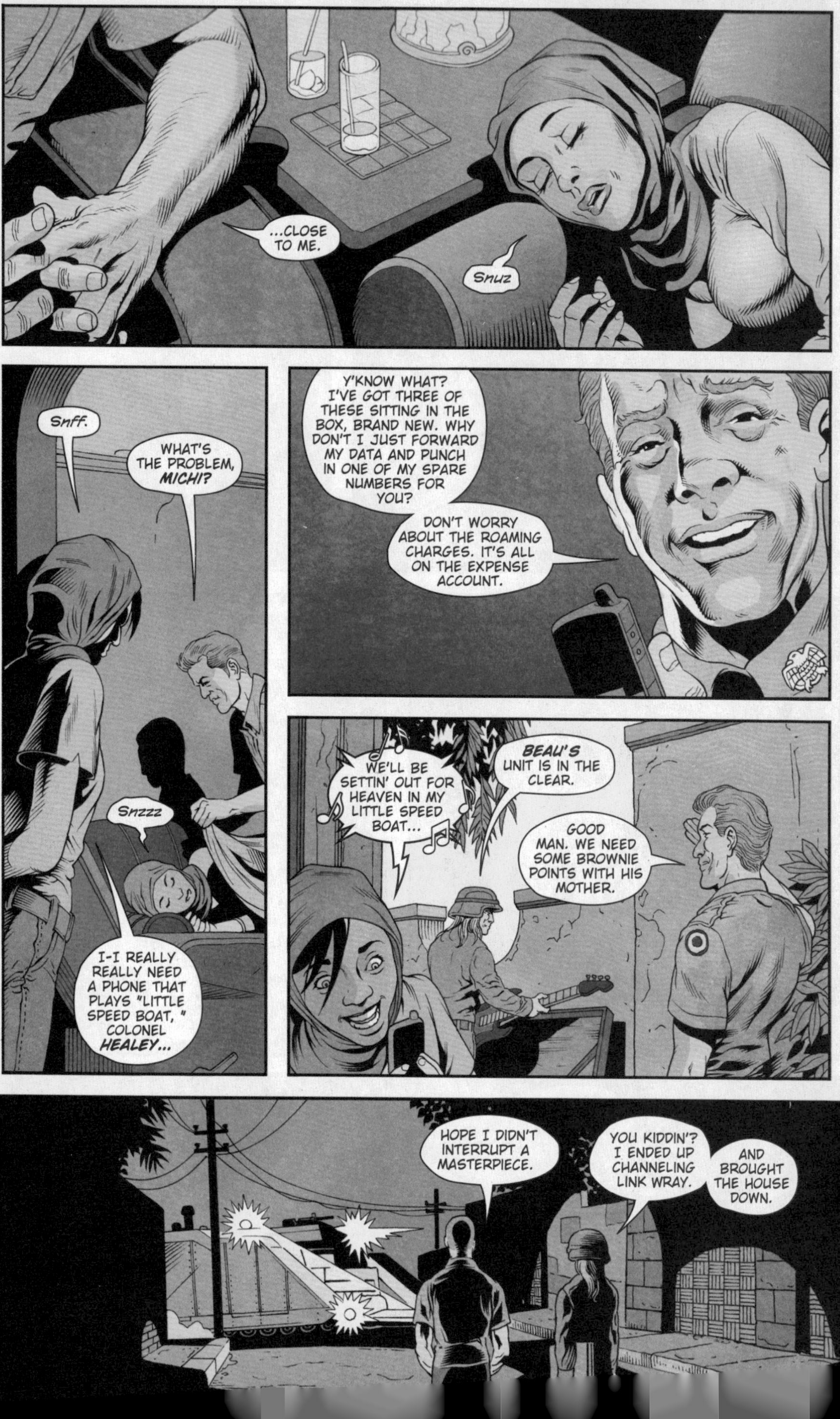
...CLOSE TO ME.
Snuz
Snff.
WHAT'S THE PROBLEM, MICHI?
Y'KNOW WHAT? I'VE GOT THREE OF THESE SITTING IN THE BOX, BRAND NEW. WHY DON'T I JUST FORWARD MY DATA AND PUNCH IN ONE OF MY SPARE NUMBERS FOR YOU?
DON'T WORRY ABOUT THE ROAMING CHARGES. IT'S ALL ON THE EXPENSE ACCOUNT.
Snzzz
I-I REALLY REALLY NEED A PHONE THAT PLAYS "LITTLE SPEED BOAT," COLONEL HEALEY...
WE'LL BE SETTIN' OUT FOR HEAVEN IN MY LITTLE SPEED BOAT...
BEAU'S UNIT IS IN THE CLEAR.
GOOD MAN. WE NEED SOME BROWNIE POINTS WITH HIS MOTHER.
HOPE I DIDN'T INTERRUPT A MASTERPIECE.
YOU KIDDIN'? I ENDED UP CHANNELING LINK WRAY.
AND BROUGHT THE HOUSE DOWN.

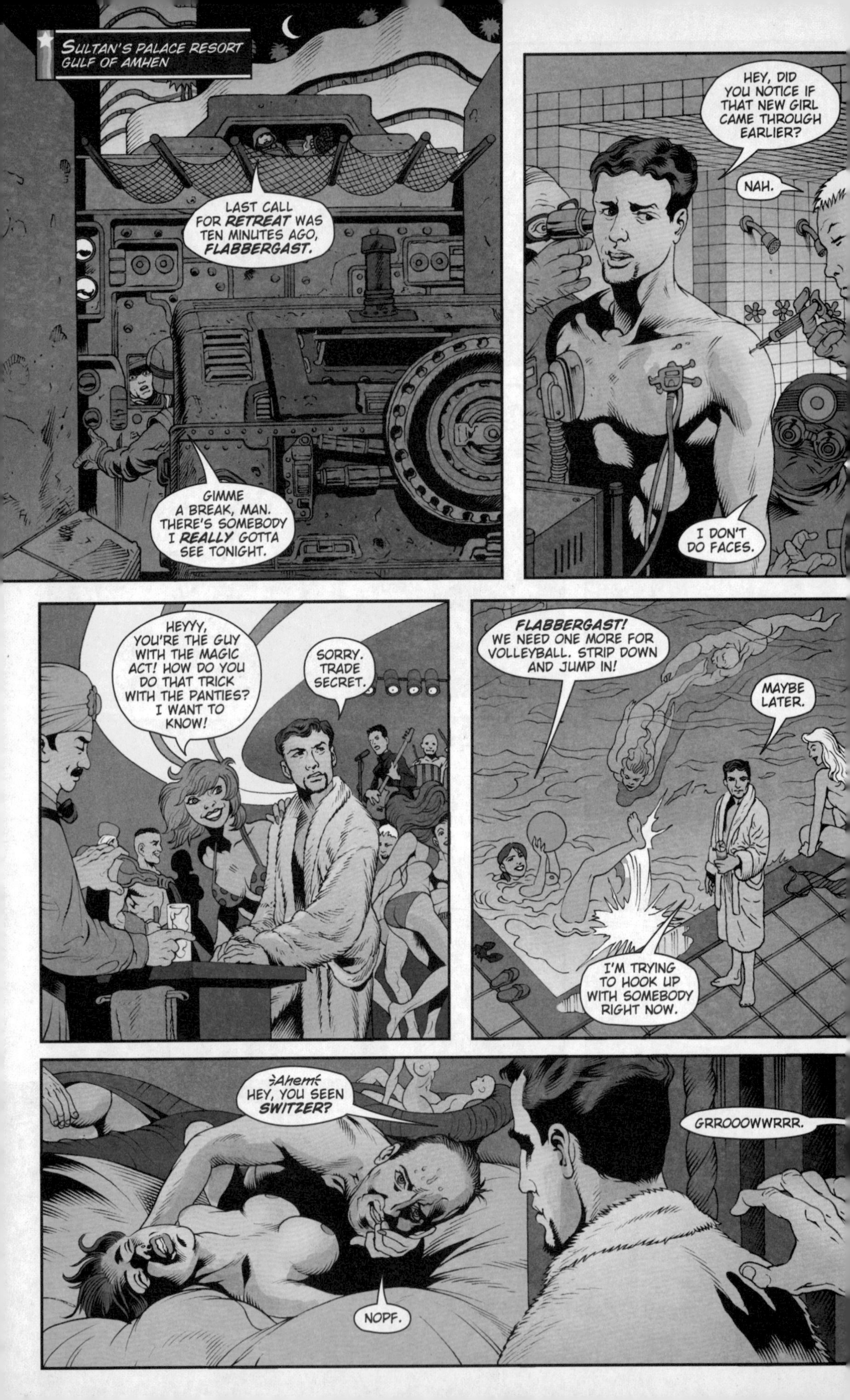
SULTAN'S PALACE RESORT
GULF OF AMHEN
LAST CALL FOR RETREAT WAS TEN MINUTES AGO, FLABBERGAST.
GIMME A BREAK, MAN. THERE'S SOMEBODY I REALLY GOTTA SEE TONIGHT.
HEY, DID YOU NOTICE IF THAT NEW GIRL CAME THROUGH EARLIER?
NAH.
I DON'T DO FACES.
HEYYY, YOU'RE THE GUY WITH THE MAGIC ACT! HOW DO YOU DO THAT TRICK WITH THE PANTIES? I WANT TO KNOW!
SORRY. TRADE SECRET.
FLABBERGAST! WE NEED ONE MORE FOR VOLLEYBALL. STRIP DOWN AND JUMP IN!
MAYBE LATER.
I'M TRYING TO HOOK UP WITH SOMEBODY RIGHT NOW.
Ahem
HEY, YOU SEEN SWITZER?
GRROOOWWRRR.
NOPF.

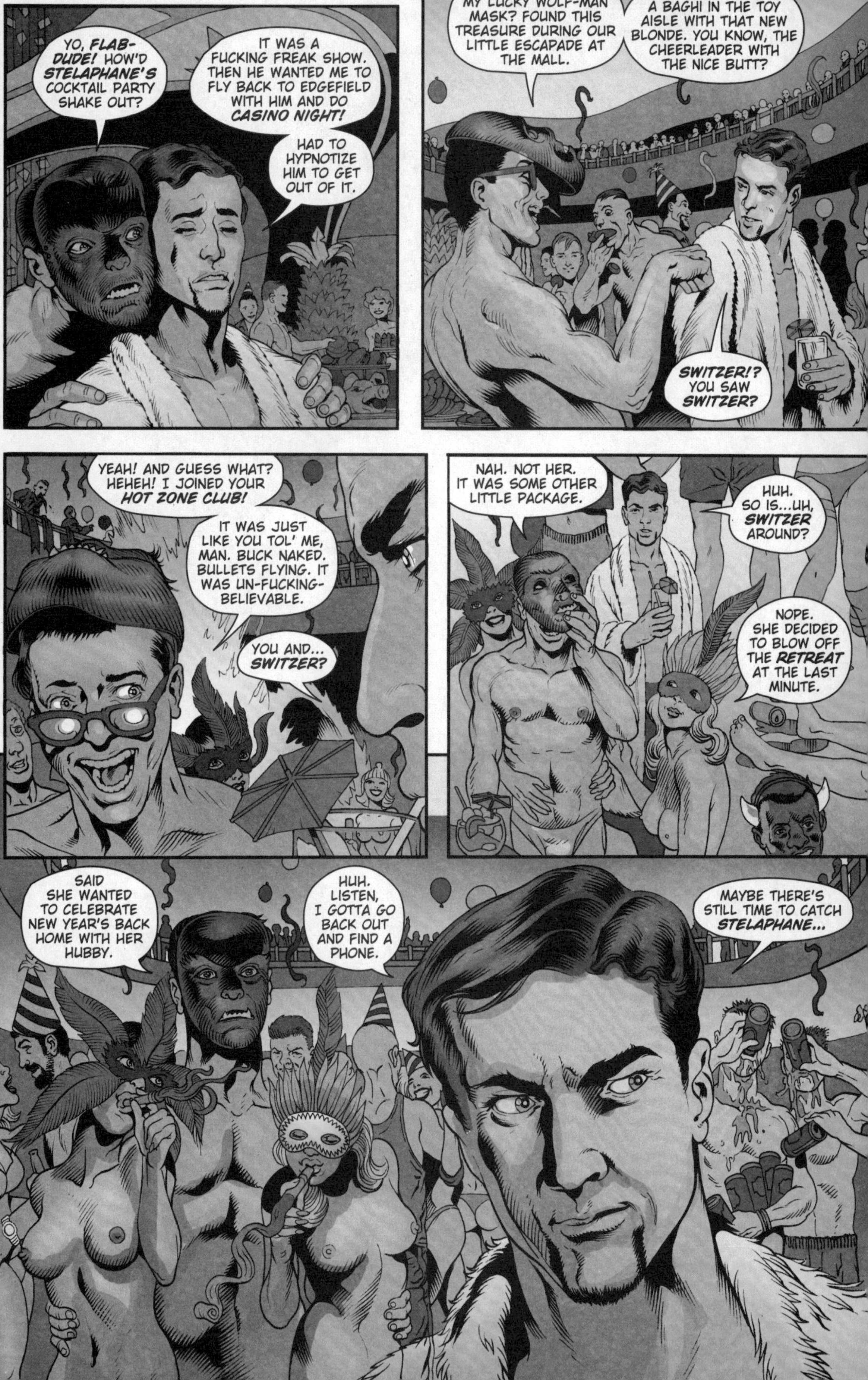

YO, FLAB-DUDE! HOW'D STELAPHANE'S COCKTAIL PARTY SHAKE OUT?
IT WAS A FUCKING FREAK SHOW. THEN HE WANTED ME TO FLY BACK TO EDGEFIELD WITH HIM AND DO CASINO NIGHT!
HAD TO HYPNOTIZE HIM TO GET OUT OF IT.
HOWD'YA LIKE MY LUCKY WOLF-MAN MASK? FOUND THIS TREASURE DURING OUR LITTLE ESCAPADE AT THE MALL.
I WAS WASTING A BAGHI IN THE TOY AISLE WITH THAT NEW BLONDE. YOU KNOW, THE CHEERLEADER WITH THE NICE BUTT?
SWITZER!? YOU SAW SWITZER?
YEAH! AND GUESS WHAT? HEHEH! I JOINED YOUR HOT ZONE CLUB!
IT WAS JUST LIKE YOU TOL' ME, MAN. BUCK NAKED. BULLETS FLYING. IT WAS UN-FUCKING-BELIEVABLE.
YOU AND... SWITZER?
NAH. NOT HER. IT WAS SOME OTHER LITTLE PACKAGE.
HUH. SO IS...UH, SWITZER AROUND?
NOPE. SHE DECIDED TO BLOW OFF THE RETREAT AT THE LAST MINUTE.
SAID SHE WANTED TO CELEBRATE NEW YEAR'S BACK HOME WITH HER HUBBY.
HUH. LISTEN, I GOTTA GO BACK OUT AND FIND A PHONE.
MAYBE THERE'S STILL TIME TO CATCH STELAPHANE...

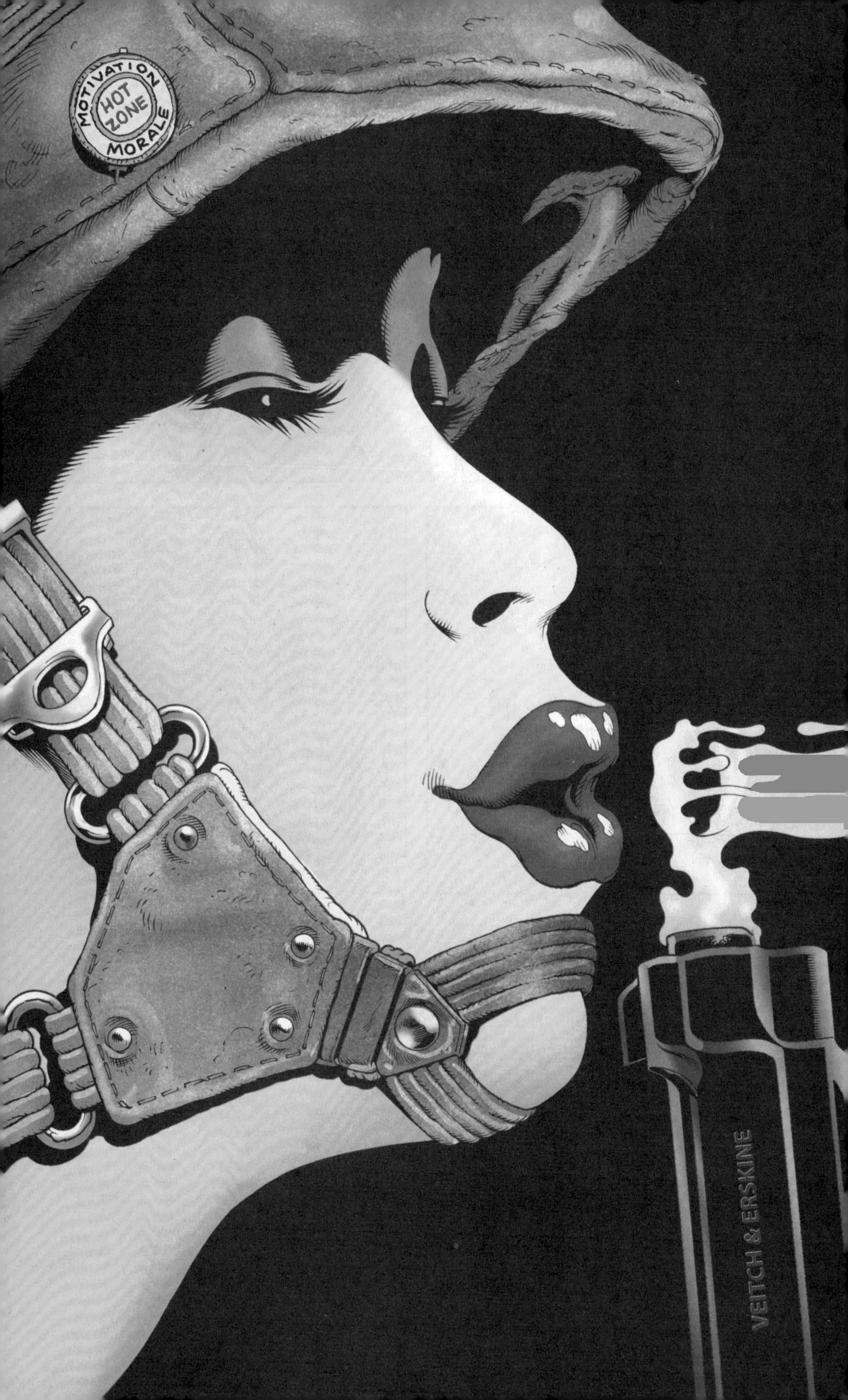
MOTIVATION
HOT ZONE
MORALE
VEITCH & ERSKINE

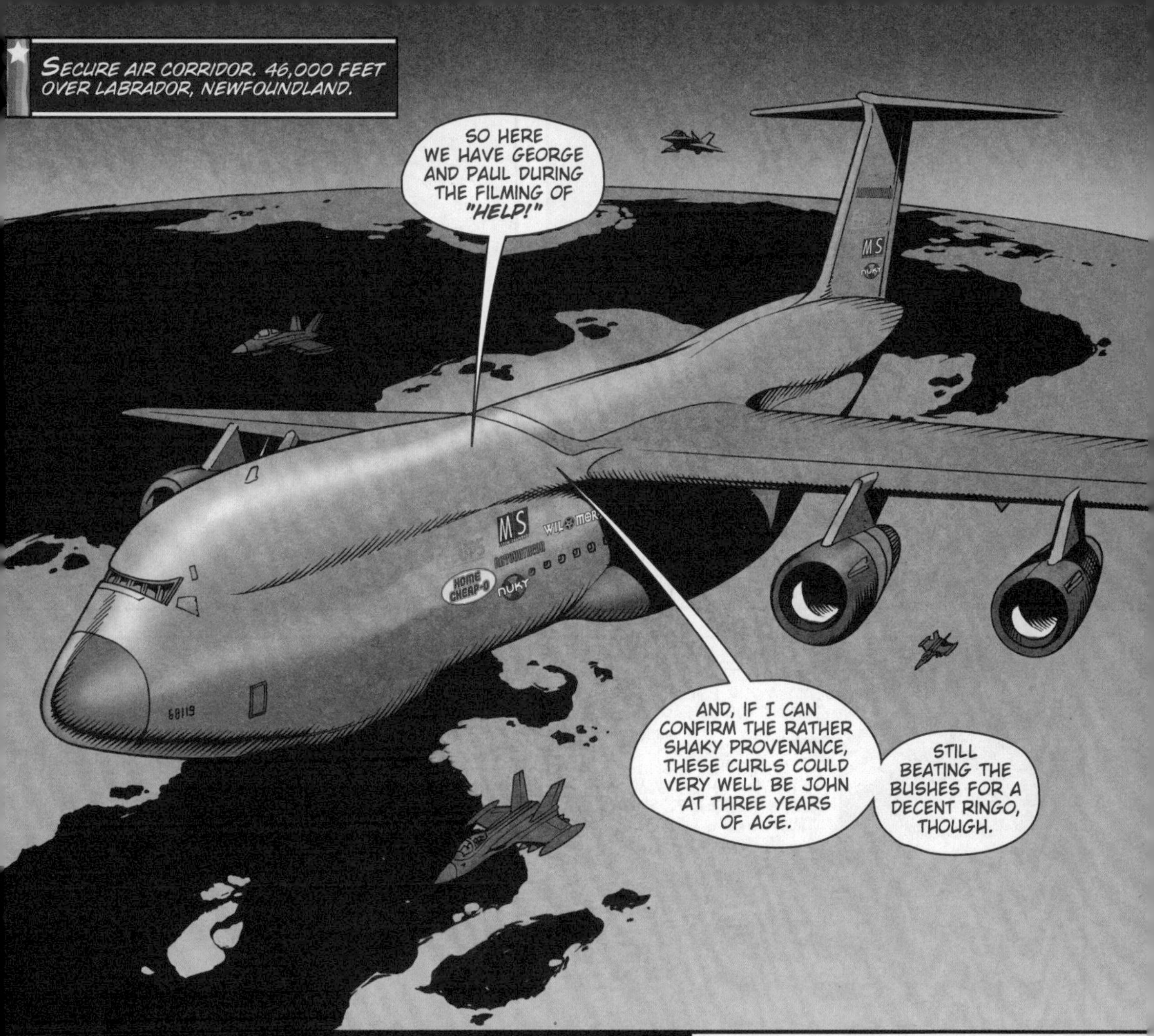
SECURE AIR CORRIDOR. 46,000 FEET OVER LABRADOR, NEWFOUNDLAND.
SO HERE WE HAVE GEORGE AND PAUL DURING THE FILMING OF "HELP!"
AND, IF I CAN CONFIRM THE RATHER SHAKY PROVENANCE, THESE CURLS COULD VERY WELL BE JOHN AT THREE YEARS OF AGE.
STILL BEATING THE BUSHES FOR A DECENT RINGO, THOUGH.

THE LADY VANISHES!

Coloring by Jose Villarrubia

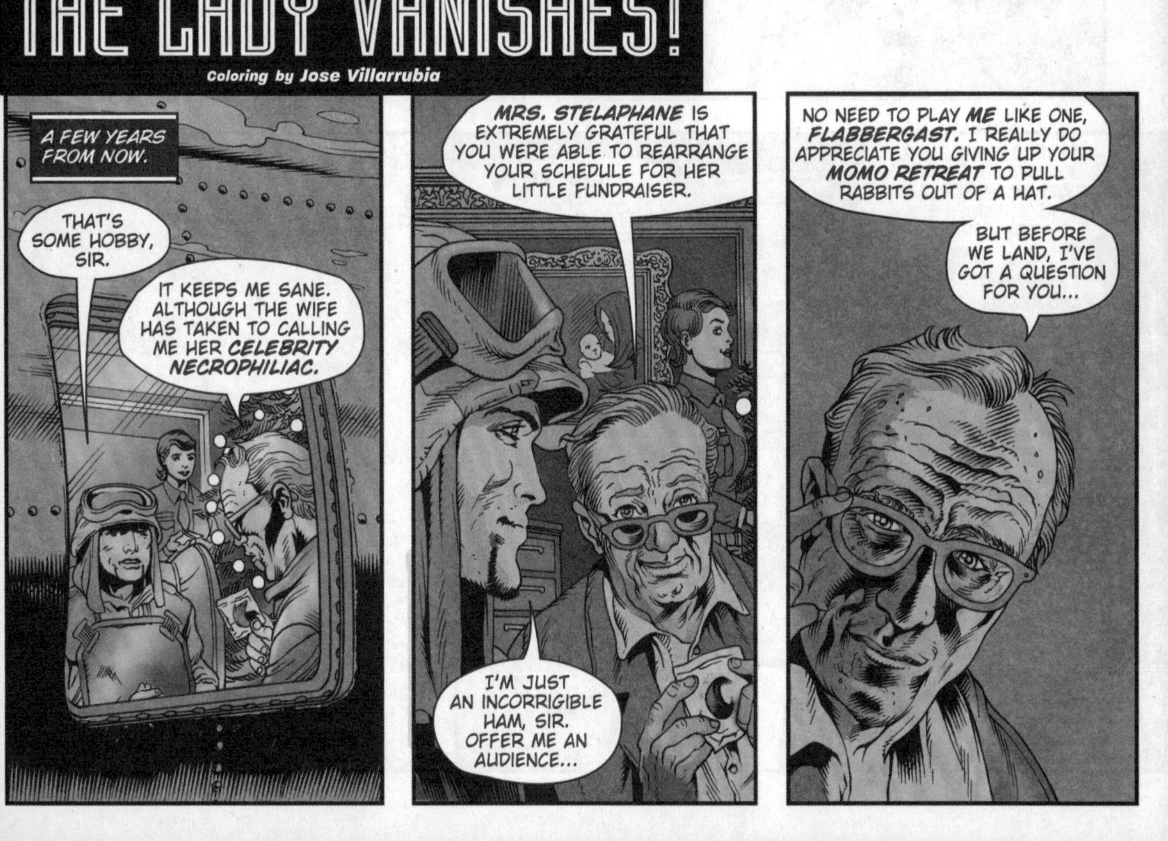
A FEW YEARS FROM NOW.
THAT'S SOME HOBBY, SIR.
IT KEEPS ME SANE. ALTHOUGH THE WIFE HAS TAKEN TO CALLING ME HER CELEBRITY NECROPHILIAC.
MRS. STELAPHANE IS EXTREMELY GRATEFUL THAT YOU WERE ABLE TO REARRANGE YOUR SCHEDULE FOR HER LITTLE FUNDRAISER.
I'M JUST AN INCORRIGIBLE HAM, SIR. OFFER ME AN AUDIENCE...
NO NEED TO PLAY ME LIKE ONE, FLABBERGAST. I REALLY DO APPRECIATE YOU GIVING UP YOUR MOMO RETREAT TO PULL RABBITS OUT OF A HAT.
BUT BEFORE WE LAND, I'VE GOT A QUESTION FOR YOU...

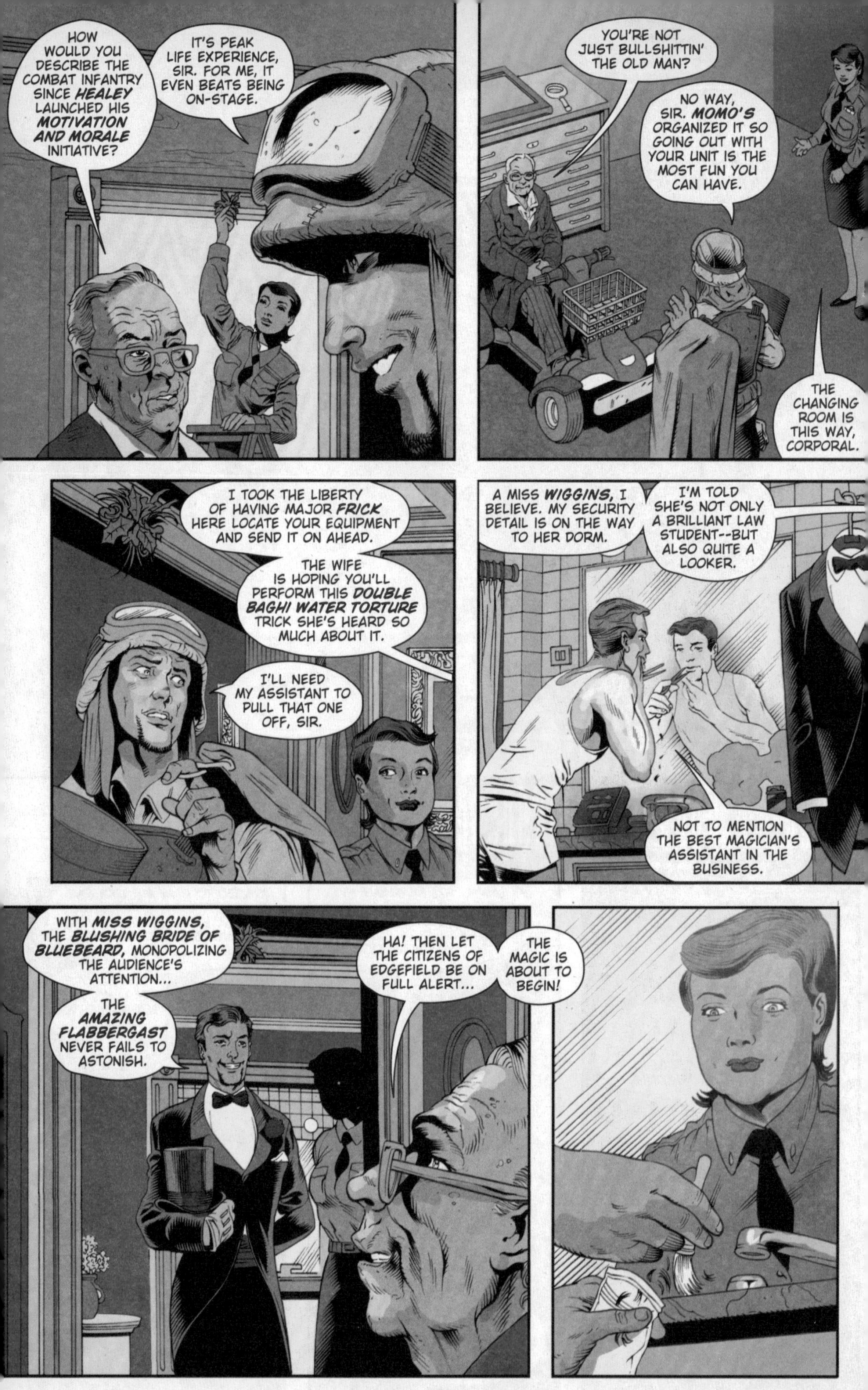
HOW WOULD YOU DESCRIBE THE COMBAT INFANTRY SINCE HEALEY LAUNCHED HIS MOTIVATION AND MORALE INITIATIVE?
IT'S PEAK LIFE EXPERIENCE, SIR. FOR ME, IT EVEN BEATS BEING ON-STAGE.
YOU'RE NOT JUST BULLSHITTIN' THE OLD MAN?
NO WAY, SIR. MOMO'S ORGANIZED IT SO GOING OUT WITH YOUR UNIT IS THE MOST FUN YOU CAN HAVE.
THE CHANGING ROOM IS THIS WAY, CORPORAL.
I TOOK THE LIBERTY OF HAVING MAJOR FRICK HERE LOCATE YOUR EQUIPMENT AND SEND IT ON AHEAD.
THE WIFE IS HOPING YOU'LL PERFORM THIS DOUBLE BAGHI WATER TORTURE TRICK SHE'S HEARD SO MUCH ABOUT IT.
I'LL NEED MY ASSISTANT TO PULL THAT ONE OFF, SIR.
A MISS WIGGINS, I BELIEVE. MY SECURITY DETAIL IS ON THE WAY TO HER DORM.
I'M TOLD SHE'S NOT ONLY A BRILLIANT LAW STUDENT--BUT ALSO QUITE A LOOKER.
NOT TO MENTION THE BEST MAGICIAN'S ASSISTANT IN THE BUSINESS.
WITH MISS WIGGINS, THE BLUSHING BRIDE OF BLUEBEARD, MONOPOLIZING THE AUDIENCE'S ATTENTION...
THE AMAZING FLABBERGAST NEVER FAILS TO ASTONISH.
HA! THEN LET THE CITIZENS OF EDGEFIELD BE ON FULL ALERT...
THE MAGIC IS ABOUT TO BEGIN!

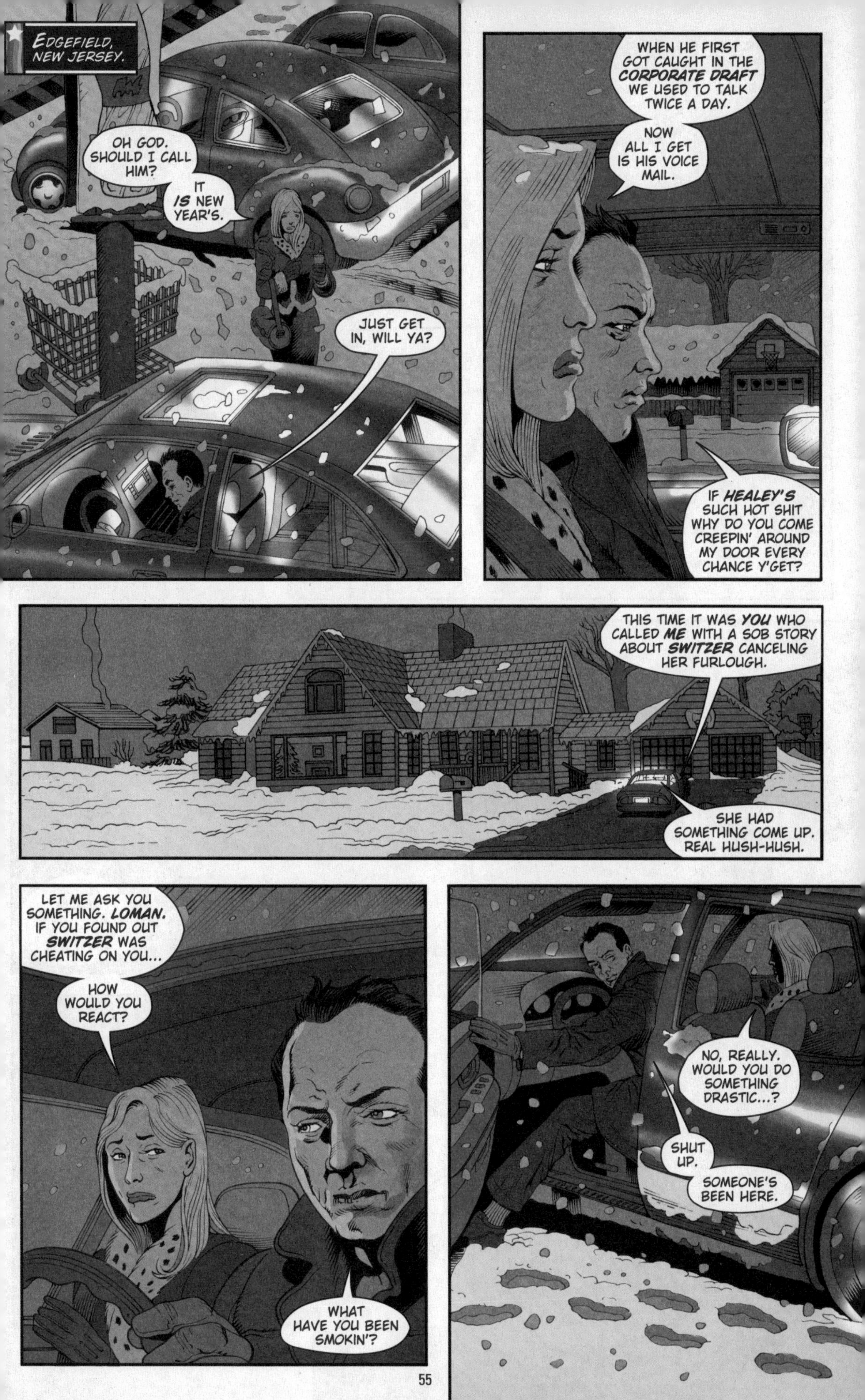
EDGEFIELD, NEW JERSEY.
OH GOD. SHOULD I CALL HIM?
IT IS NEW YEAR'S.
JUST GET IN, WILL YA?
WHEN HE FIRST GOT CAUGHT IN THE CORPORATE DRAFT WE USED TO TALK TWICE A DAY.
NOW ALL I GET IS HIS VOICE MAIL.
IF HEALEY'S SUCH HOT SHIT WHY DO YOU COME CREEPIN' AROUND MY DOOR EVERY CHANCE Y'GET?
THIS TIME IT WAS YOU WHO CALLED ME WITH A SOB STORY ABOUT SWITZER CANCELING HER FURLOUGH.
SHE HAD SOMETHING COME UP. REAL HUSH-HUSH.
LET ME ASK YOU SOMETHING, LOMAN. IF YOU FOUND OUT SWITZER WAS CHEATING ON YOU...
HOW WOULD YOU REACT?
WHAT HAVE YOU BEEN SMOKIN'?
NO, REALLY. WOULD YOU DO SOMETHING DRASTIC...?
SHUT UP.
SOMEONE'S BEEN HERE.

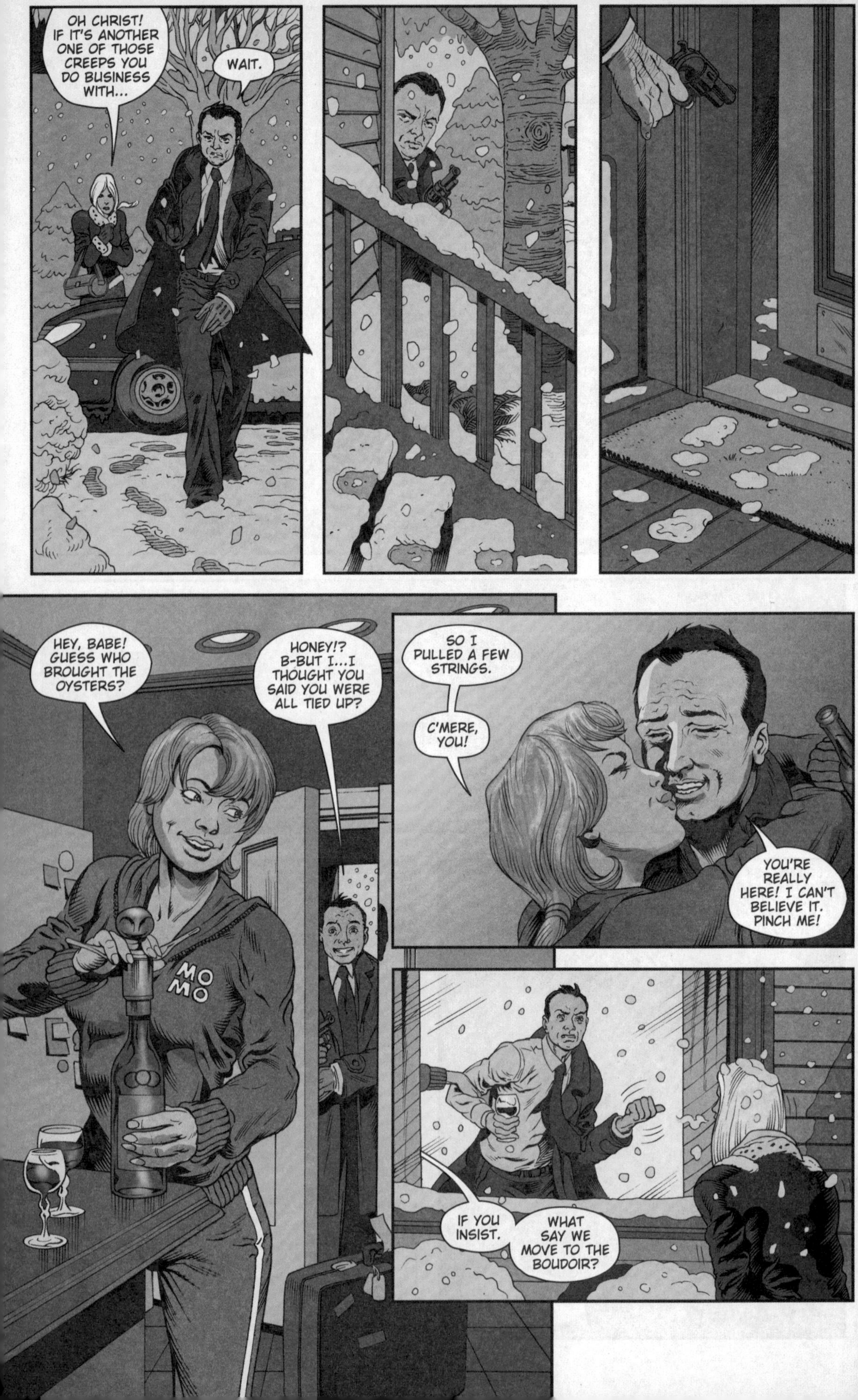
OH CHRIST! IF IT'S ANOTHER ONE OF THOSE CREEPS YOU DO BUSINESS WITH...
WAIT.
HEY, BABE! GUESS WHO BROUGHT THE OYSTERS?
HONEY!? B-BUT I...I THOUGHT YOU SAID YOU WERE ALL TIED UP?
SO I PULLED A FEW STRINGS.
C'MERE, YOU!
YOU'RE REALLY HERE! I CAN'T BELIEVE IT. PINCH ME!
WHAT SAY WE MOVE TO THE BOUDOIR?
IF YOU INSIST.
MO
MO

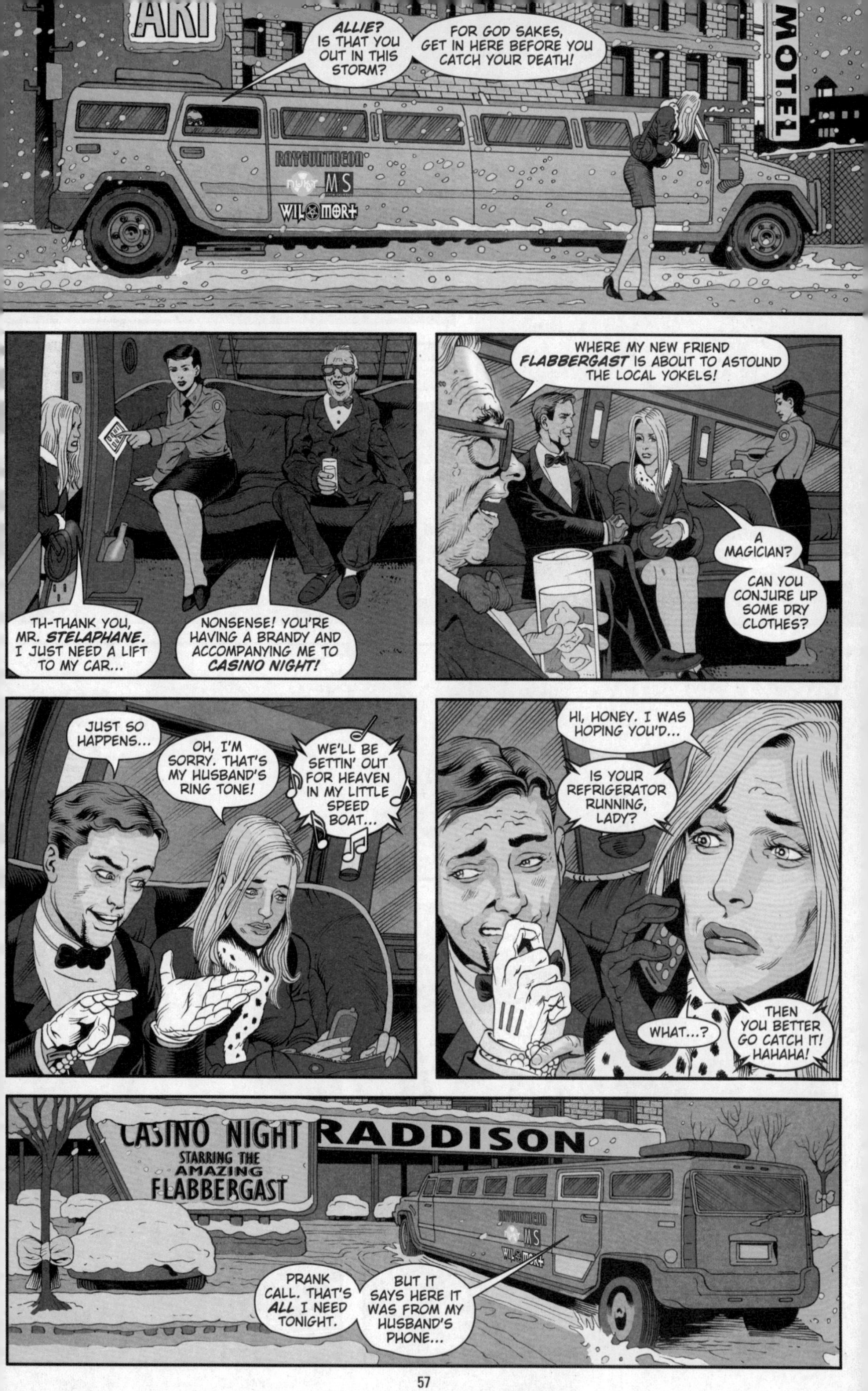
ARI
MOTEL
ALLIE? IS THAT YOU OUT IN THIS STORM?
FOR GOD SAKES, GET IN HERE BEFORE YOU CATCH YOUR DEATH!
RAYGUNTHEON
MS
WIL MORT
TH-THANK YOU, MR. STELAPHANE. I JUST NEED A LIFT TO MY CAR...
NONSENSE! YOU'RE HAVING A BRANDY AND ACCOMPANYING ME TO CASINO NIGHT!
WHERE MY NEW FRIEND FLABBERGAST IS ABOUT TO ASTOUND THE LOCAL YOKELS!
A MAGICIAN?
CAN YOU CONJURE UP SOME DRY CLOTHES?
JUST SO HAPPENS...
OH, I'M SORRY. THAT'S MY HUSBAND'S RING TONE!
WE'LL BE SETTIN' OUT FOR HEAVEN IN MY LITTLE SPEED BOAT...
HI, HONEY. I WAS HOPING YOU'D...
IS YOUR REFRIGERATOR RUNNING, LADY?
WHAT...?
THEN YOU BETTER GO CATCH IT! HAHAHA!
CASINO NIGHT STARRING THE AMAZING FLABBERGAST
RADDISON
PRANK CALL. THAT'S ALL I NEED TONIGHT.
BUT IT SAYS HERE IT WAS FROM MY HUSBAND'S PHONE...

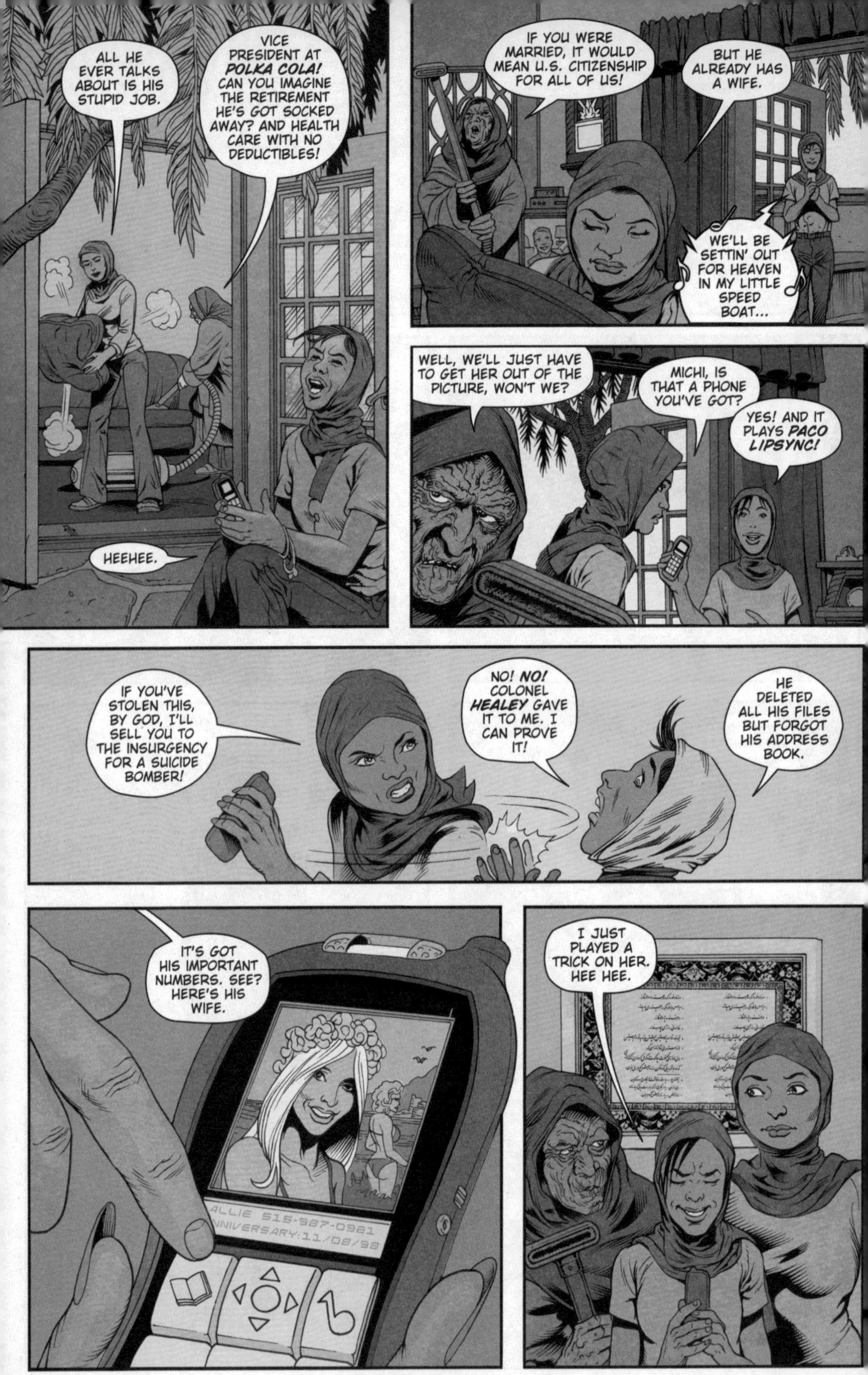
ALL HE EVER TALKS ABOUT IS HIS STUPID JOB.
VICE PRESIDENT AT POLKA COLA! CAN YOU IMAGINE THE RETIREMENT HE'S GOT SOCKED AWAY? AND HEALTH CARE WITH NO DEDUCTIBLES!
HEEHEE.
IF YOU WERE MARRIED, IT WOULD MEAN U.S. CITIZENSHIP FOR ALL OF US!
BUT HE ALREADY HAS A WIFE.
WE'LL BE SETTIN' OUT FOR HEAVEN IN MY LITTLE SPEED BOAT...
WELL, WE'LL JUST HAVE TO GET HER OUT OF THE PICTURE, WON'T WE?
MICHI, IS THAT A PHONE YOU'VE GOT?
YES! AND IT PLAYS PACO LIPSYNC!
IF YOU'VE STOLEN THIS, BY GOD, I'LL SELL YOU TO THE INSURGENCY FOR A SUICIDE BOMBER!
NO! NO! COLONEL HEALEY GAVE IT TO ME. I CAN PROVE IT!
HE DELETED ALL HIS FILES BUT FORGOT HIS ADDRESS BOOK.
IT'S GOT HIS IMPORTANT NUMBERS. SEE? HERE'S HIS WIFE.
ALLIE 515-987-0921
NNIVERSARY:11/08/98
I JUST PLAYED A TRICK ON HER. HEE HEE.

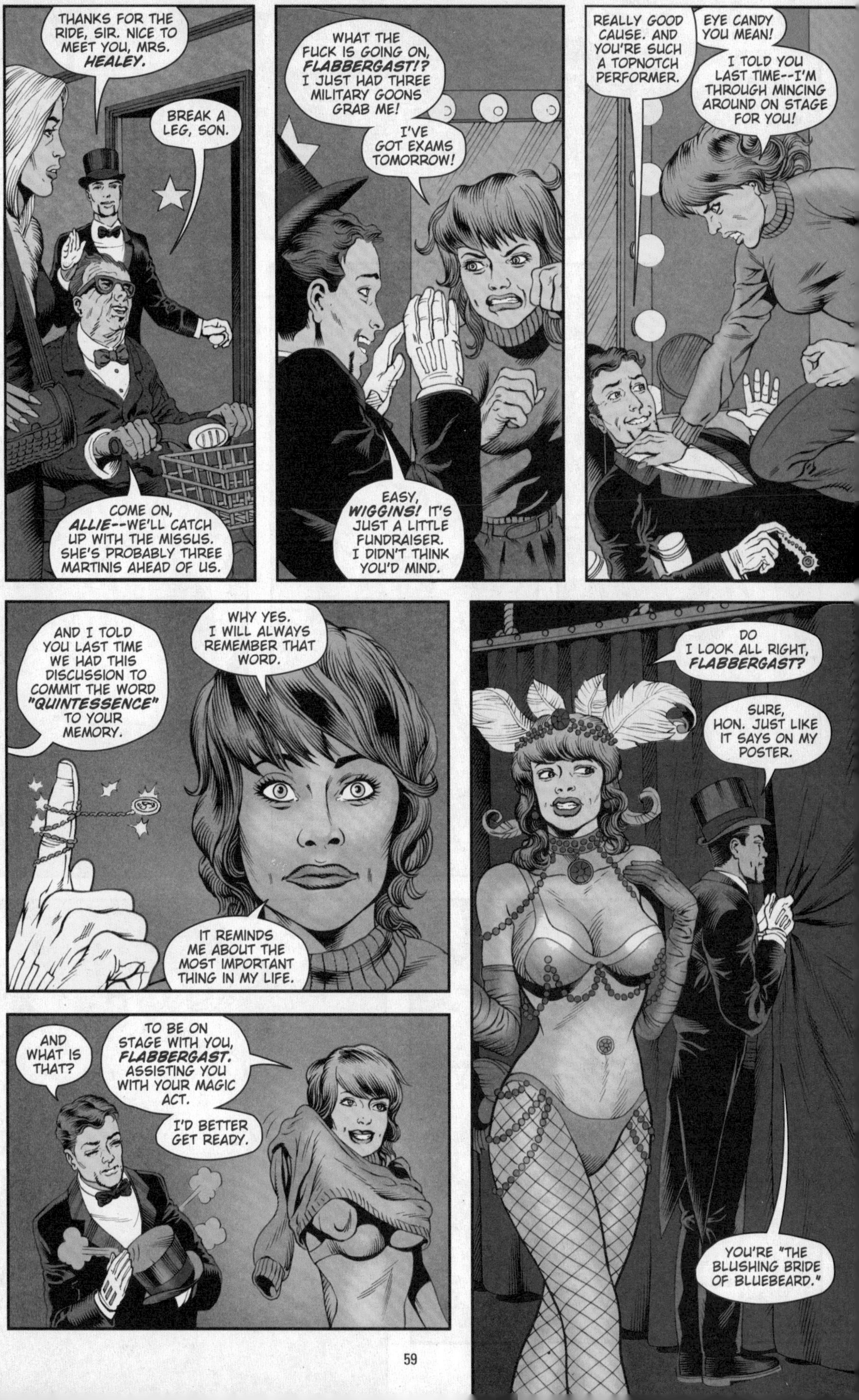
THANKS FOR THE RIDE, SIR. NICE TO MEET YOU, MRS. HEALEY.
BREAK A LEG, SON.
COME ON, ALLIE--WE'LL CATCH UP WITH THE MISSUS. SHE'S PROBABLY THREE MARTINIS AHEAD OF US.
WHAT THE FUCK IS GOING ON, FLABBERGAST!? I JUST HAD THREE MILITARY GOONS GRAB ME!
I'VE GOT EXAMS TOMORROW!
EASY, WIGGINS! IT'S JUST A LITTLE FUNDRAISER. I DIDN'T THINK YOU'D MIND.
REALLY GOOD CAUSE. AND YOU'RE SUCH A TOPNOTCH PERFORMER.
EYE CANDY YOU MEAN!
I TOLD YOU LAST TIME--I'M THROUGH MINCING AROUND ON STAGE FOR YOU!
AND I TOLD YOU LAST TIME WE HAD THIS DISCUSSION TO COMMIT THE WORD "QUINTESSENCE" TO YOUR MEMORY.
WHY YES. I WILL ALWAYS REMEMBER THAT WORD.
IT REMINDS ME ABOUT THE MOST IMPORTANT THING IN MY LIFE.
AND WHAT IS THAT?
TO BE ON STAGE WITH YOU, FLABBERGAST. ASSISTING YOU WITH YOUR MAGIC ACT.
I'D BETTER GET READY.
DO I LOOK ALL RIGHT, FLABBERGAST?
SURE, HON. JUST LIKE IT SAYS ON MY POSTER.
YOU'RE "THE BLUSHING BRIDE OF BLUEBEARD."

SO I GOTTA ASK YA SOMETHIN'.

WHY'D YOU MARRY ME?

THAT'S A LOADED QUESTION.

IT'S JUST I NEVER UNDERSTOOD WHY SOMEONE WHO HAD EVERYTHING GOING FOR THEM...

FELL FOR A BUM LIKE YOU?

WHEN WE MET, YOU WERE AN HONOR STUDENT. I WAS EIGHT YEARS OLDER WITH A FELONY RECORD.

YEAH. BUT YOU HAD SOMETHING ALL YOUR OWN.

WHAT?

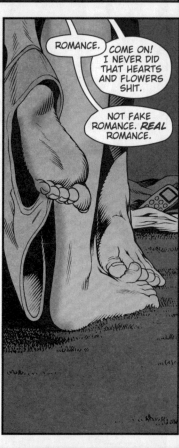

ROMANCE.

COME ON! I NEVER DID THAT HEARTS AND FLOWERS SHIT.

NOT FAKE ROMANCE. REAL ROMANCE.

LIKE THIS?

MMM. MAYBE.

WE'LL BE SETTIN' OUT FOR HEAVEN IN MY LITTLE SPEED BOAT...

OHHH, DON'T ANSWER.

I'VE GOTTA.

IT'S OLD MAN PEEBLES.

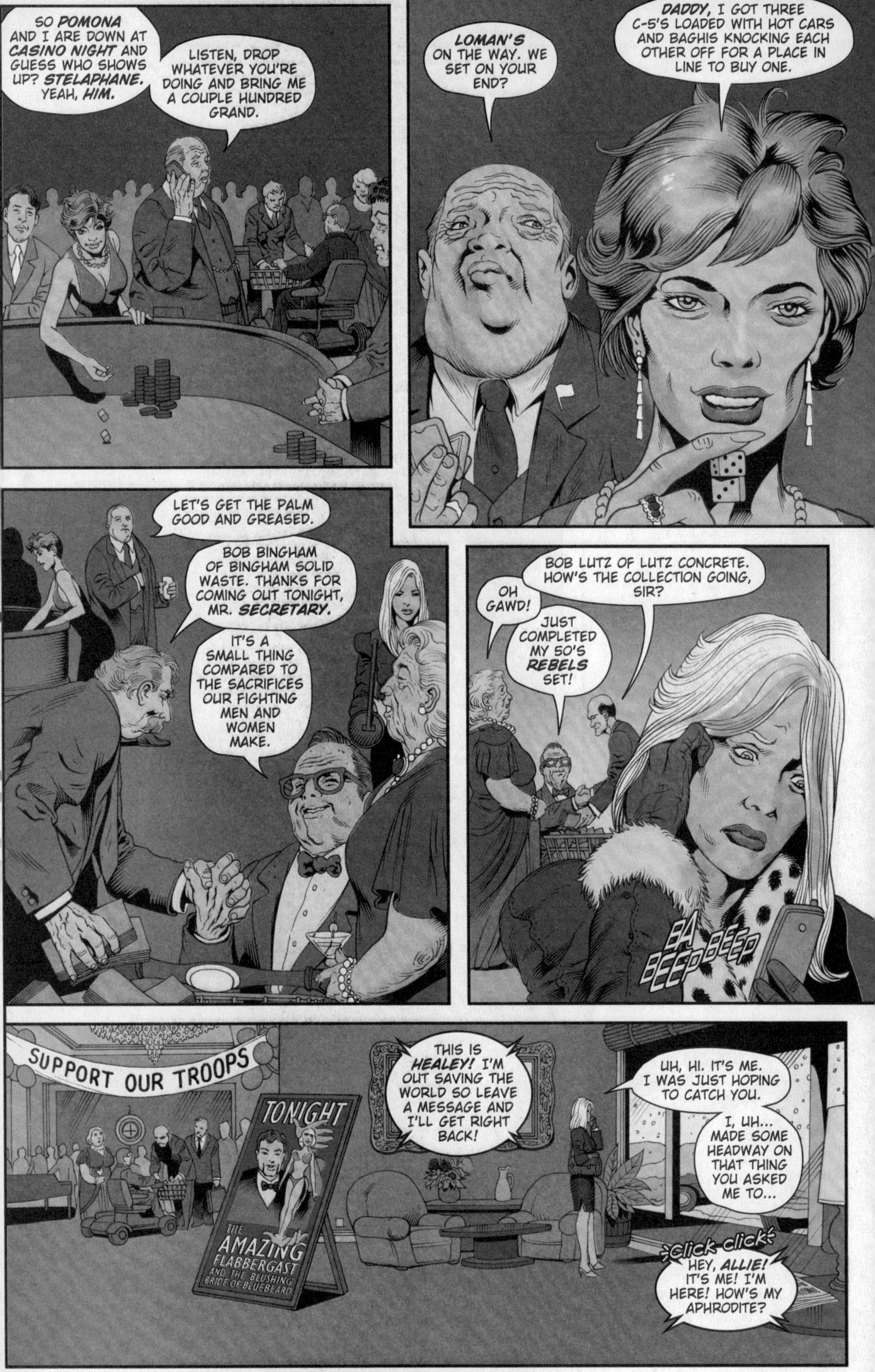
SO POMONA AND I ARE DOWN AT CASINO NIGHT AND GUESS WHO SHOWS UP? STELAPHANE. YEAH, HIM.
LISTEN, DROP WHATEVER YOU'RE DOING AND BRING ME A COUPLE HUNDRED GRAND.
LOMAN'S ON THE WAY. WE SET ON YOUR END?
DADDY, I GOT THREE C-5'S LOADED WITH HOT CARS AND BAGHIS KNOCKING EACH OTHER OFF FOR A PLACE IN LINE TO BUY ONE.
LET'S GET THE PALM GOOD AND GREASED.
BOB BINGHAM OF BINGHAM SOLID WASTE. THANKS FOR COMING OUT TONIGHT, MR. SECRETARY.
IT'S A SMALL THING COMPARED TO THE SACRIFICES OUR FIGHTING MEN AND WOMEN MAKE.
BOB LUTZ OF LUTZ CONCRETE. HOW'S THE COLLECTION GOING, SIR?
OH GAWD!
JUST COMPLETED MY 50'S REBELS SET!
BA BEEP BEEP
SUPPORT OUR TROOPS
TONIGHT
THE AMAZING FLABBERGAST AND THE BLUSHING BRIDE OF BLUEBEARD
THIS IS HEALEY! I'M OUT SAVING THE WORLD SO LEAVE A MESSAGE AND I'LL GET RIGHT BACK!
UH, HI. IT'S ME. I WAS JUST HOPING TO CATCH YOU.
I, UH... MADE SOME HEADWAY ON THAT THING YOU ASKED ME TO...
click click
HEY, ALLIE! IT'S ME! I'M HERE! HOW'S MY APHRODITE?

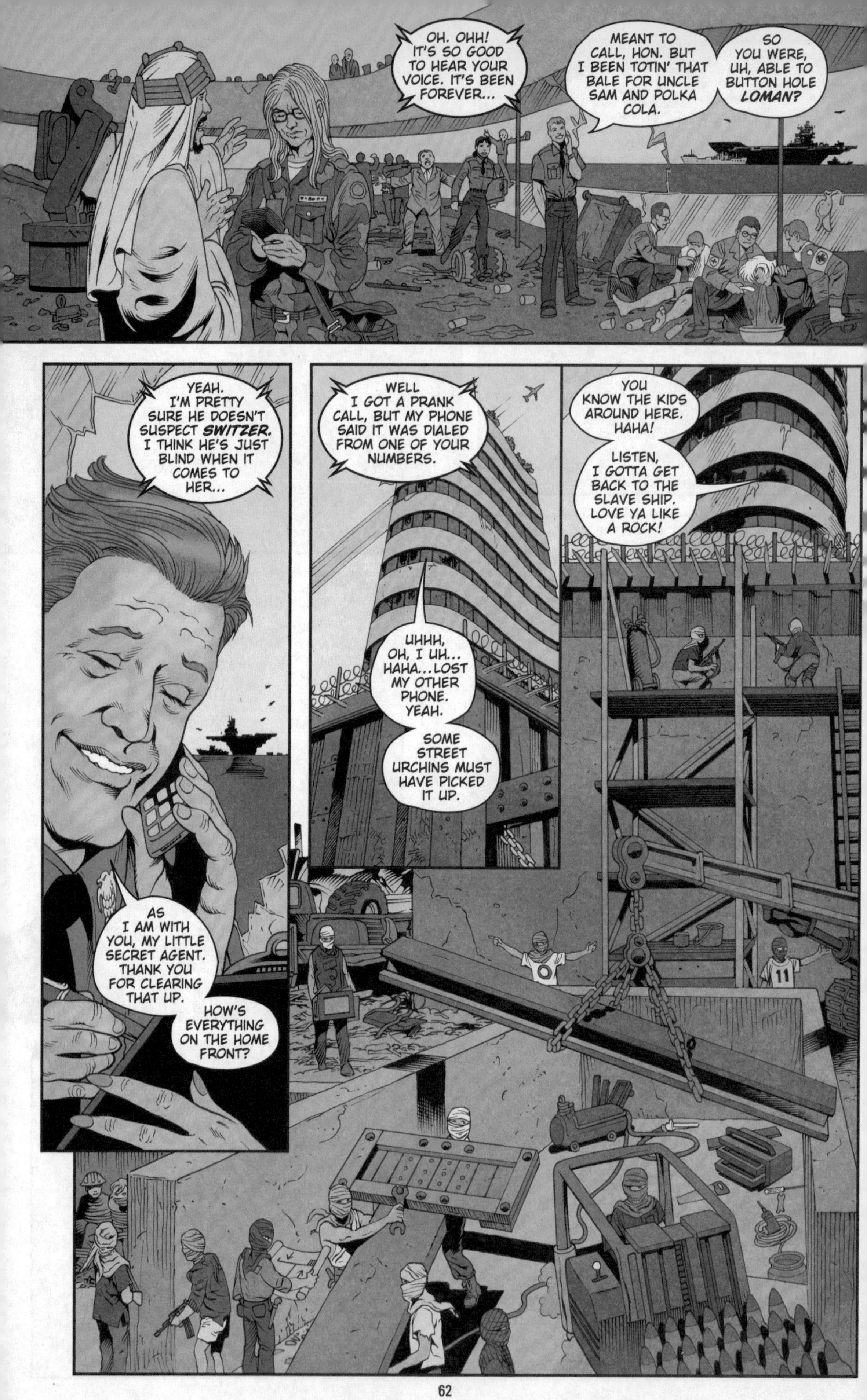
OH. OHH! IT'S SO GOOD TO HEAR YOUR VOICE. IT'S BEEN FOREVER...
MEANT TO CALL, HON. BUT I BEEN TOTIN' THAT BALE FOR UNCLE SAM AND POLKA COLA.
SO YOU WERE, UH, ABLE TO BUTTON HOLE LOMAN?
YEAH. I'M PRETTY SURE HE DOESN'T SUSPECT SWITZER. I THINK HE'S JUST BLIND WHEN IT COMES TO HER...
AS I AM WITH YOU, MY LITTLE SECRET AGENT. THANK YOU FOR CLEARING THAT UP.
HOW'S EVERYTHING ON THE HOME FRONT?
WELL I GOT A PRANK CALL, BUT MY PHONE SAID IT WAS DIALED FROM ONE OF YOUR NUMBERS.
UHHH, OH, I UH... HAHA...LOST MY OTHER PHONE. YEAH.
SOME STREET URCHINS MUST HAVE PICKED IT UP.
YOU KNOW THE KIDS AROUND HERE. HAHA!
LISTEN, I GOTTA GET BACK TO THE SLAVE SHIP. LOVE YA LIKE A ROCK!

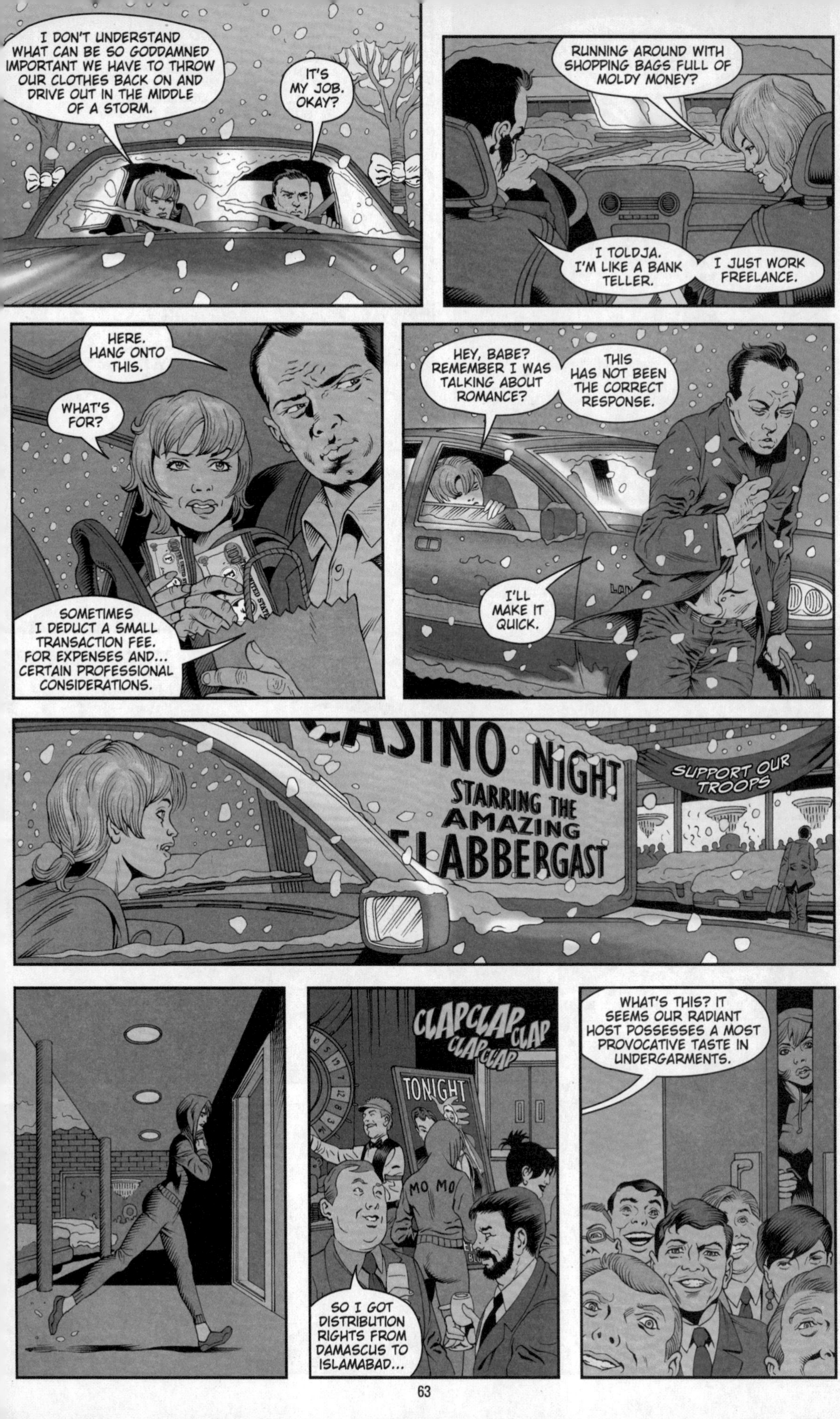
I DON'T UNDERSTAND WHAT CAN BE SO GODDAMNED IMPORTANT WE HAVE TO THROW OUR CLOTHES BACK ON AND DRIVE OUT IN THE MIDDLE OF A STORM.
IT'S MY JOB. OKAY?
RUNNING AROUND WITH SHOPPING BAGS FULL OF MOLDY MONEY?
I TOLDJA. I'M LIKE A BANK TELLER.
I JUST WORK FREELANCE.
HERE. HANG ONTO THIS.
WHAT'S FOR?
SOMETIMES I DEDUCT A SMALL TRANSACTION FEE. FOR EXPENSES AND... CERTAIN PROFESSIONAL CONSIDERATIONS.
HEY, BABE? REMEMBER I WAS TALKING ABOUT ROMANCE?
THIS HAS NOT BEEN THE CORRECT RESPONSE.
I'LL MAKE IT QUICK.
CASINO NIGHT STARRING THE AMAZING FLABBERGAST
SUPPORT OUR TROOPS
CLAPCLAP CLAP CLAP CLAP
TONIGHT
MO MO
SO I GOT DISTRIBUTION RIGHTS FROM DAMASCUS TO ISLAMABAD...
WHAT'S THIS? IT SEEMS OUR RADIANT HOST POSSESSES A MOST PROVOCATIVE TASTE IN UNDERGARMENTS.

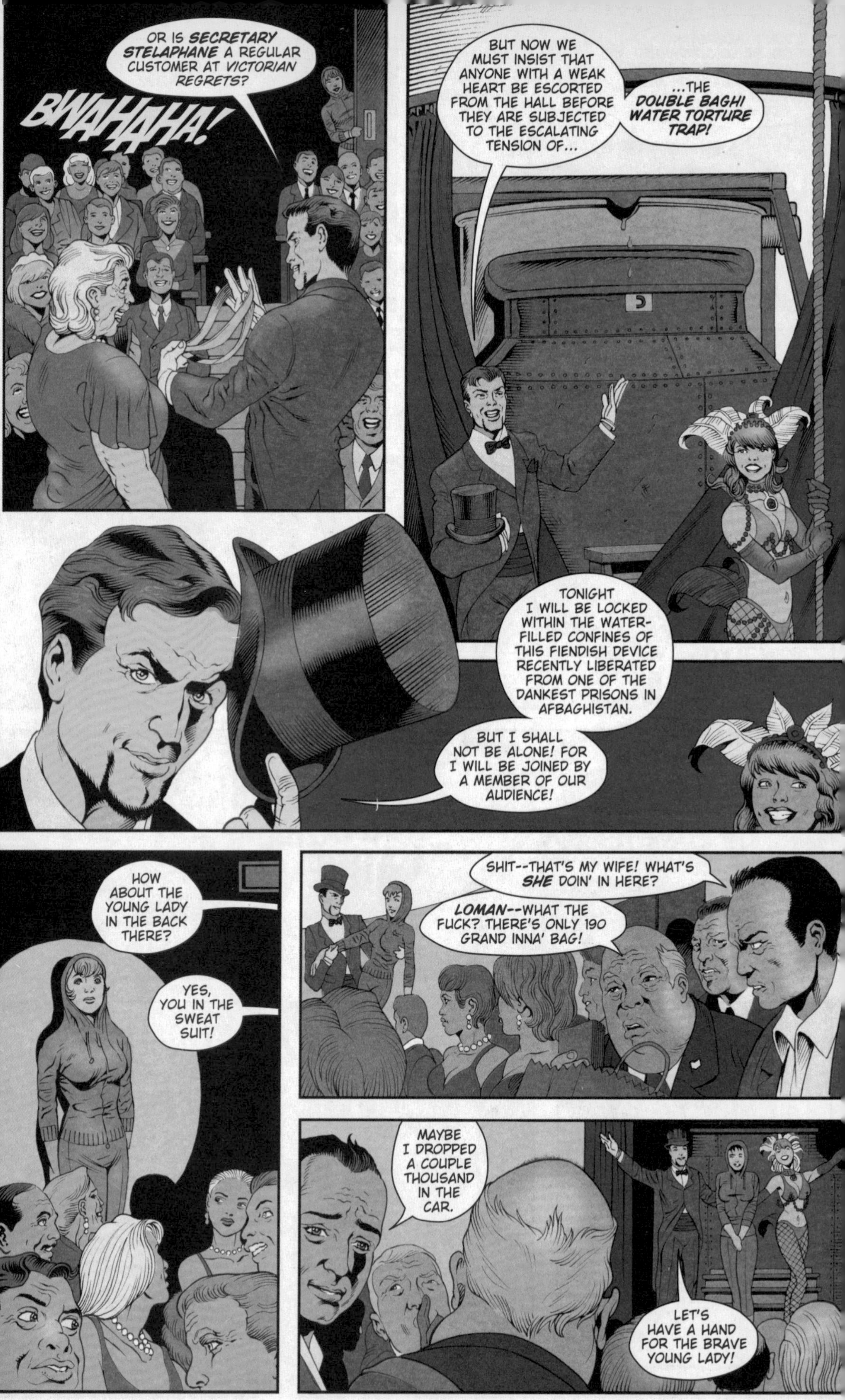

OR IS SECRETARY STELAPHANE A REGULAR CUSTOMER AT VICTORIAN REGRETS?
BWAHAHA!
BUT NOW WE MUST INSIST THAT ANYONE WITH A WEAK HEART BE ESCORTED FROM THE HALL BEFORE THEY ARE SUBJECTED TO THE ESCALATING TENSION OF...
...THE DOUBLE BAGHI WATER TORTURE TRAP!
TONIGHT I WILL BE LOCKED WITHIN THE WATER-FILLED CONFINES OF THIS FIENDISH DEVICE RECENTLY LIBERATED FROM ONE OF THE DANKEST PRISONS IN AFBAGHISTAN.
BUT I SHALL NOT BE ALONE! FOR I WILL BE JOINED BY A MEMBER OF OUR AUDIENCE!
HOW ABOUT THE YOUNG LADY IN THE BACK THERE?
YES, YOU IN THE SWEAT SUIT!
SHIT--THAT'S MY WIFE! WHAT'S SHE DOIN' IN HERE?
LOMAN--WHAT THE FUCK? THERE'S ONLY 190 GRAND INNA' BAG!
MAYBE I DROPPED A COUPLE THOUSAND IN THE CAR.
LET'S HAVE A HAND FOR THE BRAVE YOUNG LADY!

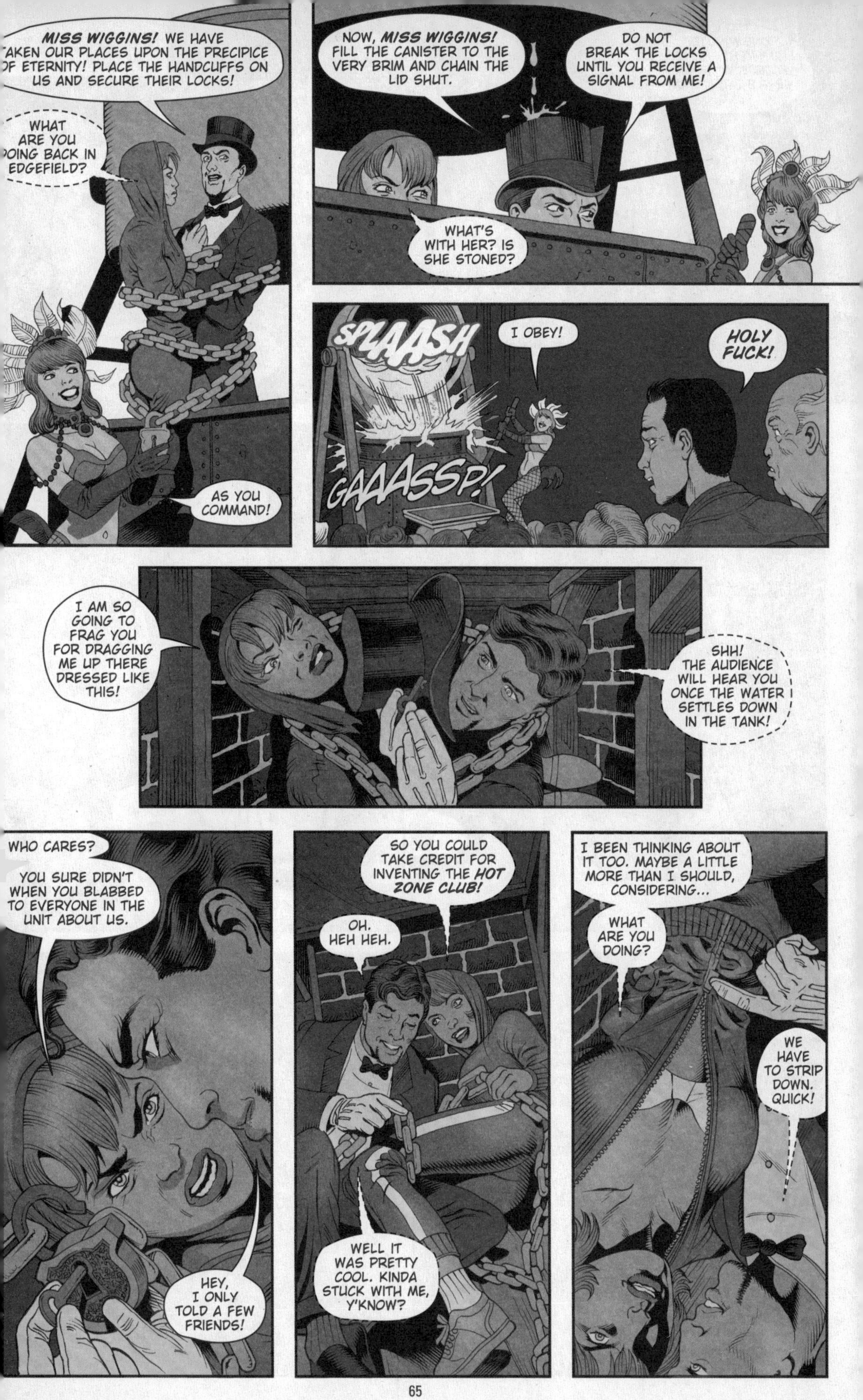
MISS WIGGINS! WE HAVE TAKEN OUR PLACES UPON THE PRECIPICE OF ETERNITY! PLACE THE HANDCUFFS ON US AND SECURE THEIR LOCKS!
WHAT ARE YOU DOING BACK IN EDGEFIELD?
AS YOU COMMAND!
NOW, MISS WIGGINS! FILL THE CANISTER TO THE VERY BRIM AND CHAIN THE LID SHUT.
DO NOT BREAK THE LOCKS UNTIL YOU RECEIVE A SIGNAL FROM ME!
WHAT'S WITH HER? IS SHE STONED?
SPLAASH
GAAASSP!
I OBEY!
HOLY FUCK!
I AM SO GOING TO FRAG YOU FOR DRAGGING ME UP THERE DRESSED LIKE THIS!
SHH! THE AUDIENCE WILL HEAR YOU ONCE THE WATER SETTLES DOWN IN THE TANK!
WHO CARES?
YOU SURE DIDN'T WHEN YOU BLABBED TO EVERYONE IN THE UNIT ABOUT US.
HEY, I ONLY TOLD A FEW FRIENDS!
SO YOU COULD TAKE CREDIT FOR INVENTING THE HOT ZONE CLUB!
OH. HEH HEH.
WELL IT WAS PRETTY COOL. KINDA STUCK WITH ME, Y'KNOW?
I BEEN THINKING ABOUT IT TOO. MAYBE A LITTLE MORE THAN I SHOULD, CONSIDERING...
WHAT ARE YOU DOING?
WE HAVE TO STRIP DOWN. QUICK!

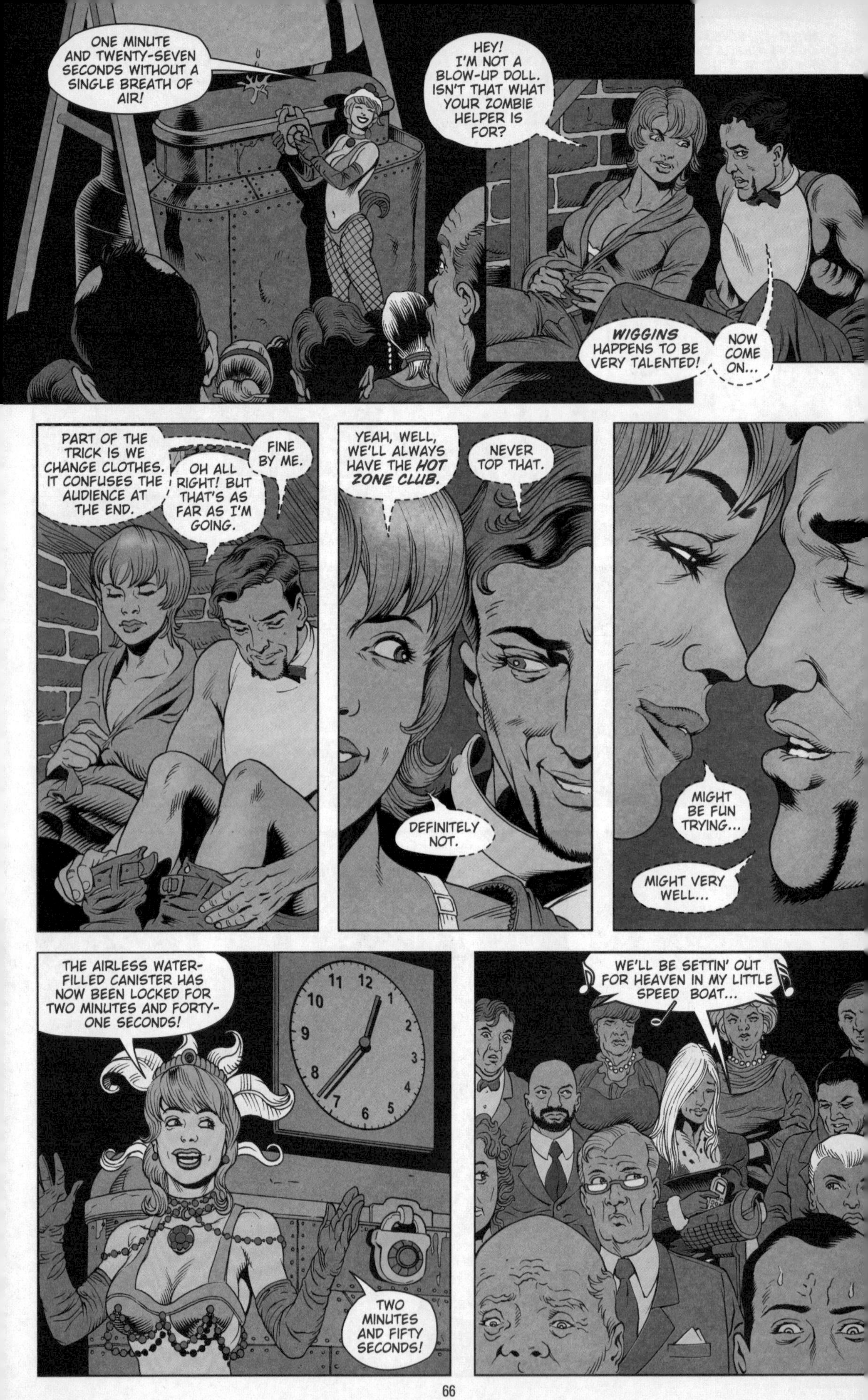
ONE MINUTE AND TWENTY-SEVEN SECONDS WITHOUT A SINGLE BREATH OF AIR!
HEY! I'M NOT A BLOW-UP DOLL. ISN'T THAT WHAT YOUR ZOMBIE HELPER IS FOR?
WIGGINS HAPPENS TO BE VERY TALENTED!
NOW COME ON...
PART OF THE TRICK IS WE CHANGE CLOTHES. IT CONFUSES THE AUDIENCE AT THE END.
FINE BY ME.
OH ALL RIGHT! BUT THAT'S AS FAR AS I'M GOING.
YEAH, WELL, WE'LL ALWAYS HAVE THE HOT ZONE CLUB.
NEVER TOP THAT.
DEFINITELY NOT.
MIGHT BE FUN TRYING...
MIGHT VERY WELL...
THE AIRLESS WATER-FILLED CANISTER HAS NOW BEEN LOCKED FOR TWO MINUTES AND FORTY-ONE SECONDS!
TWO MINUTES AND FIFTY SECONDS!
WE'LL BE SETTIN' OUT FOR HEAVEN IN MY LITTLE SPEED BOAT...

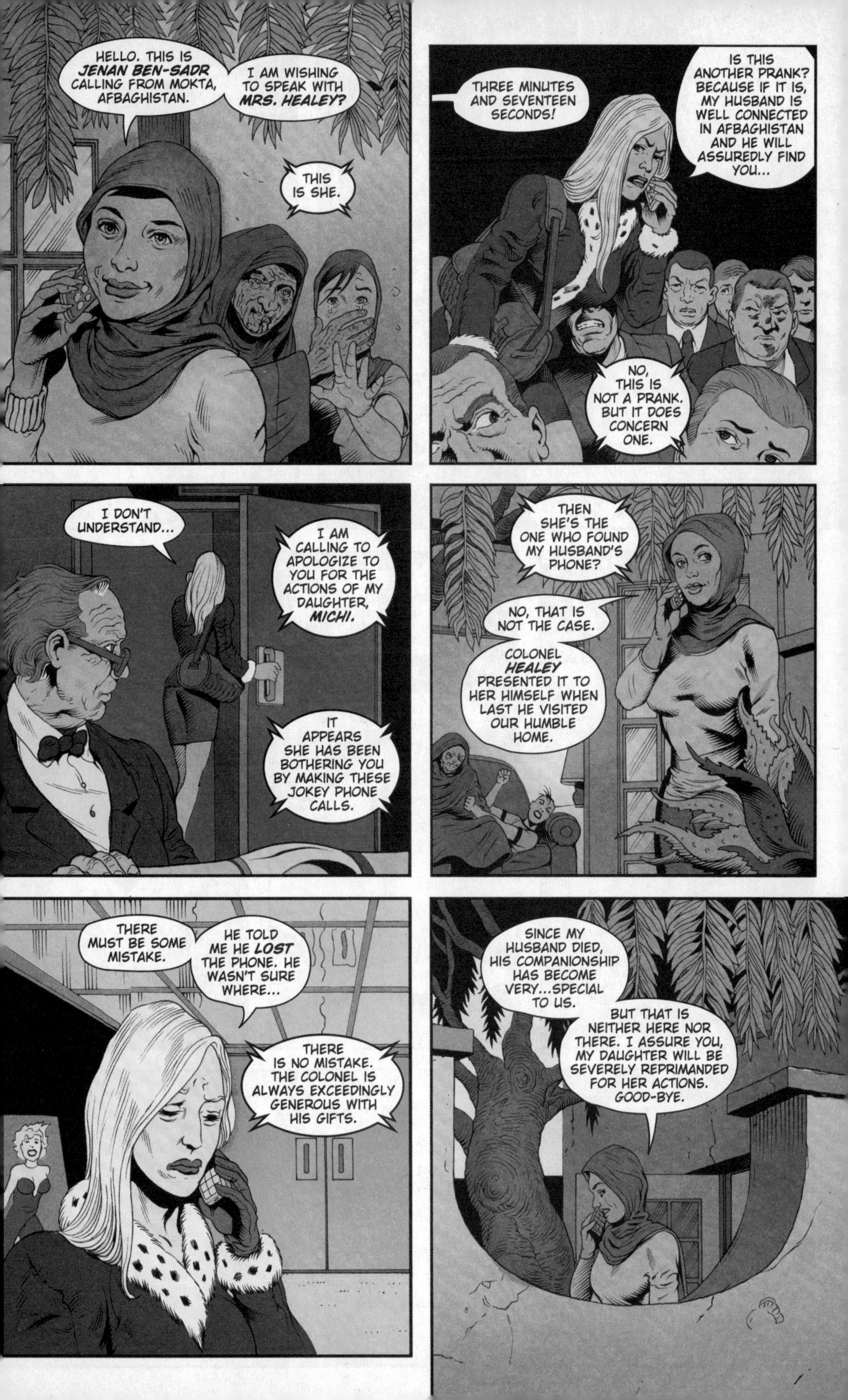
HELLO. THIS IS JENAN BEN-SADR CALLING FROM MOKTA, AFBAGHISTAN.
I AM WISHING TO SPEAK WITH MRS. HEALEY?
THIS IS SHE.
THREE MINUTES AND SEVENTEEN SECONDS!
IS THIS ANOTHER PRANK? BECAUSE IF IT IS, MY HUSBAND IS WELL CONNECTED IN AFBAGHISTAN AND HE WILL ASSUREDLY FIND YOU...
NO, THIS IS NOT A PRANK. BUT IT DOES CONCERN ONE.
I DON'T UNDERSTAND...
I AM CALLING TO APOLOGIZE TO YOU FOR THE ACTIONS OF MY DAUGHTER, MICHI.
IT APPEARS SHE HAS BEEN BOTHERING YOU BY MAKING THESE JOKEY PHONE CALLS.
THEN SHE'S THE ONE WHO FOUND MY HUSBAND'S PHONE?
NO, THAT IS NOT THE CASE.
COLONEL HEALEY PRESENTED IT TO HER HIMSELF WHEN LAST HE VISITED OUR HUMBLE HOME.
THERE MUST BE SOME MISTAKE.
HE TOLD ME HE LOST THE PHONE. HE WASN'T SURE WHERE...
THERE IS NO MISTAKE. THE COLONEL IS ALWAYS EXCEEDINGLY GENEROUS WITH HIS GIFTS.
SINCE MY HUSBAND DIED, HIS COMPANIONSHIP HAS BECOME VERY...SPECIAL TO US.
BUT THAT IS NEITHER HERE NOR THERE. I ASSURE YOU, MY DAUGHTER WILL BE SEVERELY REPRIMANDED FOR HER ACTIONS. GOOD-BYE.

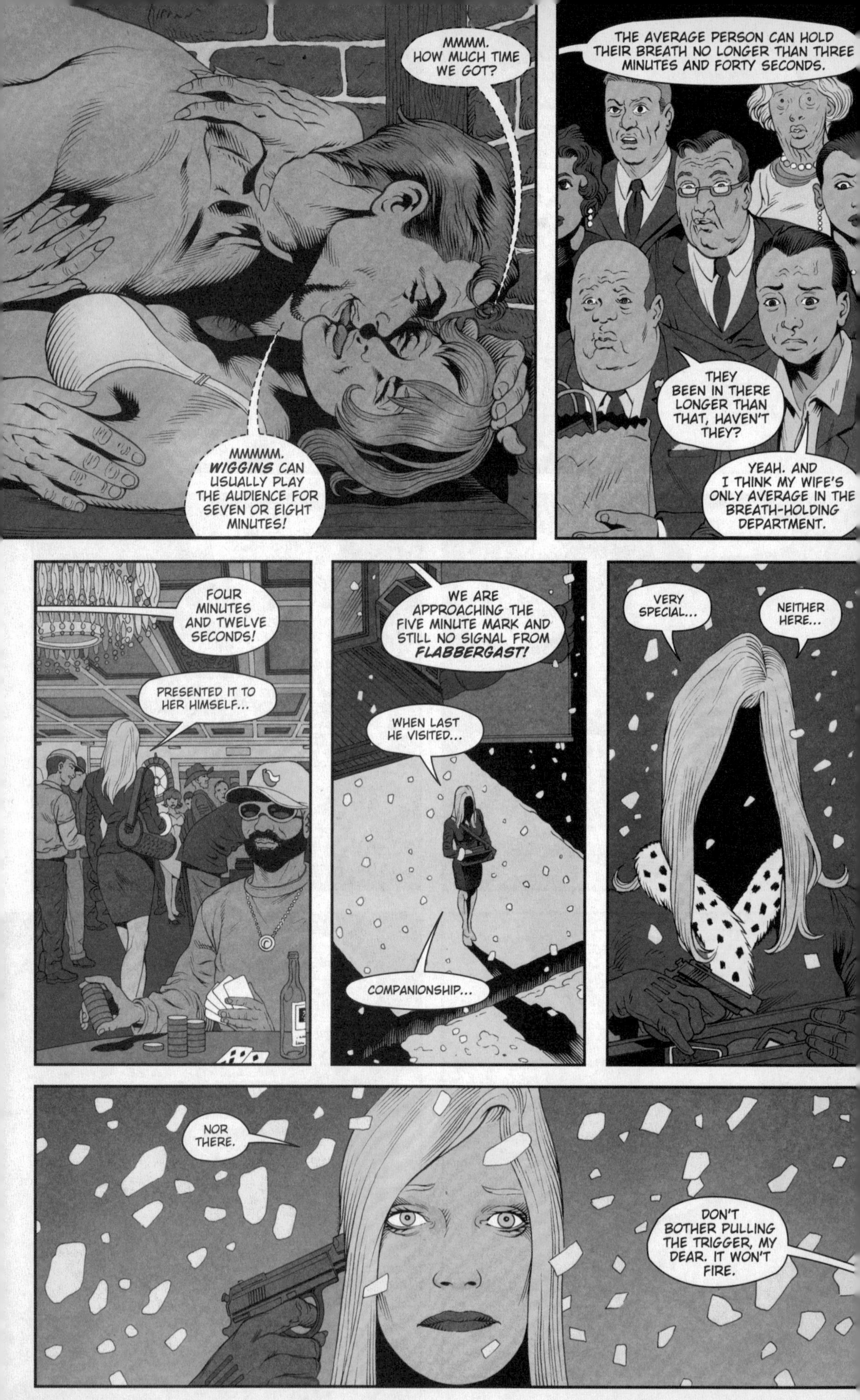
MMMM. HOW MUCH TIME WE GOT?
MMMMM. WIGGINS CAN USUALLY PLAY THE AUDIENCE FOR SEVEN OR EIGHT MINUTES!
THE AVERAGE PERSON CAN HOLD THEIR BREATH NO LONGER THAN THREE MINUTES AND FORTY SECONDS.
THEY BEEN IN THERE LONGER THAN THAT, HAVEN'T THEY?
YEAH. AND I THINK MY WIFE'S ONLY AVERAGE IN THE BREATH-HOLDING DEPARTMENT.
FOUR MINUTES AND TWELVE SECONDS!
PRESENTED IT TO HER HIMSELF...
WE ARE APPROACHING THE FIVE MINUTE MARK AND STILL NO SIGNAL FROM FLABBERGAST!
WHEN LAST HE VISITED...
COMPANIONSHIP...
VERY SPECIAL...
NEITHER HERE...
NOR THERE.
DON'T BOTHER PULLING THE TRIGGER, MY DEAR. IT WON'T FIRE.

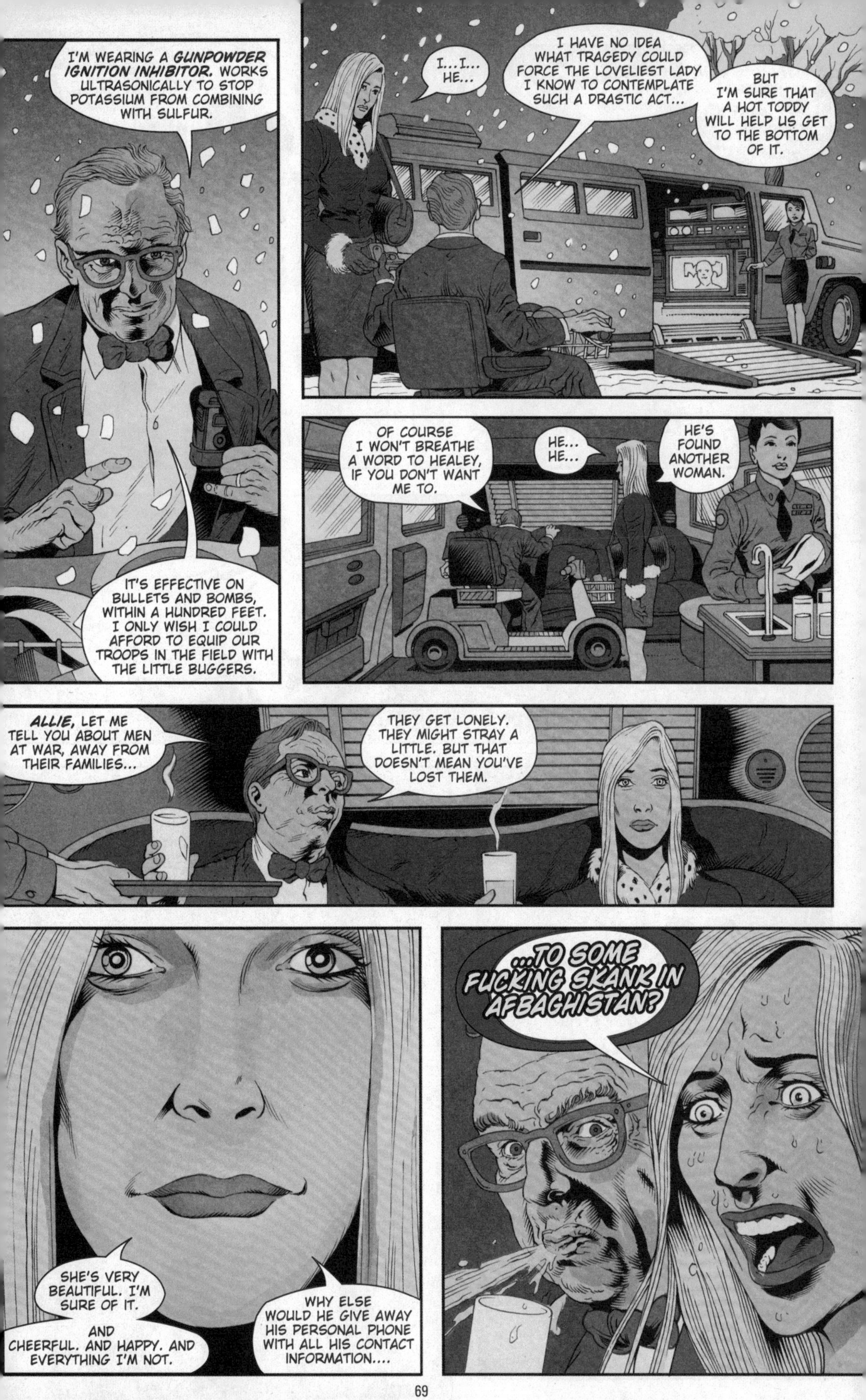
I'M WEARING A GUNPOWDER IGNITION INHIBITOR. WORKS ULTRASONICALLY TO STOP POTASSIUM FROM COMBINING WITH SULFUR.
IT'S EFFECTIVE ON BULLETS AND BOMBS, WITHIN A HUNDRED FEET. I ONLY WISH I COULD AFFORD TO EQUIP OUR TROOPS IN THE FIELD WITH THE LITTLE BUGGERS.
I...I... HE...
I HAVE NO IDEA WHAT TRAGEDY COULD FORCE THE LOVELIEST LADY I KNOW TO CONTEMPLATE SUCH A DRASTIC ACT...
BUT I'M SURE THAT A HOT TODDY WILL HELP US GET TO THE BOTTOM OF IT.
OF COURSE I WON'T BREATHE A WORD TO HEALEY, IF YOU DON'T WANT ME TO.
HE... HE...
HE'S FOUND ANOTHER WOMAN.
ALLIE, LET ME TELL YOU ABOUT MEN AT WAR, AWAY FROM THEIR FAMILIES...
THEY GET LONELY. THEY MIGHT STRAY A LITTLE. BUT THAT DOESN'T MEAN YOU'VE LOST THEM.
SHE'S VERY BEAUTIFUL. I'M SURE OF IT.
AND CHEERFUL. AND HAPPY. AND EVERYTHING I'M NOT.
WHY ELSE WOULD HE GIVE AWAY HIS PERSONAL PHONE WITH ALL HIS CONTACT INFORMATION....
...TO SOME FUCKING SKANK IN AFBAGHISTAN?

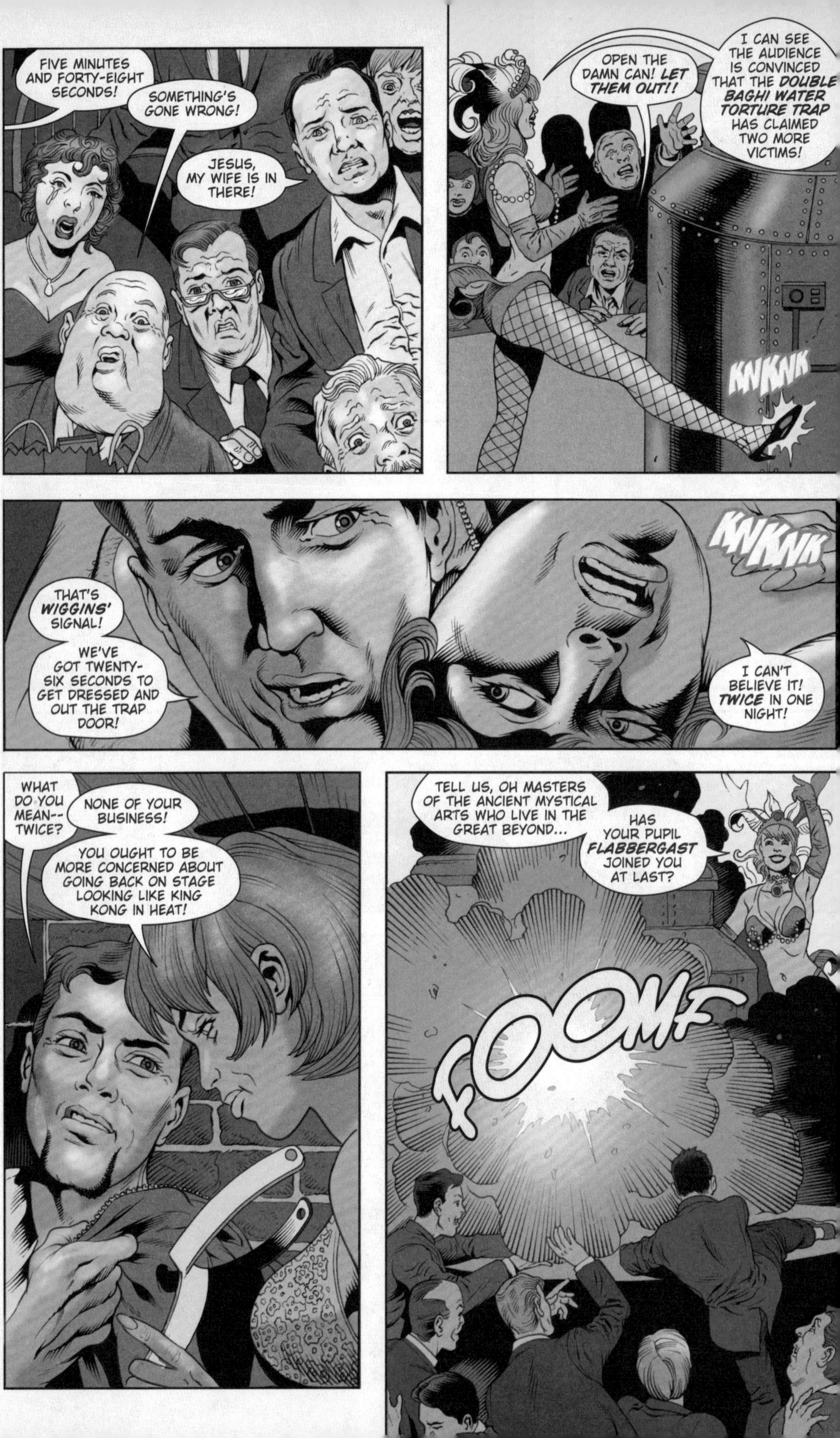
FIVE MINUTES AND FORTY-EIGHT SECONDS!
SOMETHING'S GONE WRONG!
JESUS, MY WIFE IS IN THERE!
OPEN THE DAMN CAN! LET THEM OUT!!
I CAN SEE THE AUDIENCE IS CONVINCED THAT THE DOUBLE BAGHI WATER TORTURE TRAP HAS CLAIMED TWO MORE VICTIMS!
KNKNK
KNKNK
THAT'S WIGGINS' SIGNAL!
WE'VE GOT TWENTY-SIX SECONDS TO GET DRESSED AND OUT THE TRAP DOOR!
I CAN'T BELIEVE IT! TWICE IN ONE NIGHT!
WHAT DO YOU MEAN--TWICE?
NONE OF YOUR BUSINESS!
YOU OUGHT TO BE MORE CONCERNED ABOUT GOING BACK ON STAGE LOOKING LIKE KING KONG IN HEAT!
TELL US, OH MASTERS OF THE ANCIENT MYSTICAL ARTS WHO LIVE IN THE GREAT BEYOND...
HAS YOUR PUPIL FLABBERGAST JOINED YOU AT LAST?
FOOMF

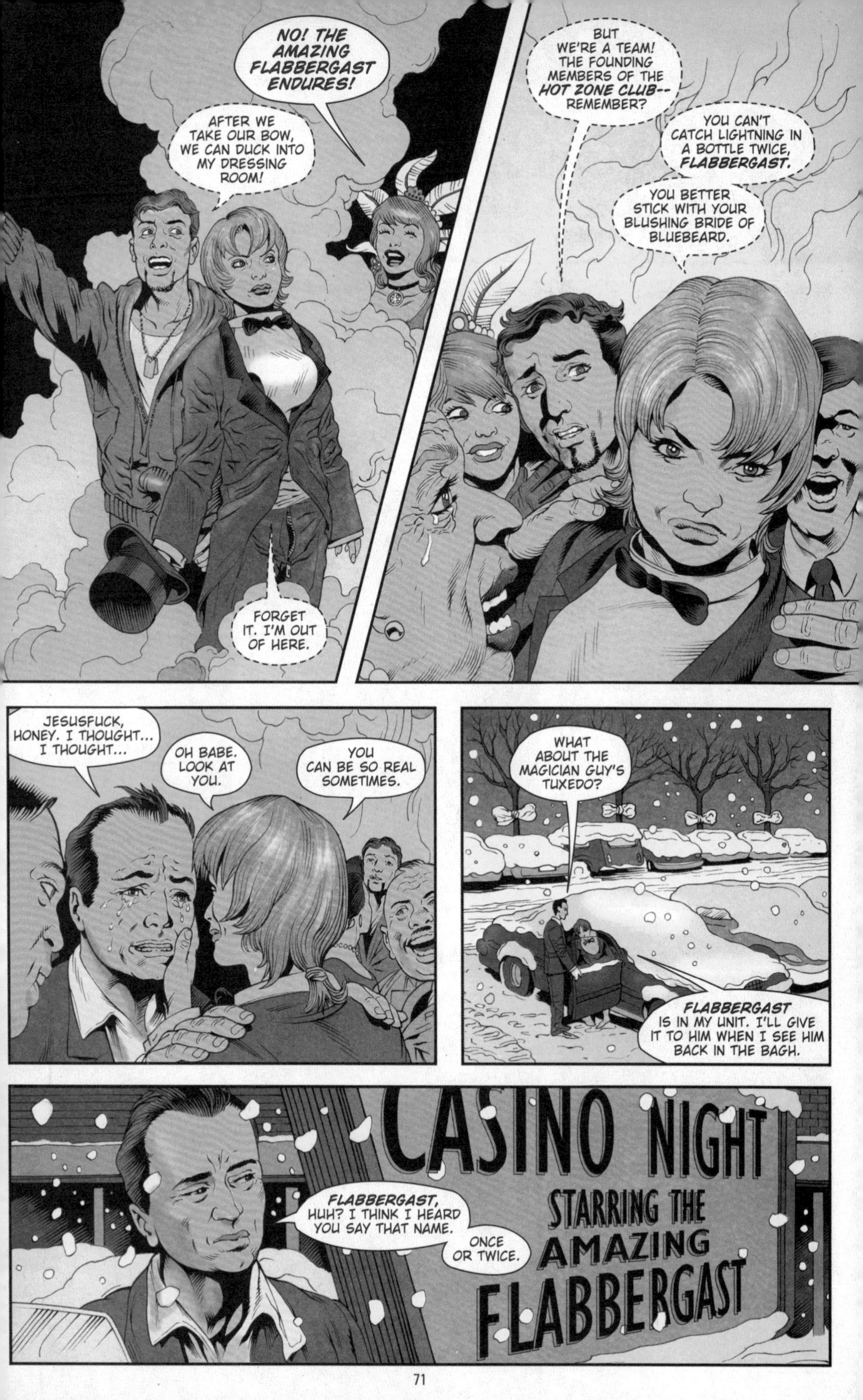
NO! THE AMAZING FLABBERGAST ENDURES!
AFTER WE TAKE OUR BOW, WE CAN DUCK INTO MY DRESSING ROOM!
FORGET IT. I'M OUT OF HERE.
BUT WE'RE A TEAM! THE FOUNDING MEMBERS OF THE HOT ZONE CLUB-- REMEMBER?
YOU CAN'T CATCH LIGHTNING IN A BOTTLE TWICE, FLABBERGAST.
YOU BETTER STICK WITH YOUR BLUSHING BRIDE OF BLUEBEARD.
JESUSFUCK, HONEY. I THOUGHT... I THOUGHT...
OH BABE. LOOK AT YOU.
YOU CAN BE SO REAL SOMETIMES.
WHAT ABOUT THE MAGICIAN GUY'S TUXEDO?
FLABBERGAST IS IN MY UNIT. I'LL GIVE IT TO HIM WHEN I SEE HIM BACK IN THE BAGH.
CASINO NIGHT
STARRING THE AMAZING FLABBERGAST
FLABBERGAST, HUH? I THINK I HEARD YOU SAY THAT NAME.
ONCE OR TWICE.

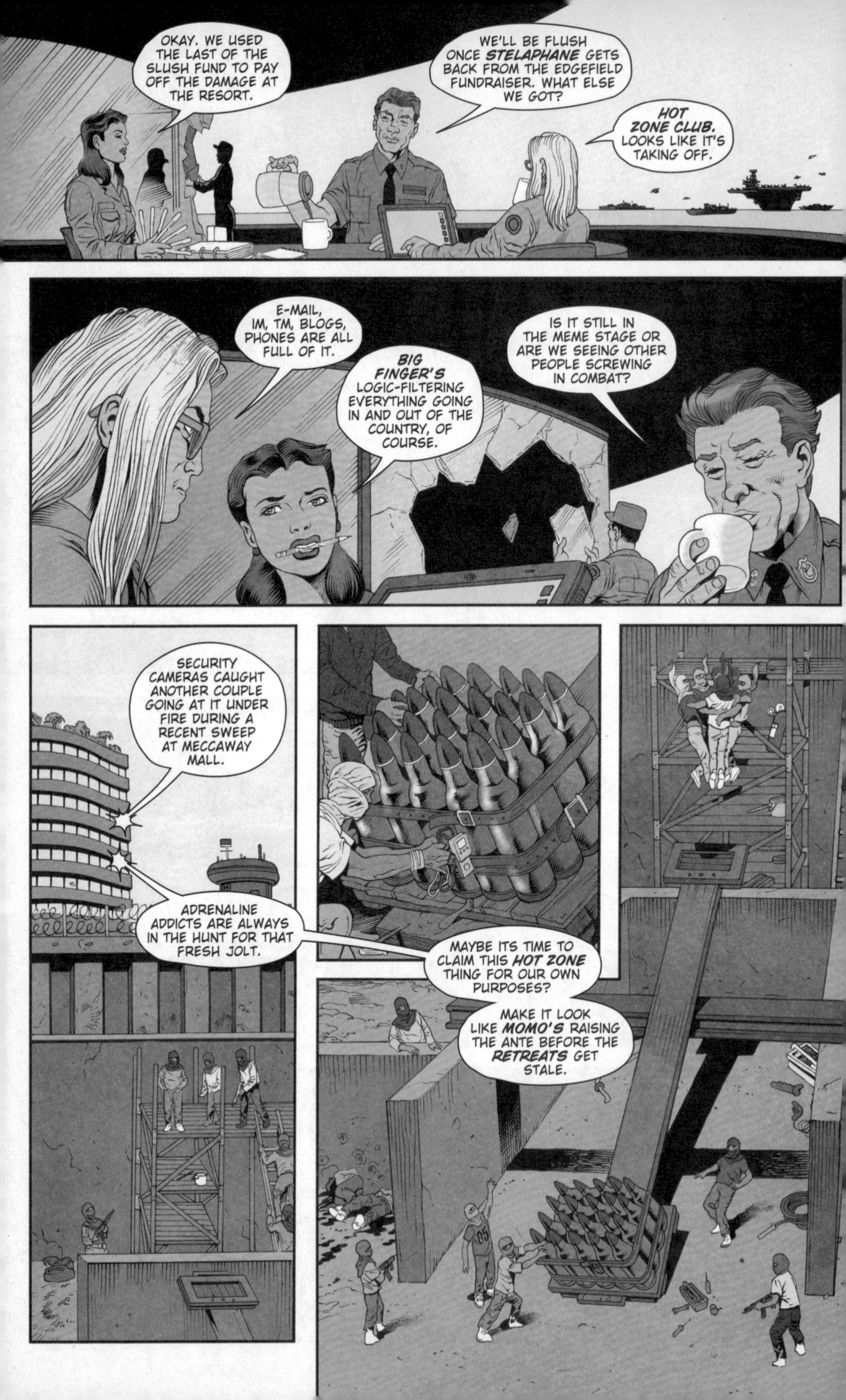
OKAY. WE USED THE LAST OF THE SLUSH FUND TO PAY OFF THE DAMAGE AT THE RESORT.
WE'LL BE FLUSH ONCE STELAPHANE GETS BACK FROM THE EDGEFIELD FUNDRAISER. WHAT ELSE WE GOT?
HOT ZONE CLUB. LOOKS LIKE IT'S TAKING OFF.
E-MAIL, IM, TM, BLOGS, PHONES ARE ALL FULL OF IT.
BIG FINGER'S LOGIC-FILTERING EVERYTHING GOING IN AND OUT OF THE COUNTRY, OF COURSE.
IS IT STILL IN THE MEME STAGE OR ARE WE SEEING OTHER PEOPLE SCREWING IN COMBAT?
SECURITY CAMERAS CAUGHT ANOTHER COUPLE GOING AT IT UNDER FIRE DURING A RECENT SWEEP AT MECCAWAY MALL.
ADRENALINE ADDICTS ARE ALWAYS IN THE HUNT FOR THAT FRESH JOLT.
MAYBE ITS TIME TO CLAIM THIS HOT ZONE THING FOR OUR OWN PURPOSES?
MAKE IT LOOK LIKE MOMO'S RAISING THE ANTE BEFORE THE RETREATS GET STALE.

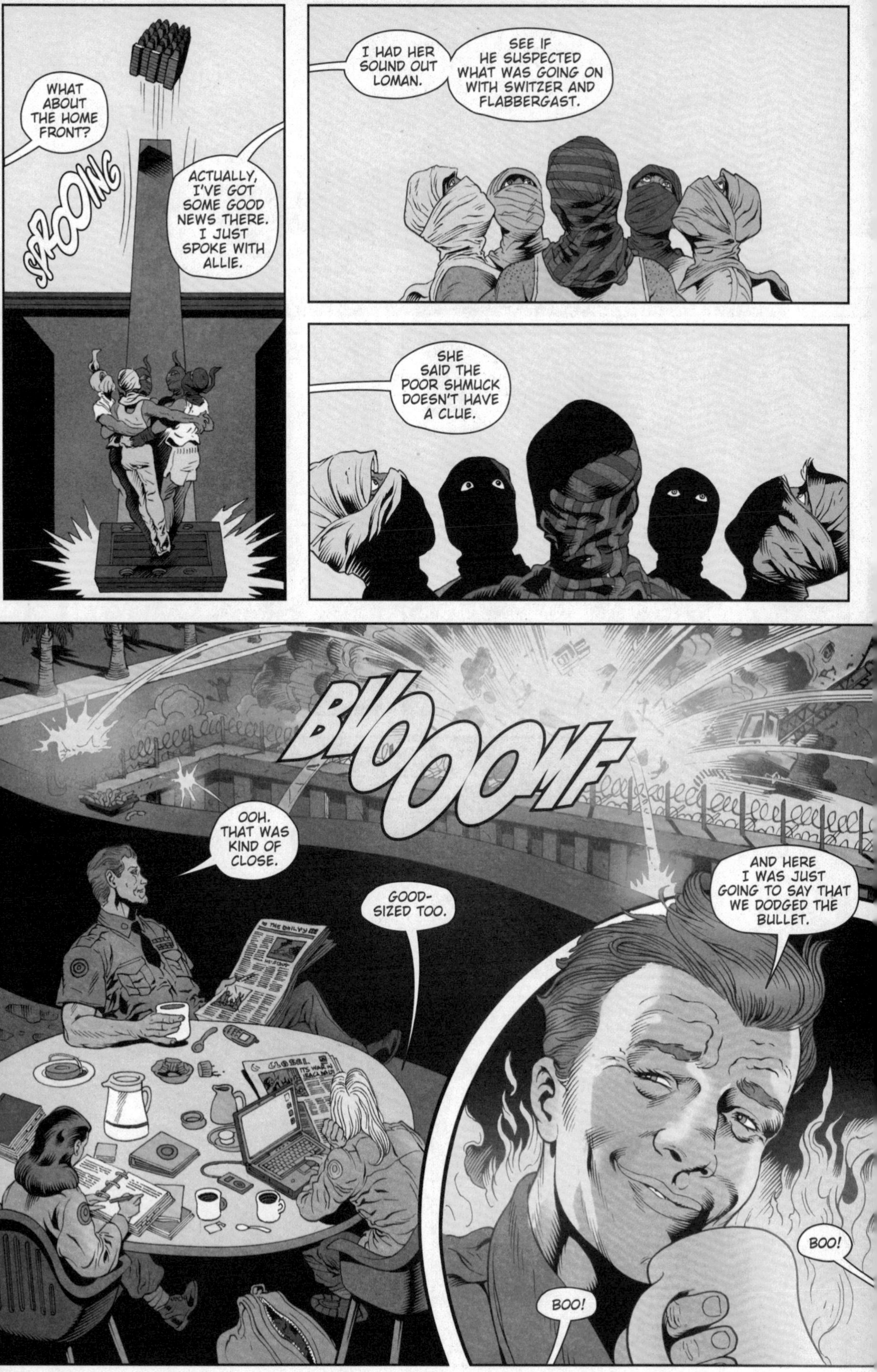
WHAT ABOUT THE HOME FRONT?
SPROOING
ACTUALLY, I'VE GOT SOME GOOD NEWS THERE. I JUST SPOKE WITH ALLIE.
I HAD HER SOUND OUT LOMAN.
SEE IF HE SUSPECTED WHAT WAS GOING ON WITH SWITZER AND FLABBERGAST.
SHE SAID THE POOR SHMUCK DOESN'T HAVE A CLUE.
BVOOOOMF
OOH. THAT WAS KIND OF CLOSE.
GOOD-SIZED TOO.
AND HERE I WAS JUST GOING TO SAY THAT WE DODGED THE BULLET.
BOO!
BOO!

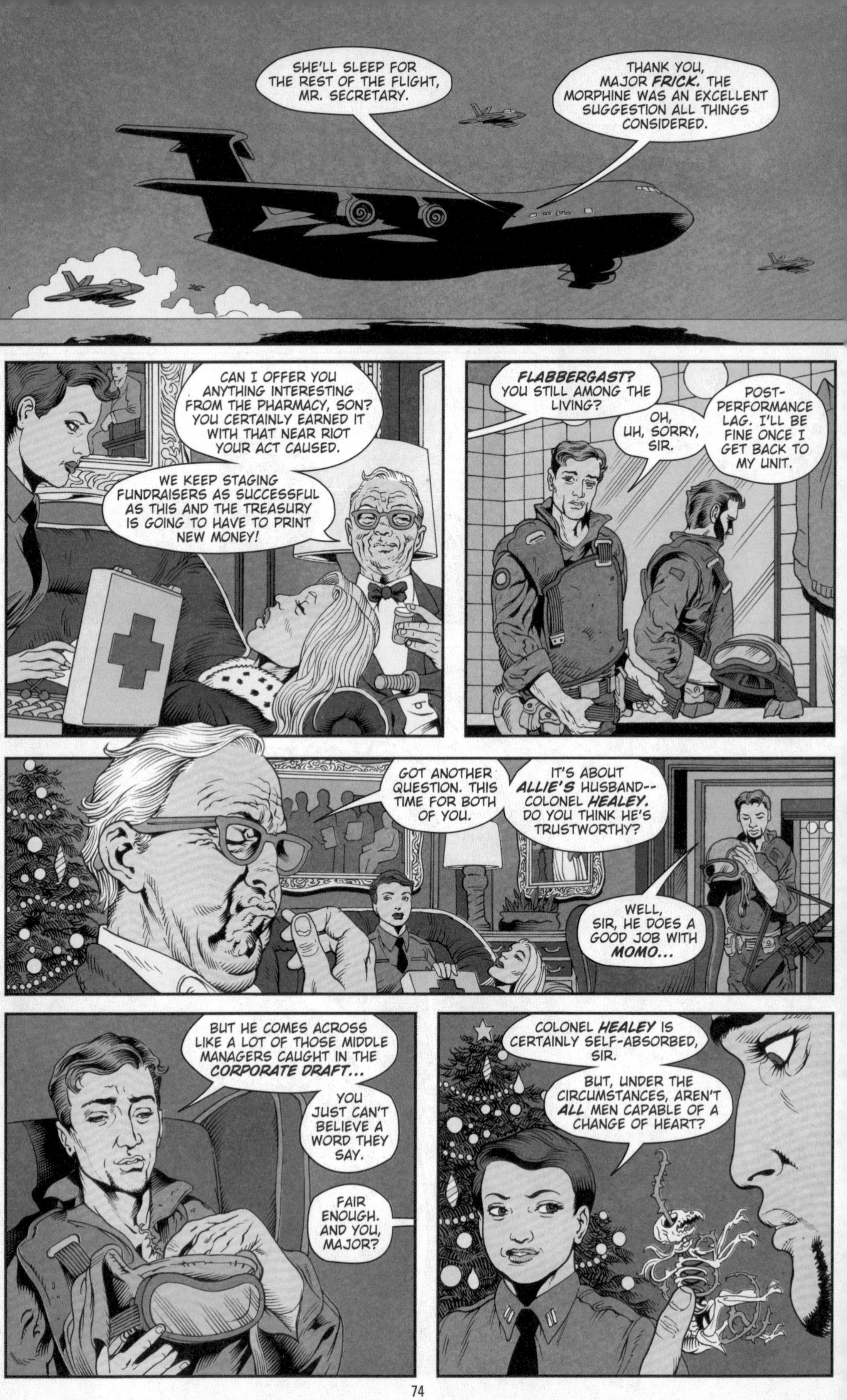
SHE'LL SLEEP FOR THE REST OF THE FLIGHT, MR. SECRETARY.
THANK YOU, MAJOR FRICK. THE MORPHINE WAS AN EXCELLENT SUGGESTION ALL THINGS CONSIDERED.
CAN I OFFER YOU ANYTHING INTERESTING FROM THE PHARMACY, SON? YOU CERTAINLY EARNED IT WITH THAT NEAR RIOT YOUR ACT CAUSED.
WE KEEP STAGING FUNDRAISERS AS SUCCESSFUL AS THIS AND THE TREASURY IS GOING TO HAVE TO PRINT NEW MONEY!
FLABBERGAST? YOU STILL AMONG THE LIVING?
OH, UH, SORRY, SIR.
POST-PERFORMANCE LAG. I'LL BE FINE ONCE I GET BACK TO MY UNIT.
GOT ANOTHER QUESTION. THIS TIME FOR BOTH OF YOU.
IT'S ABOUT ALLIE'S HUSBAND-- COLONEL HEALEY. DO YOU THINK HE'S TRUSTWORTHY?
WELL, SIR, HE DOES A GOOD JOB WITH MOMO...
BUT HE COMES ACROSS LIKE A LOT OF THOSE MIDDLE MANAGERS CAUGHT IN THE CORPORATE DRAFT...
YOU JUST CAN'T BELIEVE A WORD THEY SAY.
FAIR ENOUGH. AND YOU, MAJOR?
COLONEL HEALEY IS CERTAINLY SELF-ABSORBED, SIR.
BUT, UNDER THE CIRCUMSTANCES, AREN'T ALL MEN CAPABLE OF A CHANGE OF HEART?

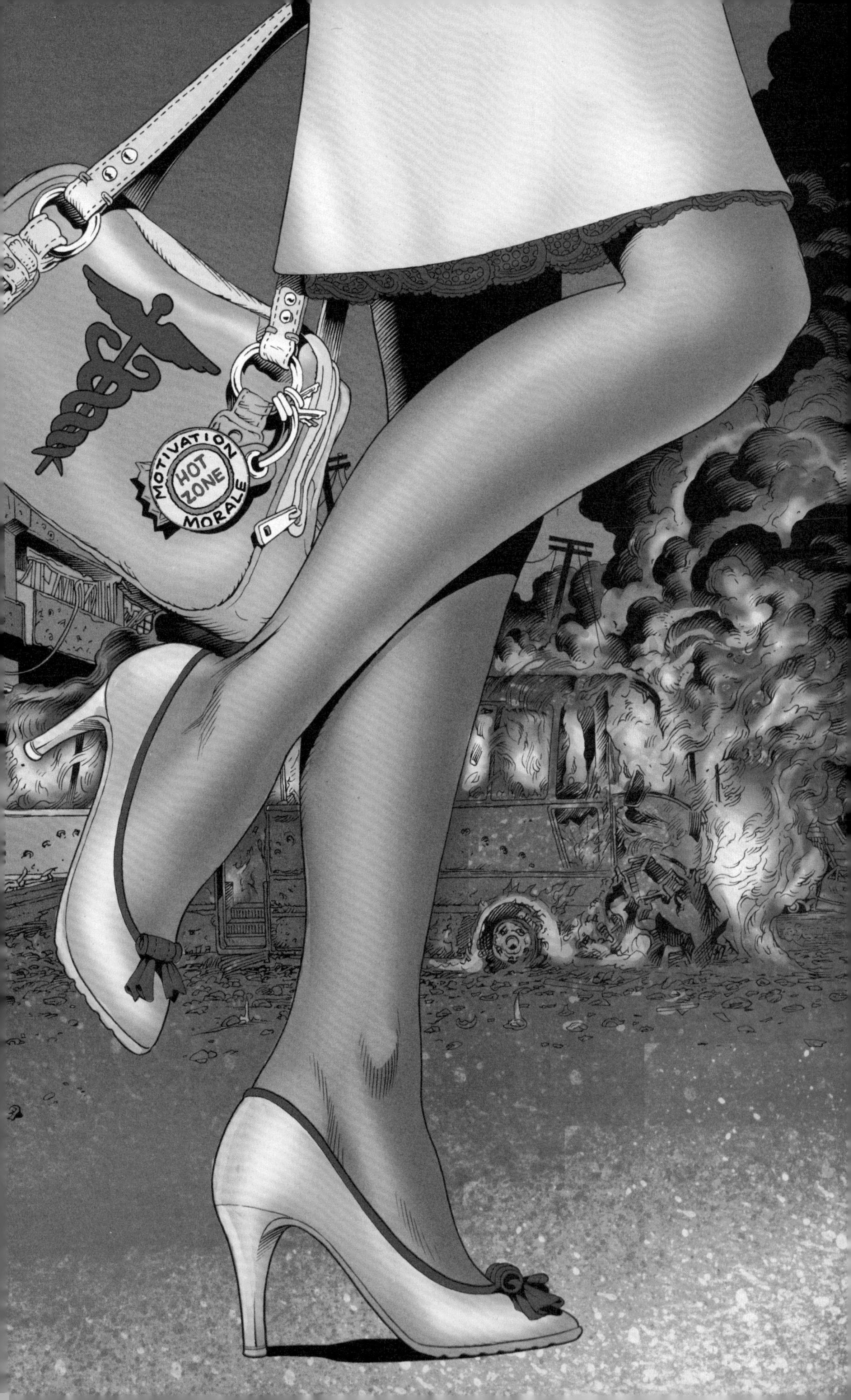
MOTIVATION
HOT ZONE
MORALE

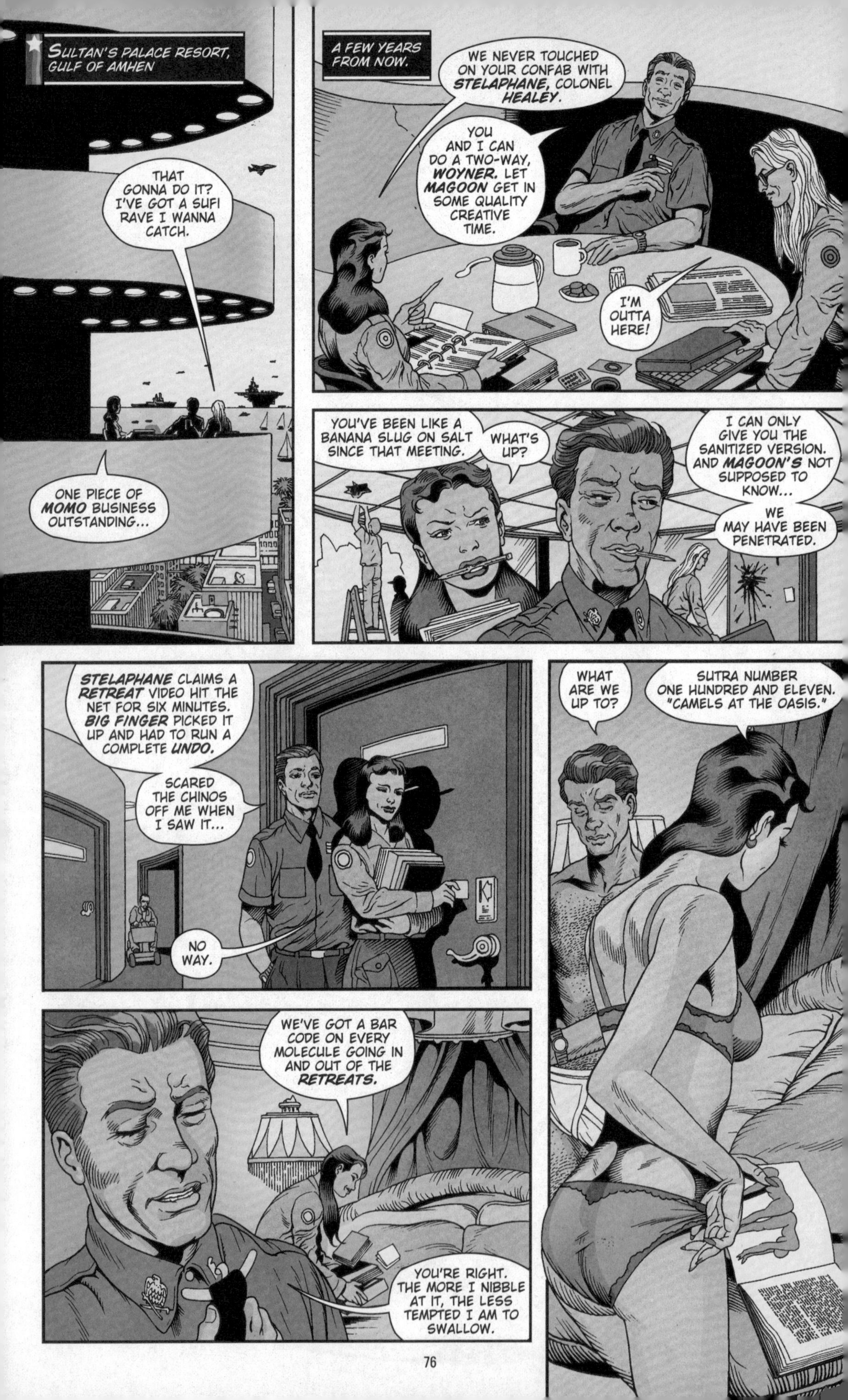
SULTAN'S PALACE RESORT, GULF OF AMHEN
THAT GONNA DO IT? I'VE GOT A SUFI RAVE I WANNA CATCH.
ONE PIECE OF MOMO BUSINESS OUTSTANDING...
A FEW YEARS FROM NOW.
WE NEVER TOUCHED ON YOUR CONFAB WITH STELAPHANE, COLONEL HEALEY.
YOU AND I CAN DO A TWO-WAY, WOYNER. LET MAGOON GET IN SOME QUALITY CREATIVE TIME.
I'M OUTTA HERE!
YOU'VE BEEN LIKE A BANANA SLUG ON SALT SINCE THAT MEETING.
WHAT'S UP?
I CAN ONLY GIVE YOU THE SANITIZED VERSION. AND MAGOON'S NOT SUPPOSED TO KNOW...
WE MAY HAVE BEEN PENETRATED.
STELAPHANE CLAIMS A RETREAT VIDEO HIT THE NET FOR SIX MINUTES. BIG FINGER PICKED IT UP AND HAD TO RUN A COMPLETE UNDO.
SCARED THE CHINOS OFF ME WHEN I SAW IT...
NO WAY.
WE'VE GOT A BAR CODE ON EVERY MOLECULE GOING IN AND OUT OF THE RETREATS.
YOU'RE RIGHT. THE MORE I NIBBLE AT IT, THE LESS TEMPTED I AM TO SWALLOW.
WHAT ARE WE UP TO?
SUTRA NUMBER ONE HUNDRED AND ELEVEN. "CAMELS AT THE OASIS."

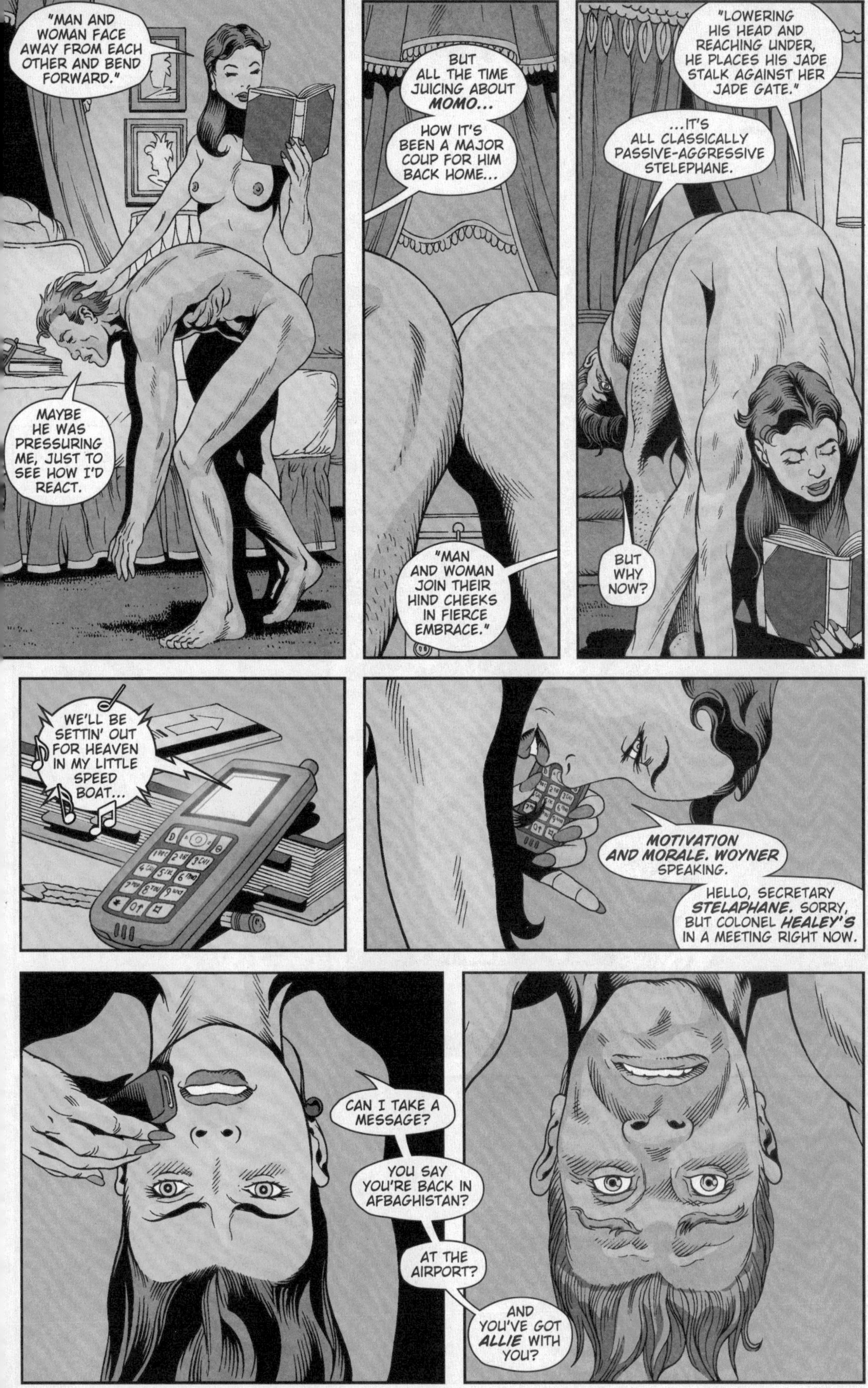
"MAN AND WOMAN FACE AWAY FROM EACH OTHER AND BEND FORWARD."
MAYBE HE WAS PRESSURING ME, JUST TO SEE HOW I'D REACT.
BUT ALL THE TIME JUICING ABOUT MOMO...
HOW IT'S BEEN A MAJOR COUP FOR HIM BACK HOME...
"MAN AND WOMAN JOIN THEIR HIND CHEEKS IN FIERCE EMBRACE."
"LOWERING HIS HEAD AND REACHING UNDER, HE PLACES HIS JADE STALK AGAINST HER JADE GATE."
...IT'S ALL CLASSICALLY PASSIVE-AGGRESSIVE STELEPHANE.
BUT WHY NOW?
WE'LL BE SETTIN' OUT FOR HEAVEN IN MY LITTLE SPEED BOAT...
MOTIVATION AND MORALE. WOYNER SPEAKING.
HELLO, SECRETARY STELAPHANE. SORRY, BUT COLONEL HEALEY'S IN A MEETING RIGHT NOW.
CAN I TAKE A MESSAGE?
YOU SAY YOU'RE BACK IN AFBAGHISTAN?
AT THE AIRPORT?
AND YOU'VE GOT ALLIE WITH YOU?

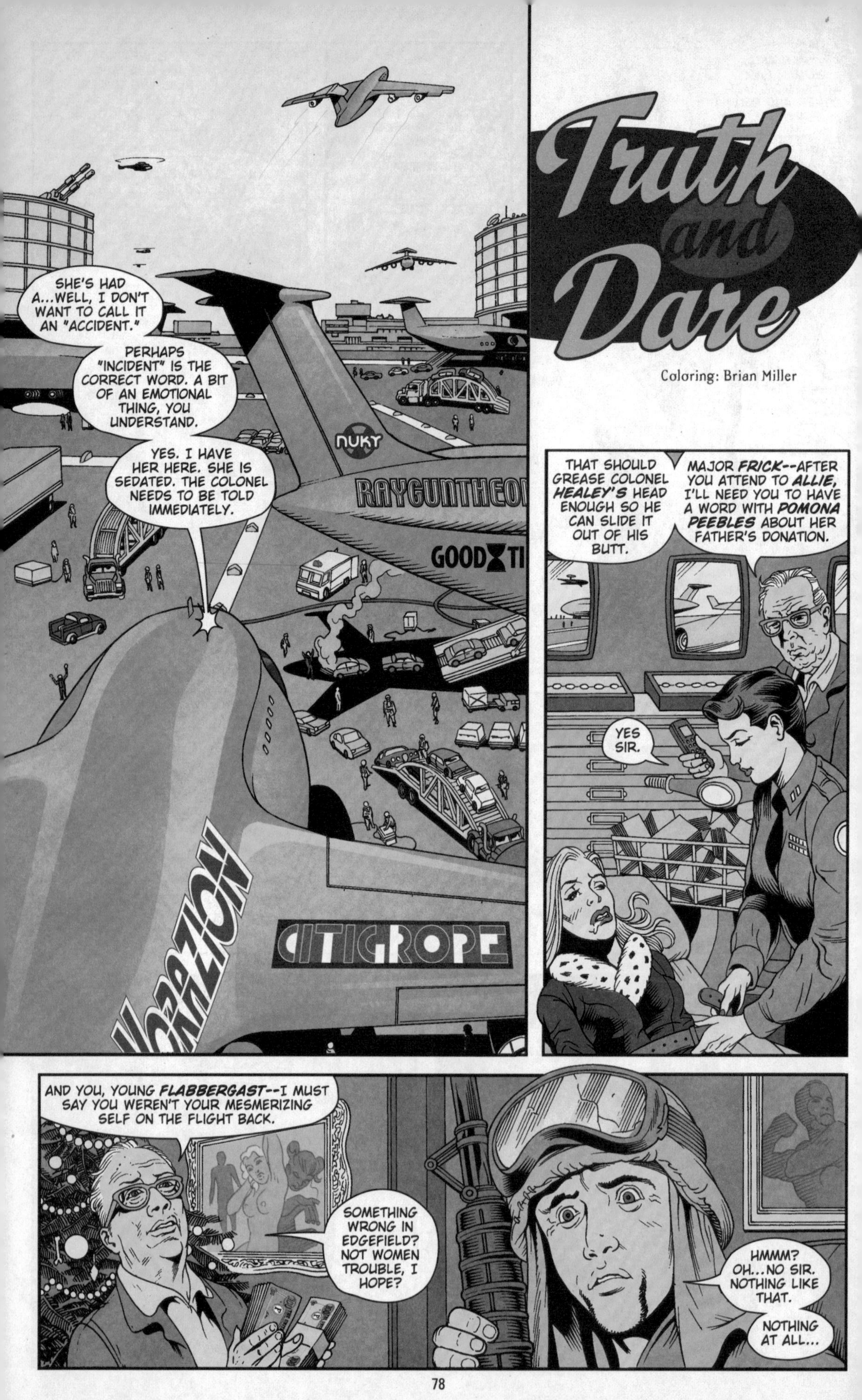

Truth and Dare
Coloring: Brian Miller
SHE'S HAD A...WELL, I DON'T WANT TO CALL IT AN "ACCIDENT."
PERHAPS "INCIDENT" IS THE CORRECT WORD. A BIT OF AN EMOTIONAL THING, YOU UNDERSTAND.
YES. I HAVE HER HERE. SHE IS SEDATED. THE COLONEL NEEDS TO BE TOLD IMMEDIATELY.
NUKY
RAYGUNTHEO
GOOD
CITIGROPE
THAT SHOULD GREASE COLONEL HEALEY'S HEAD ENOUGH SO HE CAN SLIDE IT OUT OF HIS BUTT.
MAJOR FRICK--AFTER YOU ATTEND TO ALLIE, I'LL NEED YOU TO HAVE A WORD WITH POMONA PEEBLES ABOUT HER FATHER'S DONATION.
YES SIR.
AND YOU, YOUNG FLABBERGAST--I MUST SAY YOU WEREN'T YOUR MESMERIZING SELF ON THE FLIGHT BACK.
SOMETHING WRONG IN EDGEFIELD? NOT WOMEN TROUBLE, I HOPE?
HMMM? OH...NO SIR. NOTHING LIKE THAT.
NOTHING AT ALL...

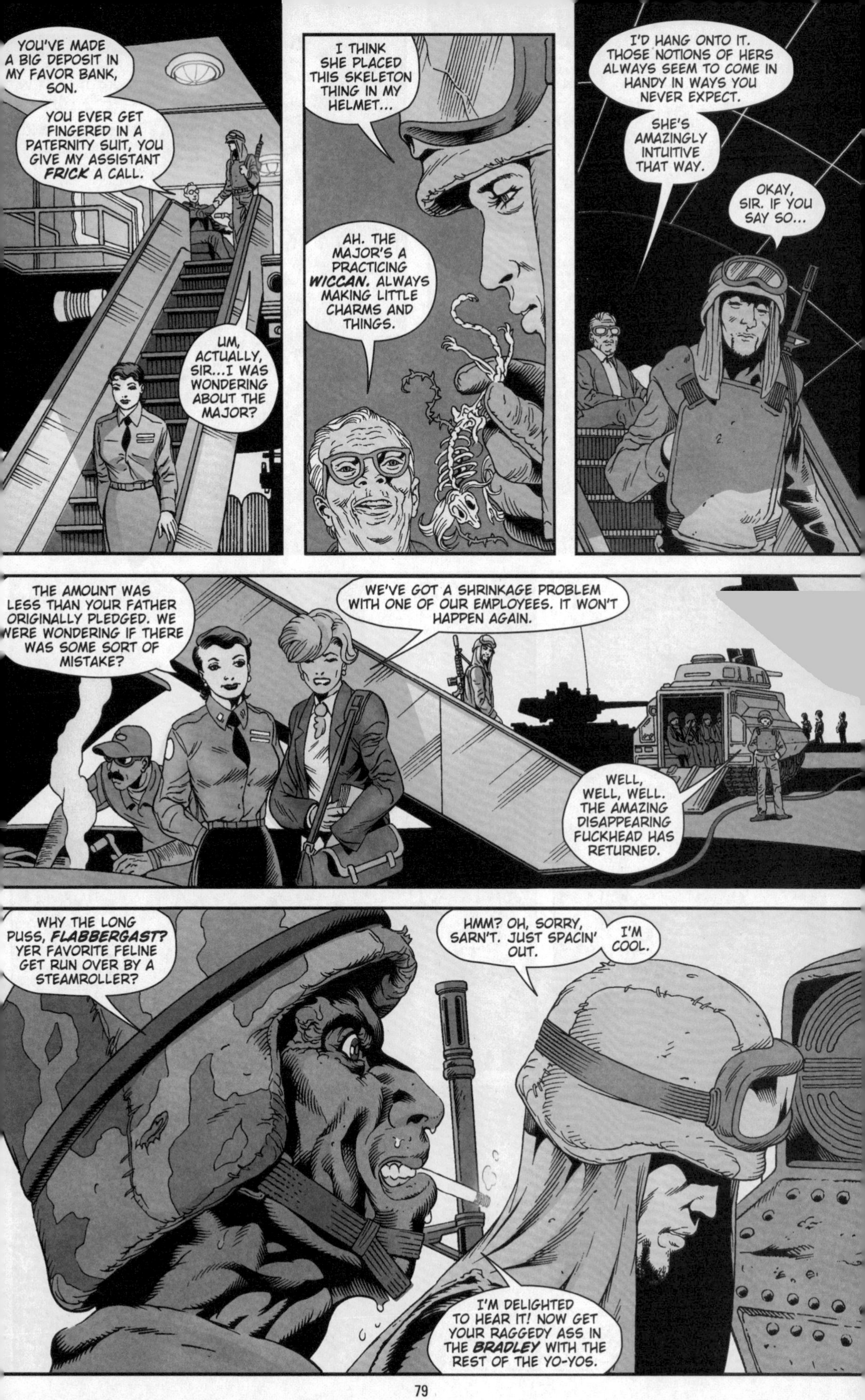

YOU'VE MADE A BIG DEPOSIT IN MY FAVOR BANK, SON.
YOU EVER GET FINGERED IN A PATERNITY SUIT, YOU GIVE MY ASSISTANT FRICK A CALL.
UM, ACTUALLY, SIR...I WAS WONDERING ABOUT THE MAJOR?
I THINK SHE PLACED THIS SKELETON THING IN MY HELMET...
AH. THE MAJOR'S A PRACTICING WICCAN. ALWAYS MAKING LITTLE CHARMS AND THINGS.
I'D HANG ONTO IT. THOSE NOTIONS OF HERS ALWAYS SEEM TO COME IN HANDY IN WAYS YOU NEVER EXPECT.
SHE'S AMAZINGLY INTUITIVE THAT WAY.
OKAY, SIR. IF YOU SAY SO...
THE AMOUNT WAS LESS THAN YOUR FATHER ORIGINALLY PLEDGED. WE WERE WONDERING IF THERE WAS SOME SORT OF MISTAKE?
WE'VE GOT A SHRINKAGE PROBLEM WITH ONE OF OUR EMPLOYEES. IT WON'T HAPPEN AGAIN.
WELL, WELL, WELL. THE AMAZING DISAPPEARING FUCKHEAD HAS RETURNED.
WHY THE LONG PUSS, FLABBERGAST? YER FAVORITE FELINE GET RUN OVER BY A STEAMROLLER?
HMM? OH, SORRY, SARN'T. JUST SPACIN' OUT.
I'M COOL.
I'M DELIGHTED TO HEAR IT! NOW GET YOUR RAGGEDY ASS IN THE BRADLEY WITH THE REST OF THE YO-YOS.

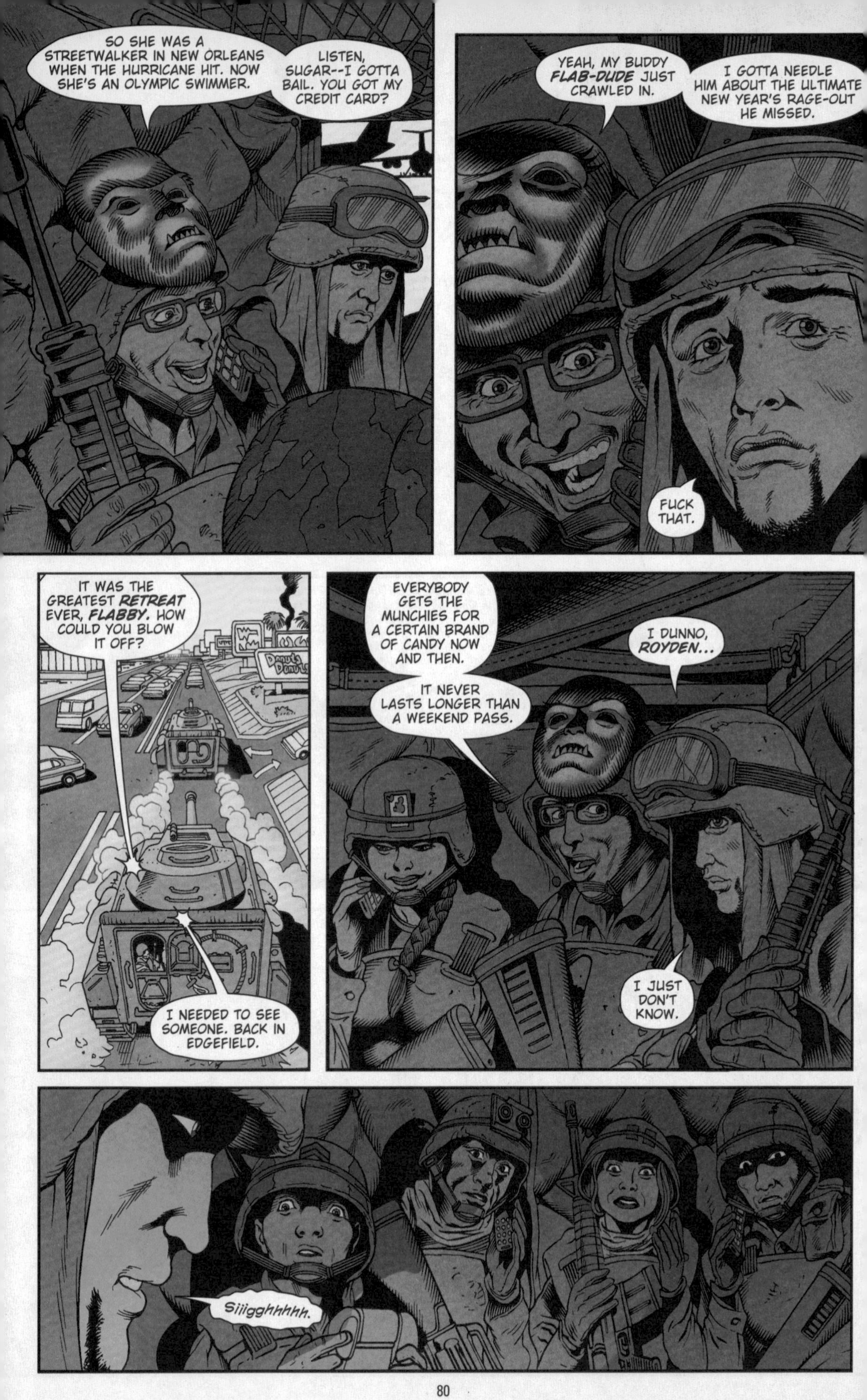
SO SHE WAS A STREETWALKER IN NEW ORLEANS WHEN THE HURRICANE HIT. NOW SHE'S AN OLYMPIC SWIMMER.
LISTEN, SUGAR--I GOTTA BAIL. YOU GOT MY CREDIT CARD?
YEAH, MY BUDDY FLAB-DUDE JUST CRAWLED IN.
I GOTTA NEEDLE HIM ABOUT THE ULTIMATE NEW YEAR'S RAGE-OUT HE MISSED.
FUCK THAT.
IT WAS THE GREATEST RETREAT EVER, FLABBY. HOW COULD YOU BLOW IT OFF?
I NEEDED TO SEE SOMEONE. BACK IN EDGEFIELD.
EVERYBODY GETS THE MUNCHIES FOR A CERTAIN BRAND OF CANDY NOW AND THEN.
IT NEVER LASTS LONGER THAN A WEEKEND PASS.
I DUNNO, ROYDEN...
I JUST DON'T KNOW.
Siiigghhhhh.

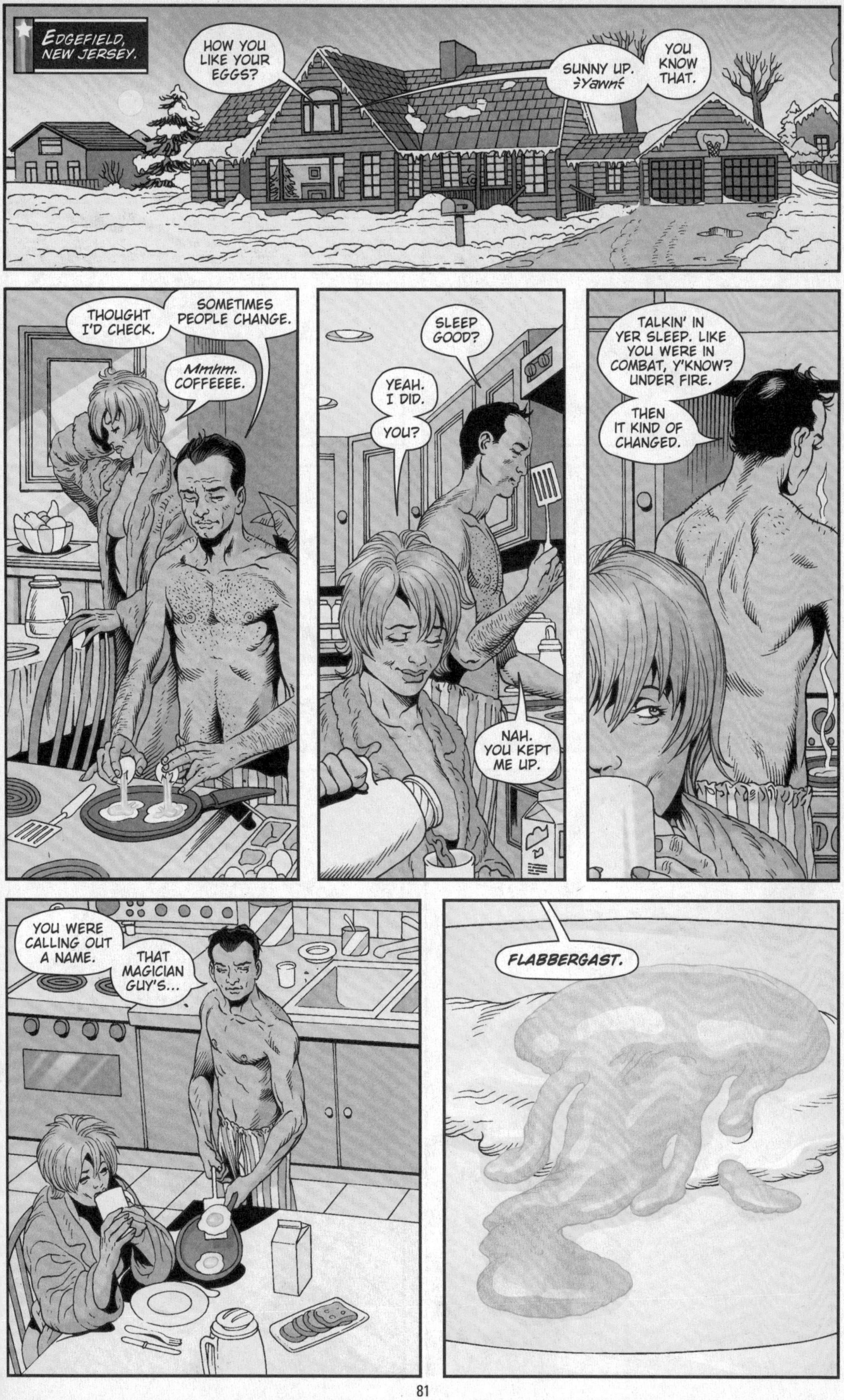
EDGEFIELD, NEW JERSEY.
HOW YOU LIKE YOUR EGGS?
SUNNY UP. ;Yawn;
YOU KNOW THAT.
THOUGHT I'D CHECK.
SOMETIMES PEOPLE CHANGE.
Mmhm. COFFEEEE.
SLEEP GOOD?
YEAH. I DID.
YOU?
NAH. YOU KEPT ME UP.
TALKIN' IN YER SLEEP. LIKE YOU WERE IN COMBAT, Y'KNOW? UNDER FIRE.
THEN IT KIND OF CHANGED.
YOU WERE CALLING OUT A NAME.
THAT MAGICIAN GUY'S...
FLABBERGAST.

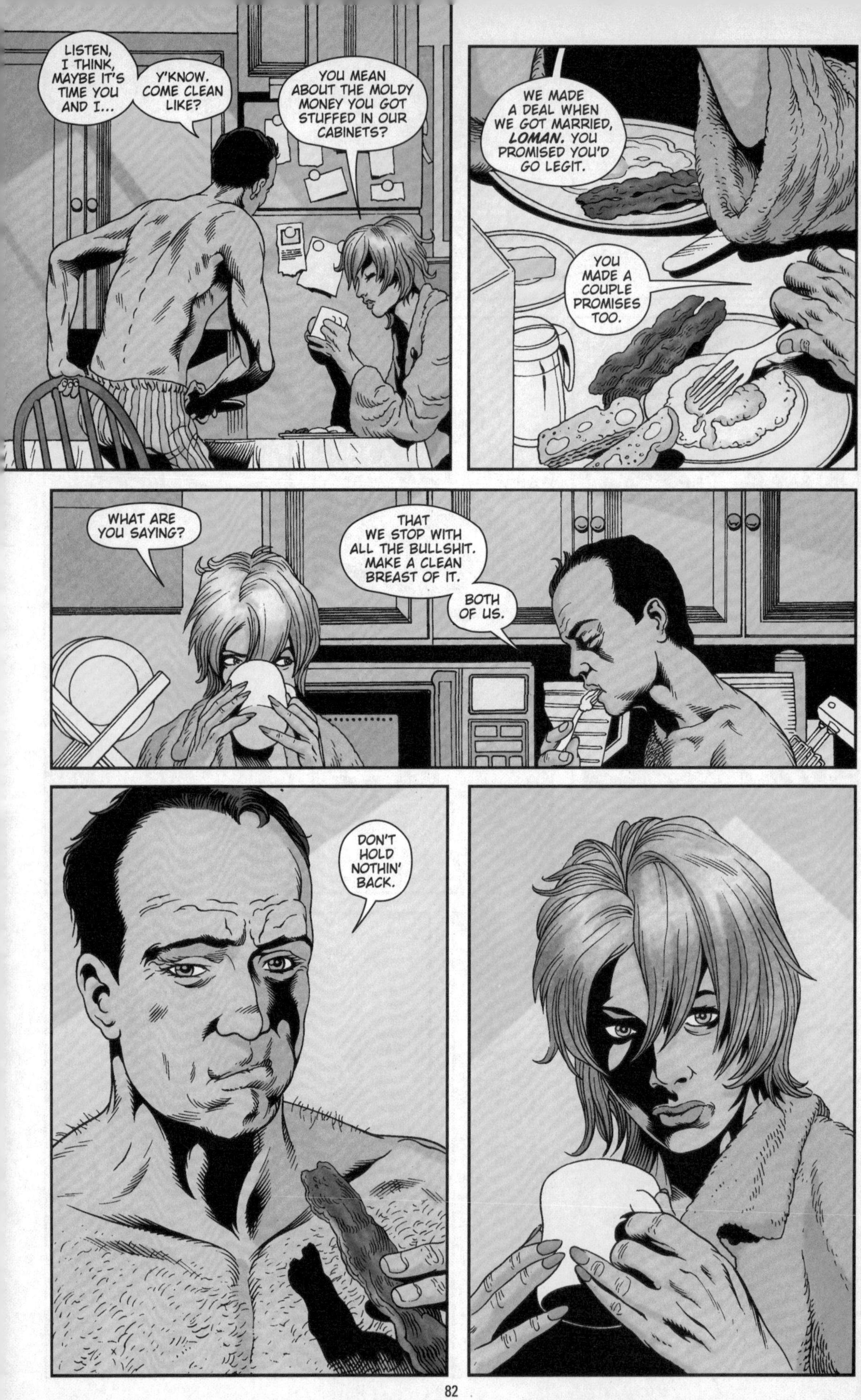
LISTEN, I THINK, MAYBE IT'S TIME YOU AND I...
Y'KNOW. COME CLEAN LIKE?
YOU MEAN ABOUT THE MOLDY MONEY YOU GOT STUFFED IN OUR CABINETS?
WE MADE A DEAL WHEN WE GOT MARRIED, **LOMAN.** YOU PROMISED YOU'D GO LEGIT.
YOU MADE A COUPLE PROMISES TOO.
WHAT ARE YOU SAYING?
THAT WE STOP WITH ALL THE BULLSHIT. MAKE A CLEAN BREAST OF IT.
BOTH OF US.
DON'T HOLD NOTHIN' BACK.

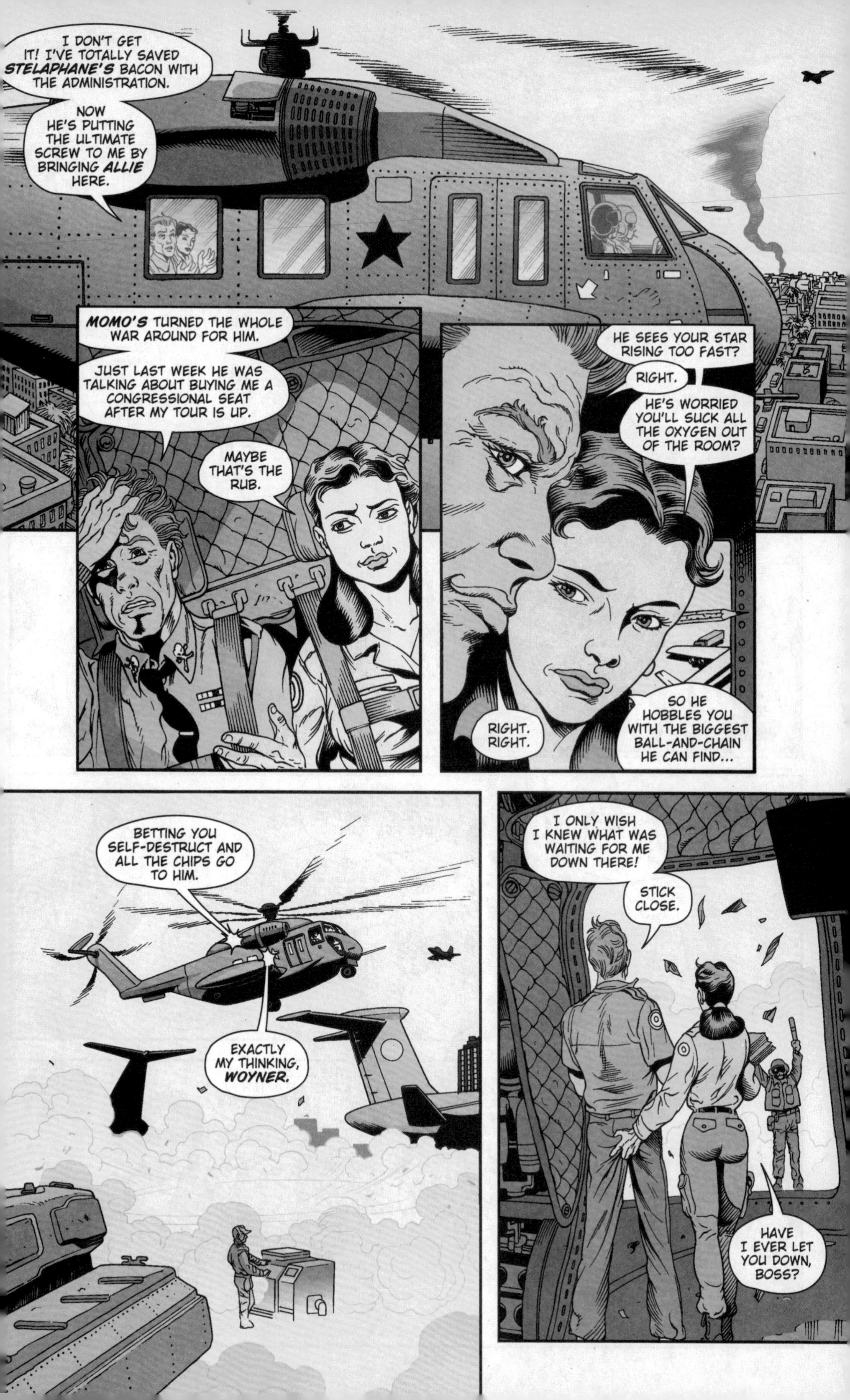
I DON'T GET IT! I'VE TOTALLY SAVED STELAPHANE'S BACON WITH THE ADMINISTRATION.
NOW HE'S PUTTING THE ULTIMATE SCREW TO ME BY BRINGING ALLIE HERE.
MOMO'S TURNED THE WHOLE WAR AROUND FOR HIM.
JUST LAST WEEK HE WAS TALKING ABOUT BUYING ME A CONGRESSIONAL SEAT AFTER MY TOUR IS UP.
MAYBE THAT'S THE RUB.
HE SEES YOUR STAR RISING TOO FAST?
RIGHT.
HE'S WORRIED YOU'LL SUCK ALL THE OXYGEN OUT OF THE ROOM?
RIGHT. RIGHT.
SO HE HOBBLES YOU WITH THE BIGGEST BALL-AND-CHAIN HE CAN FIND...
BETTING YOU SELF-DESTRUCT AND ALL THE CHIPS GO TO HIM.
EXACTLY MY THINKING, WOYNER.
I ONLY WISH I KNEW WHAT WAS WAITING FOR ME DOWN THERE!
STICK CLOSE.
HAVE I EVER LET YOU DOWN, BOSS?

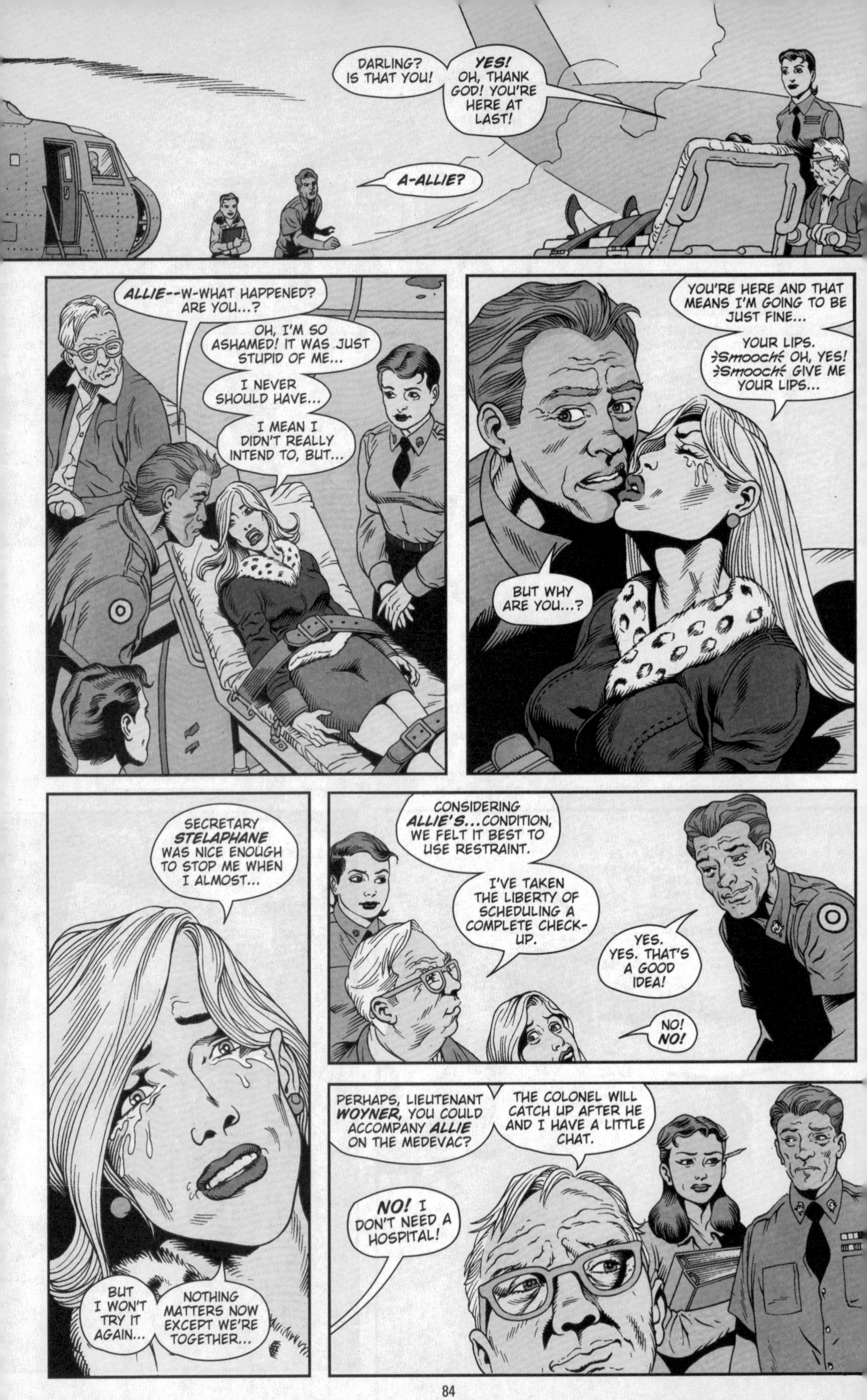
DARLING? IS THAT YOU!
YES! OH, THANK GOD! YOU'RE HERE AT LAST!
A-ALLIE?
ALLIE--W-WHAT HAPPENED? ARE YOU...?
OH, I'M SO ASHAMED! IT WAS JUST STUPID OF ME...
I NEVER SHOULD HAVE...
I MEAN I DIDN'T REALLY INTEND TO, BUT...
YOU'RE HERE AND THAT MEANS I'M GOING TO BE JUST FINE...
YOUR LIPS. Smooch OH, YES! Smooch GIVE ME YOUR LIPS...
BUT WHY ARE YOU...?
SECRETARY STELAPHANE WAS NICE ENOUGH TO STOP ME WHEN I ALMOST...
NOTHING MATTERS NOW EXCEPT WE'RE TOGETHER...
BUT I WON'T TRY IT AGAIN...
CONSIDERING ALLIE'S...CONDITION, WE FELT IT BEST TO USE RESTRAINT.
I'VE TAKEN THE LIBERTY OF SCHEDULING A COMPLETE CHECK-UP.
YES. YES. THAT'S A GOOD IDEA!
NO! NO!
PERHAPS, LIEUTENANT WOYNER, YOU COULD ACCOMPANY ALLIE ON THE MEDEVAC?
THE COLONEL WILL CATCH UP AFTER HE AND I HAVE A LITTLE CHAT.
NO! I DON'T NEED A HOSPITAL!

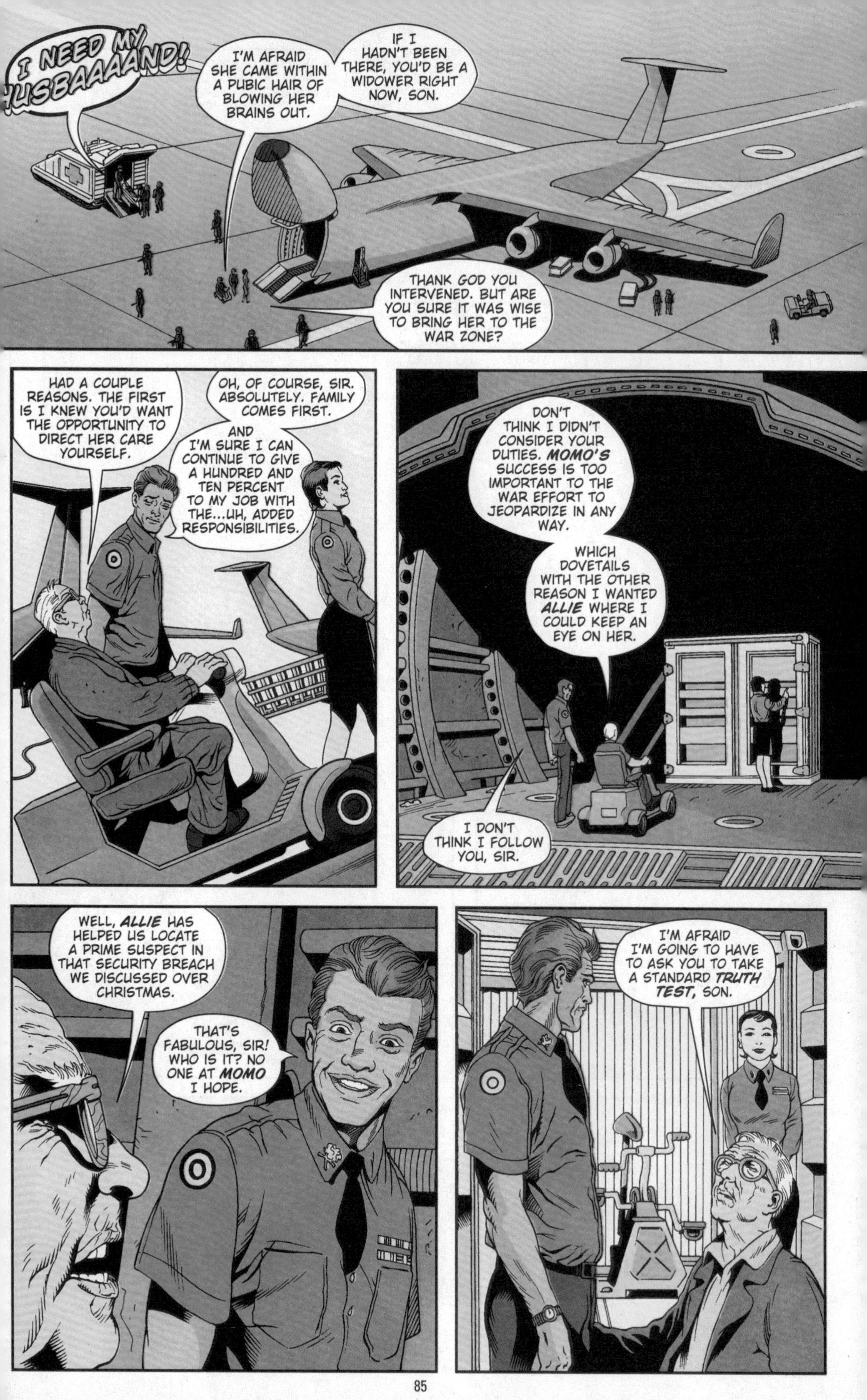
I NEED MY HUSBAAAAND!
I'M AFRAID SHE CAME WITHIN A PUBIC HAIR OF BLOWING HER BRAINS OUT.
IF I HADN'T BEEN THERE, YOU'D BE A WIDOWER RIGHT NOW, SON.
THANK GOD YOU INTERVENED. BUT ARE YOU SURE IT WAS WISE TO BRING HER TO THE WAR ZONE?
HAD A COUPLE REASONS. THE FIRST IS I KNEW YOU'D WANT THE OPPORTUNITY TO DIRECT HER CARE YOURSELF.
OH, OF COURSE, SIR. ABSOLUTELY. FAMILY COMES FIRST.
AND I'M SURE I CAN CONTINUE TO GIVE A HUNDRED AND TEN PERCENT TO MY JOB WITH THE...UH, ADDED RESPONSIBILITIES.
DON'T THINK I DIDN'T CONSIDER YOUR DUTIES. MOMO'S SUCCESS IS TOO IMPORTANT TO THE WAR EFFORT TO JEOPARDIZE IN ANY WAY.
WHICH DOVETAILS WITH THE OTHER REASON I WANTED ALLIE WHERE I COULD KEEP AN EYE ON HER.
I DON'T THINK I FOLLOW YOU, SIR.
WELL, ALLIE HAS HELPED US LOCATE A PRIME SUSPECT IN THAT SECURITY BREACH WE DISCUSSED OVER CHRISTMAS.
THAT'S FABULOUS, SIR! WHO IS IT? NO ONE AT MOMO I HOPE.
I'M AFRAID I'M GOING TO HAVE TO ASK YOU TO TAKE A STANDARD TRUTH TEST, SON.

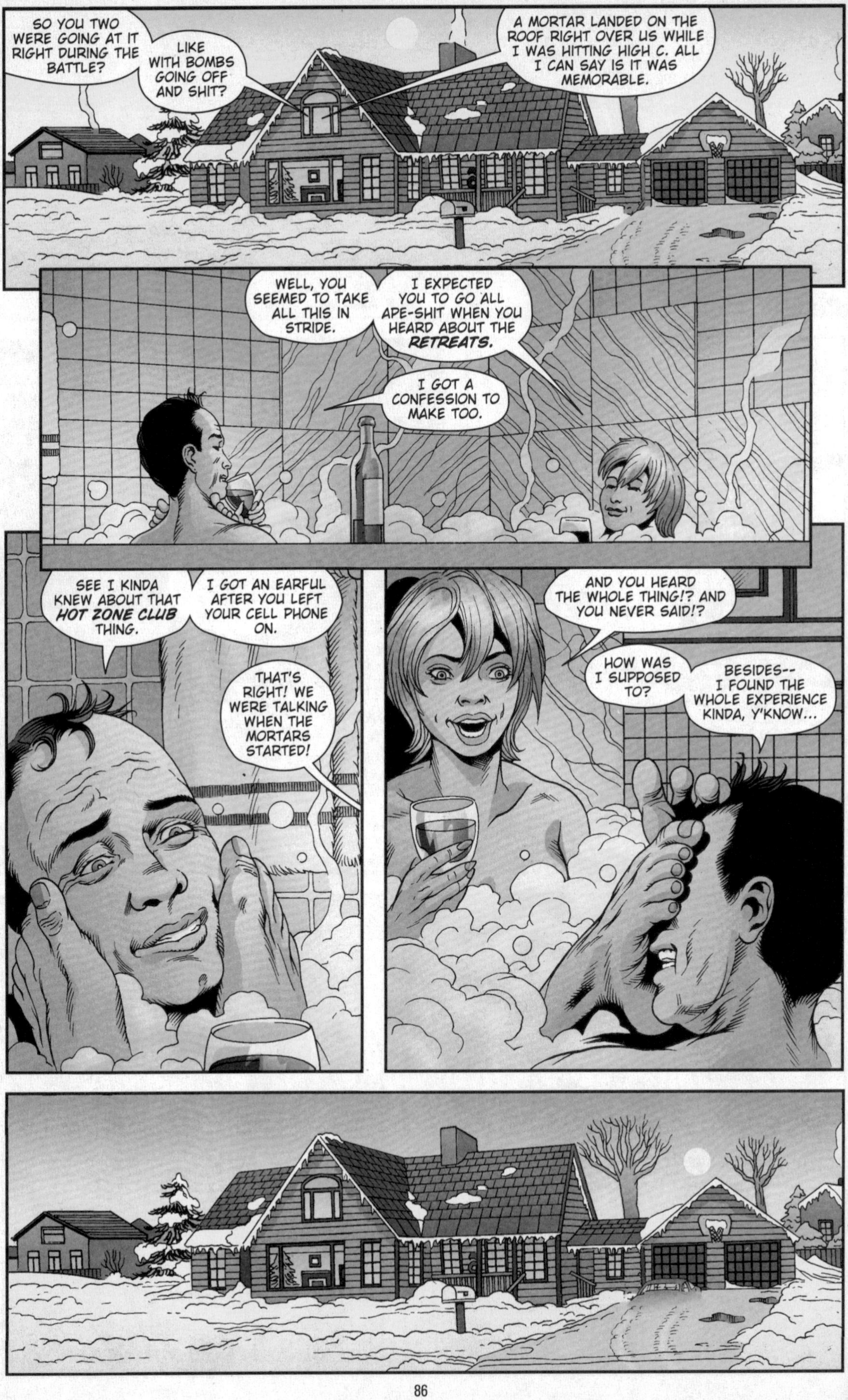
SO YOU TWO WERE GOING AT IT RIGHT DURING THE BATTLE?
LIKE WITH BOMBS GOING OFF AND SHIT?
A MORTAR LANDED ON THE ROOF RIGHT OVER US WHILE I WAS HITTING HIGH C. ALL I CAN SAY IS IT WAS MEMORABLE.
WELL, YOU SEEMED TO TAKE ALL THIS IN STRIDE.
I EXPECTED YOU TO GO ALL APE-SHIT WHEN YOU HEARD ABOUT THE RETREATS.
I GOT A CONFESSION TO MAKE TOO.
SEE I KINDA KNEW ABOUT THAT HOT ZONE CLUB THING.
I GOT AN EARFUL AFTER YOU LEFT YOUR CELL PHONE ON.
THAT'S RIGHT! WE WERE TALKING WHEN THE MORTARS STARTED!
AND YOU HEARD THE WHOLE THING!? AND YOU NEVER SAID!?
HOW WAS I SUPPOSED TO?
BESIDES-- I FOUND THE WHOLE EXPERIENCE KINDA, Y'KNOW...

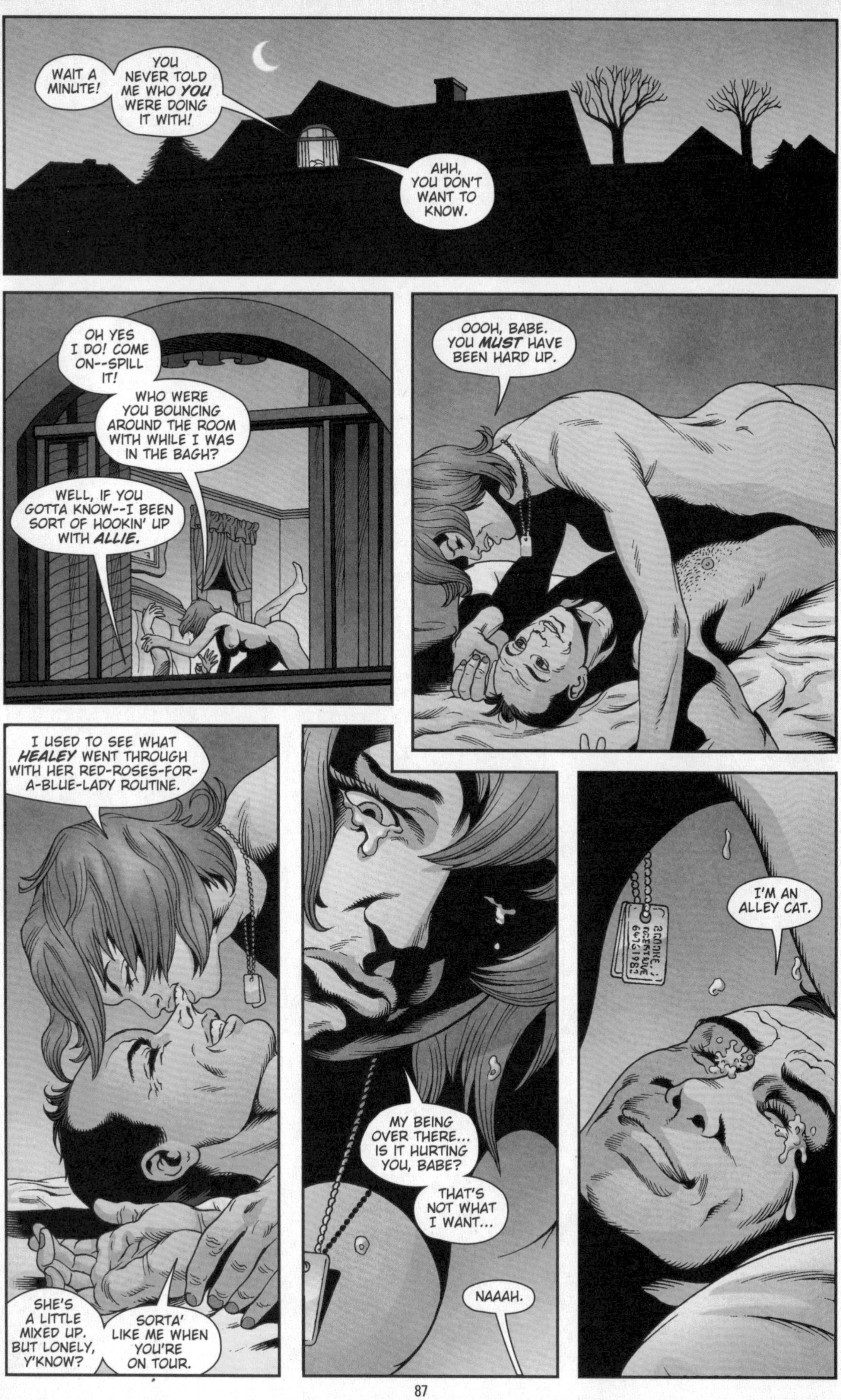
WAIT A MINUTE!
YOU NEVER TOLD ME WHO *YOU* WERE DOING IT WITH!
AHH, YOU DON'T WANT TO KNOW.
OH YES I DO! COME ON--SPILL IT!
WHO WERE YOU BOUNCING AROUND THE ROOM WITH WHILE I WAS IN THE BAGH?
WELL, IF YOU GOTTA KNOW--I BEEN SORT OF HOOKIN' UP WITH *ALLIE.*
OOOH, BABE. YOU *MUST* HAVE BEEN HARD UP.
I USED TO SEE WHAT *HEALEY* WENT THROUGH WITH HER RED-ROSES-FOR-A-BLUE-LADY ROUTINE.
SHE'S A LITTLE MIXED UP. BUT LONELY, Y'KNOW?
SORTA' LIKE ME WHEN YOU'RE ON TOUR.
MY BEING OVER THERE... IS IT HURTING YOU, BABE?
THAT'S NOT WHAT I WANT...
NAAAH.
I'M AN ALLEY CAT.

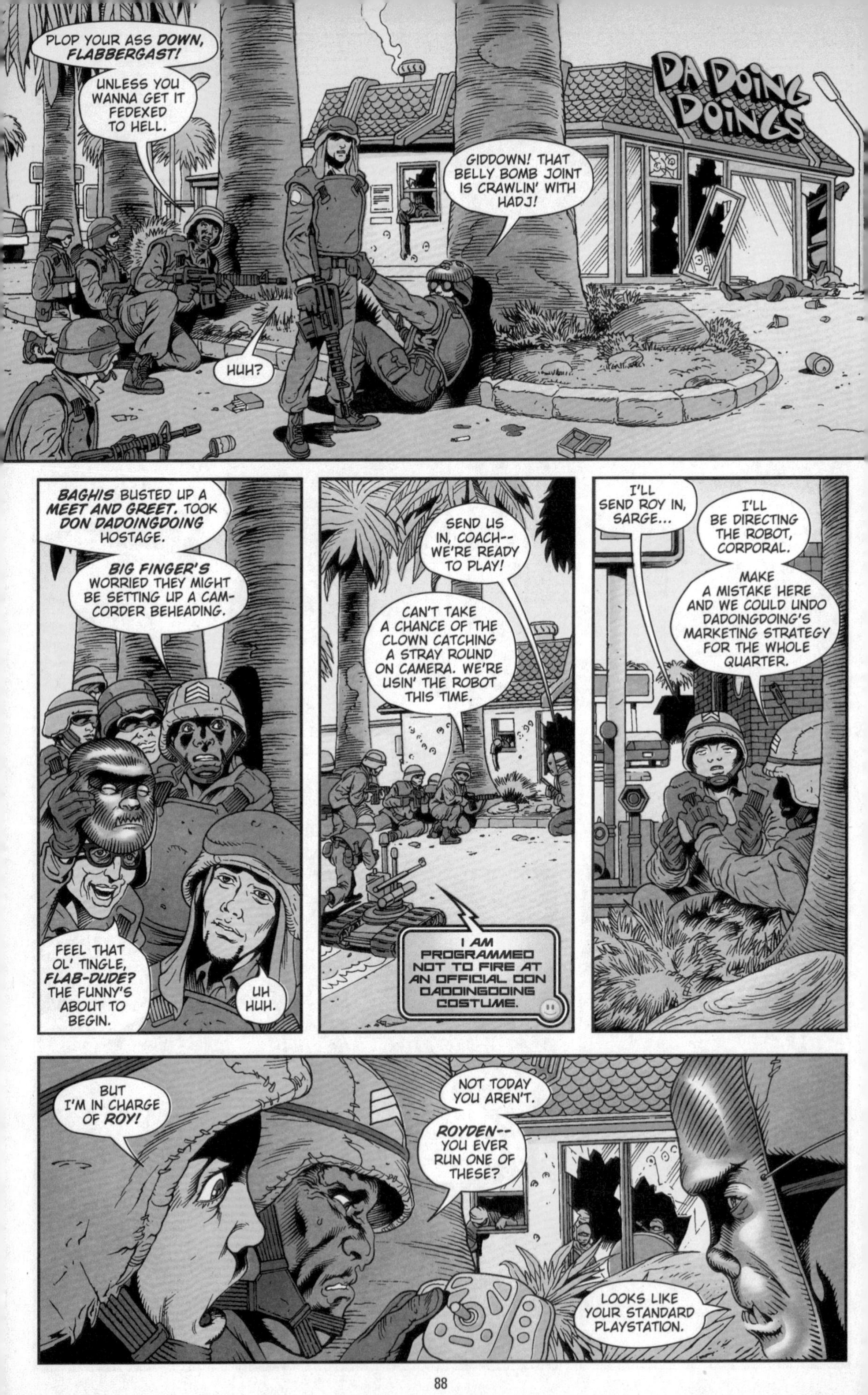
PLOP YOUR ASS DOWN, FLABBERGAST!
UNLESS YOU WANNA GET IT FEDEXED TO HELL.
DA DOING DOINGS
GIDDOWN! THAT BELLY BOMB JOINT IS CRAWLIN' WITH HADJ!
HUH?
BAGHIS BUSTED UP A MEET AND GREET. TOOK DON DADOINGDOING HOSTAGE.
BIG FINGER'S WORRIED THEY MIGHT BE SETTING UP A CAMCORDER BEHEADING.
FEEL THAT OL' TINGLE, FLAB-DUDE? THE FUNNY'S ABOUT TO BEGIN.
UH HUH.
SEND US IN, COACH-- WE'RE READY TO PLAY!
CAN'T TAKE A CHANCE OF THE CLOWN CATCHING A STRAY ROUND ON CAMERA. WE'RE USIN' THE ROBOT THIS TIME.
I AM PROGRAMMED NOT TO FIRE AT AN OFFICIAL DON DADOINGDOING COSTUME.
I'LL SEND ROY IN, SARGE...
I'LL BE DIRECTING THE ROBOT, CORPORAL.
MAKE A MISTAKE HERE AND WE COULD UNDO DADOINGDOING'S MARKETING STRATEGY FOR THE WHOLE QUARTER.
BUT I'M IN CHARGE OF ROY!
NOT TODAY YOU AREN'T.
ROYDEN-- YOU EVER RUN ONE OF THESE?
LOOKS LIKE YOUR STANDARD PLAYSTATION.

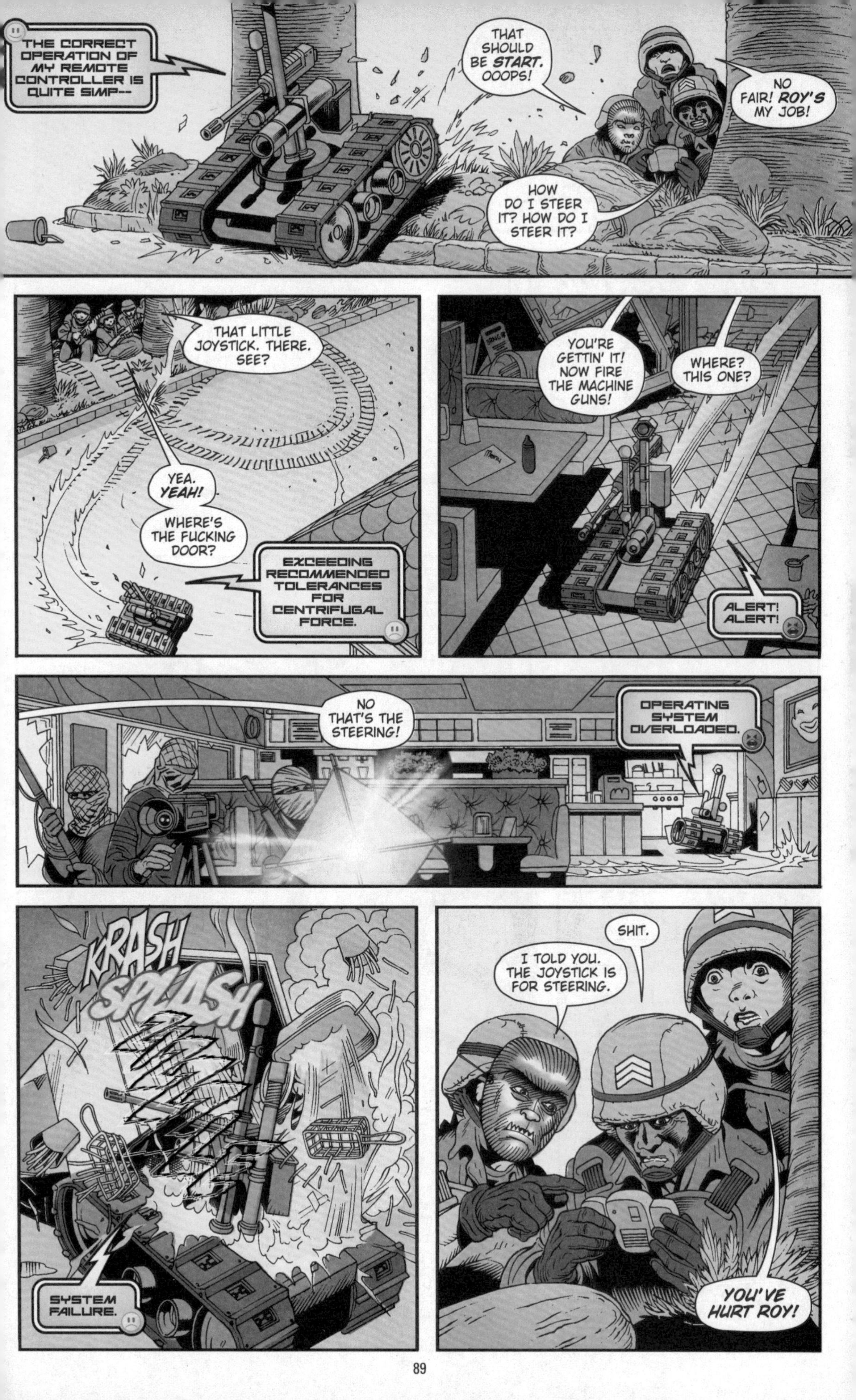
THE CORRECT OPERATION OF MY REMOTE CONTROLLER IS QUITE SIMP--
THAT SHOULD BE **START.** OOOPS!
NO FAIR! **ROY'S** MY JOB!
HOW DO I STEER IT? HOW DO I STEER IT?
THAT LITTLE JOYSTICK. THERE. SEE?
YEA. **YEAH!**
WHERE'S THE FUCKING DOOR?
EXCEEDING RECOMMENDED TOLERANCES FOR CENTRIFUGAL FORCE.
YOU'RE GETTIN' IT! NOW FIRE THE MACHINE GUNS!
WHERE? THIS ONE?
ALERT! ALERT!
NO THAT'S THE STEERING!
OPERATING SYSTEM OVERLOADED.
KRASH
SPLASH
SYSTEM FAILURE.
SHIT.
I TOLD YOU. THE JOYSTICK IS FOR STEERING.
YOU'VE HURT ROY!

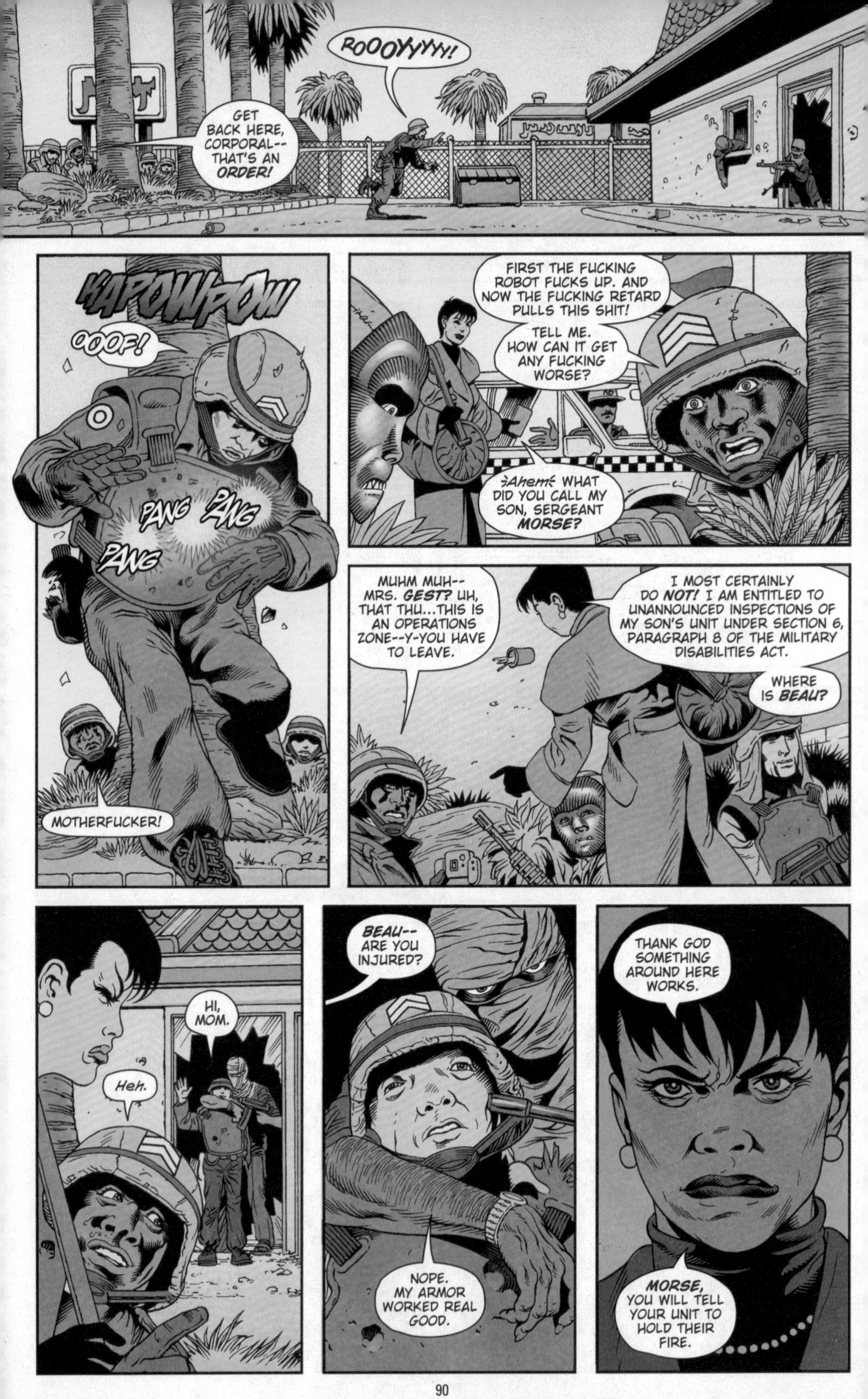
ROOOYYYYY!
GET BACK HERE, CORPORAL-- THAT'S AN ORDER!
KAPOWPOW
OOOF!
PANG PANG
PANG
MOTHERFUCKER!
FIRST THE FUCKING ROBOT FUCKS UP. AND NOW THE FUCKING RETARD PULLS THIS SHIT!
TELL ME. HOW CAN IT GET ANY FUCKING WORSE?
Ahem WHAT DID YOU CALL MY SON, SERGEANT MORSE?
MUHM MUH-- MRS. GEST? UH, THAT THU...THIS IS AN OPERATIONS ZONE--Y-YOU HAVE TO LEAVE.
I MOST CERTAINLY DO NOT! I AM ENTITLED TO UNANNOUNCED INSPECTIONS OF MY SON'S UNIT UNDER SECTION 6, PARAGRAPH 8 OF THE MILITARY DISABILITIES ACT.
WHERE IS BEAU?
HI, MOM.
Heh.
BEAU-- ARE YOU INJURED?
NOPE. MY ARMOR WORKED REAL GOOD.
THANK GOD SOMETHING AROUND HERE WORKS.
MORSE, YOU WILL TELL YOUR UNIT TO HOLD THEIR FIRE.

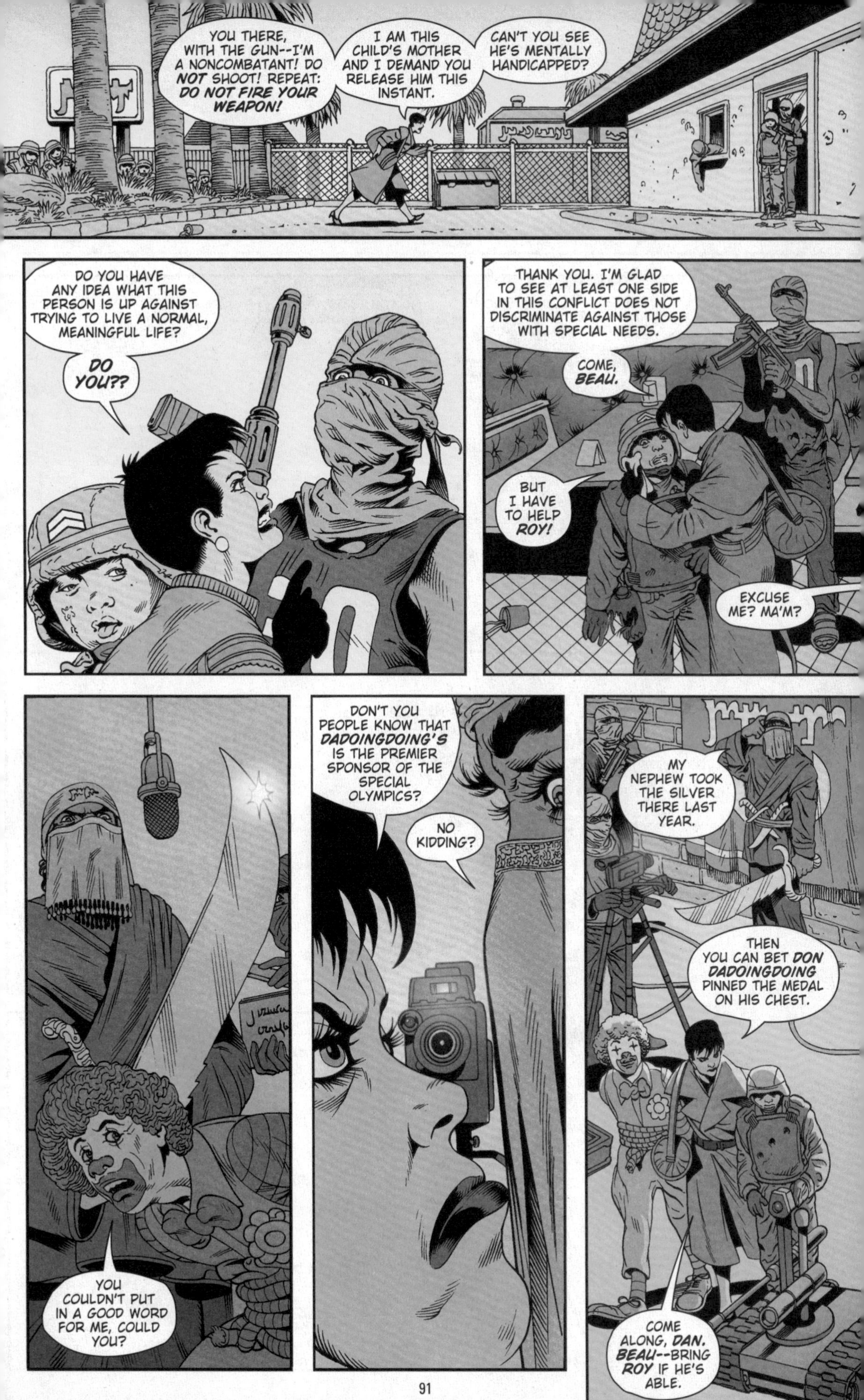
YOU THERE, WITH THE GUN--I'M A NONCOMBATANT! DO NOT SHOOT! REPEAT: DO NOT FIRE YOUR WEAPON!
I AM THIS CHILD'S MOTHER AND I DEMAND YOU RELEASE HIM THIS INSTANT.
CAN'T YOU SEE HE'S MENTALLY HANDICAPPED?
DO YOU HAVE ANY IDEA WHAT THIS PERSON IS UP AGAINST TRYING TO LIVE A NORMAL, MEANINGFUL LIFE?
DO YOU??
THANK YOU. I'M GLAD TO SEE AT LEAST ONE SIDE IN THIS CONFLICT DOES NOT DISCRIMINATE AGAINST THOSE WITH SPECIAL NEEDS.
COME, BEAU.
BUT I HAVE TO HELP ROY!
EXCUSE ME? MA'M?
YOU COULDN'T PUT IN A GOOD WORD FOR ME, COULD YOU?
DON'T YOU PEOPLE KNOW THAT DADOINGDOING'S IS THE PREMIER SPONSOR OF THE SPECIAL OLYMPICS?
NO KIDDING?
MY NEPHEW TOOK THE SILVER THERE LAST YEAR.
THEN YOU CAN BET DON DADOINGDOING PINNED THE MEDAL ON HIS CHEST.
COME ALONG, DAN. BEAU--BRING ROY IF HE'S ABLE.

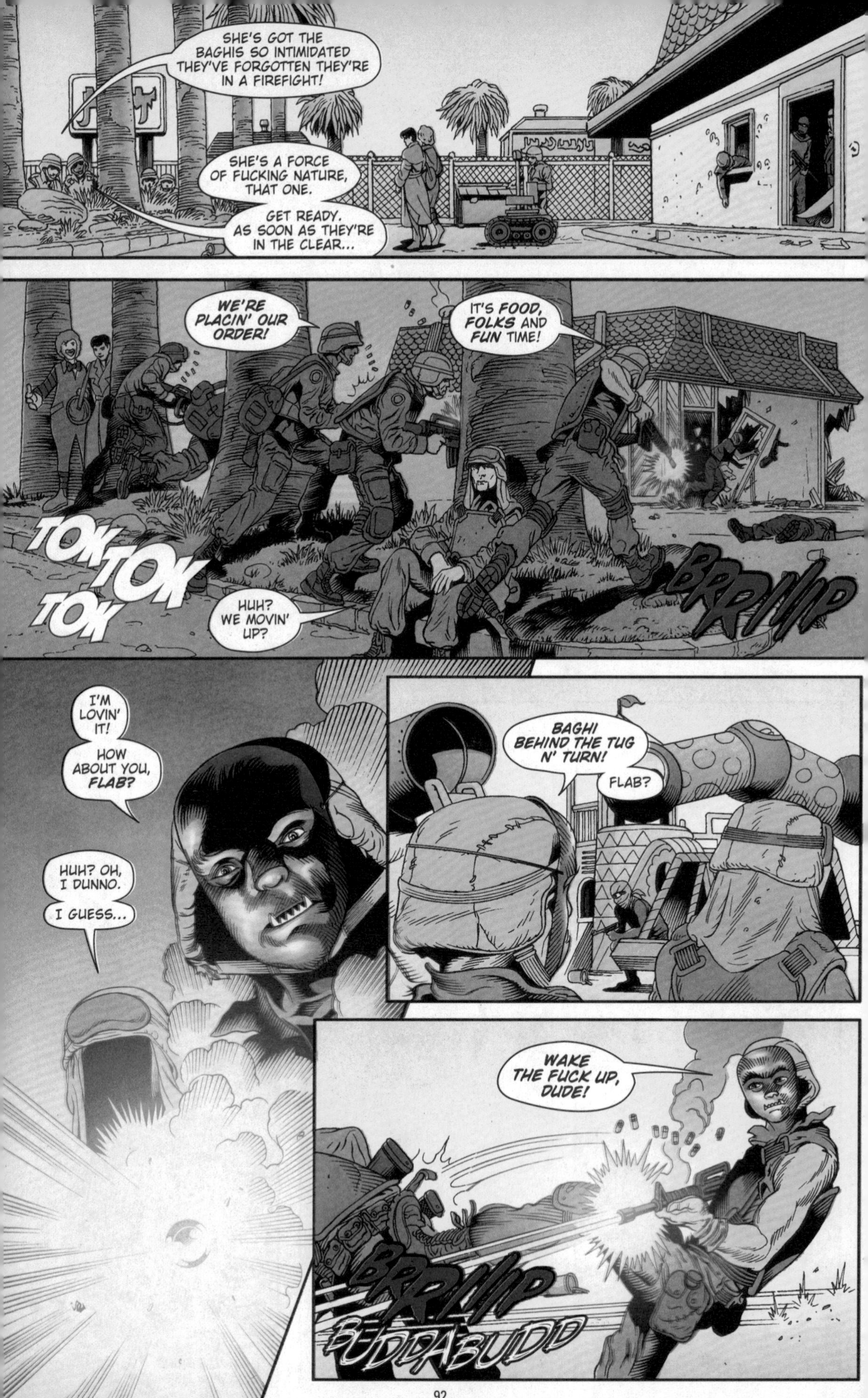
SHE'S GOT THE BAGHIS SO INTIMIDATED THEY'VE FORGOTTEN THEY'RE IN A FIREFIGHT!
SHE'S A FORCE OF FUCKING NATURE, THAT ONE.
GET READY. AS SOON AS THEY'RE IN THE CLEAR...
WE'RE PLACIN' OUR ORDER!
IT'S FOOD, FOLKS AND FUN TIME!
TOK TOK TOK
HUH? WE MOVIN' UP?
BRRIIIP
I'M LOVIN' IT!
HOW ABOUT YOU, FLAB?
HUH? OH, I DUNNO.
I GUESS...
BAGHI BEHIND THE TUG N' TURN!
FLAB?
WAKE THE FUCK UP, DUDE!
BRRIIIP
BUDDABUDD

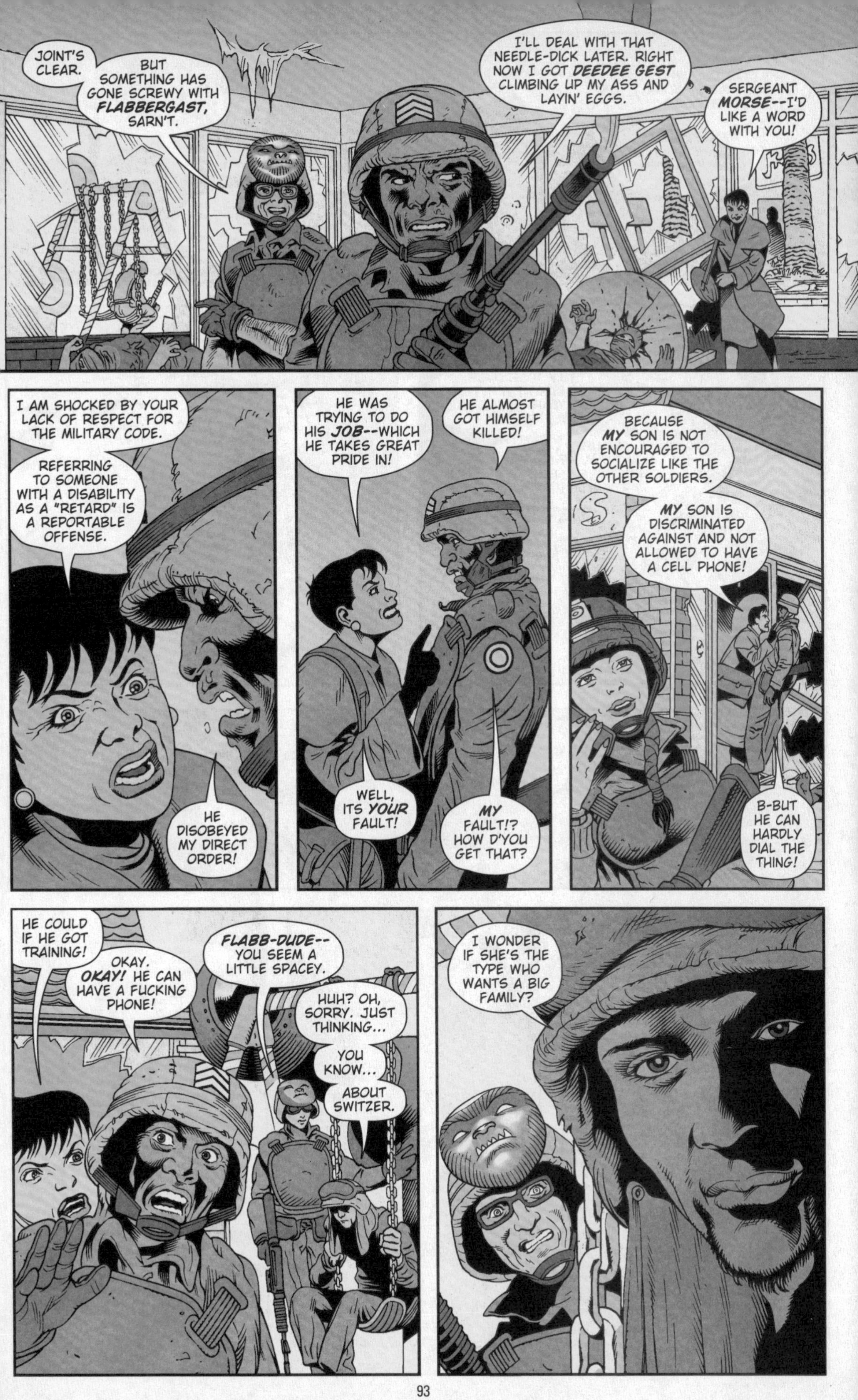
JOINT'S CLEAR.
BUT SOMETHING HAS GONE SCREWY WITH FLABBERGAST, SARN'T.
I'LL DEAL WITH THAT NEEDLE-DICK LATER. RIGHT NOW I GOT DEEDEE GEST CLIMBING UP MY ASS AND LAYIN' EGGS.
SERGEANT MORSE--I'D LIKE A WORD WITH YOU!
I AM SHOCKED BY YOUR LACK OF RESPECT FOR THE MILITARY CODE.
REFERRING TO SOMEONE WITH A DISABILITY AS A "RETARD" IS A REPORTABLE OFFENSE.
HE DISOBEYED MY DIRECT ORDER!
HE WAS TRYING TO DO HIS JOB--WHICH HE TAKES GREAT PRIDE IN!
HE ALMOST GOT HIMSELF KILLED!
WELL, ITS YOUR FAULT!
MY FAULT!? HOW D'YOU GET THAT?
BECAUSE MY SON IS NOT ENCOURAGED TO SOCIALIZE LIKE THE OTHER SOLDIERS.
MY SON IS DISCRIMINATED AGAINST AND NOT ALLOWED TO HAVE A CELL PHONE!
B-BUT HE CAN HARDLY DIAL THE THING!
HE COULD IF HE GOT TRAINING!
OKAY. OKAY! HE CAN HAVE A FUCKING PHONE!
FLABB-DUDE-- YOU SEEM A LITTLE SPACEY.
HUH? OH, SORRY. JUST THINKING...
YOU KNOW...
ABOUT SWITZER.
I WONDER IF SHE'S THE TYPE WHO WANTS A BIG FAMILY?

I WASN'T THE ONLY ONE WHO CAUGHT WIND OF YOUR *HOT ZONE CLUB.*

HEALEY CALLED *ALLIE* ASKIN' IF I KNEW WHAT WAS GOING ON.

IT'S JUST *MOMO.* THEY WATCH US LIKE HAWKS.

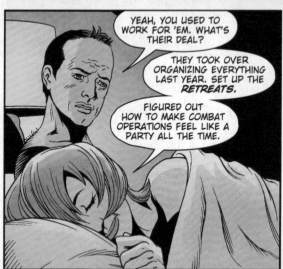

YEAH, YOU USED TO WORK FOR 'EM. WHAT'S THEIR DEAL?

THEY TOOK OVER ORGANIZING EVERYTHING LAST YEAR. SET UP THE *RETREATS.*

FIGURED OUT HOW TO MAKE COMBAT OPERATIONS FEEL LIKE A PARTY ALL THE TIME.

I GUESS I DON'T DIG THE PART ABOUT PEOPLE GETTING BLOWN AWAY.

IT'S WAR, BABE. ONLY WAY TO END IT IS TO WIN.

ARE YOU SURE YOU'RE COOL WITH THIS?

ME GOING BACK TO THE BAGH?

WHO AM I TO SLOW YOU DOWN?

I BETTER CHECK ON *ALLIE.*

SHE'S GONE OFF THE DEEP END WITH THE PILLS MORE THAN ONCE.

NOT PICKING UP. NO VOICE MAIL EITHER.

I BET SHE'S ESCAPED TO SOME EXOTIC LOCALE...

...JUST TO DO SOMETHING REALLY WILD AND CRAZY TO HER HUSBAND.

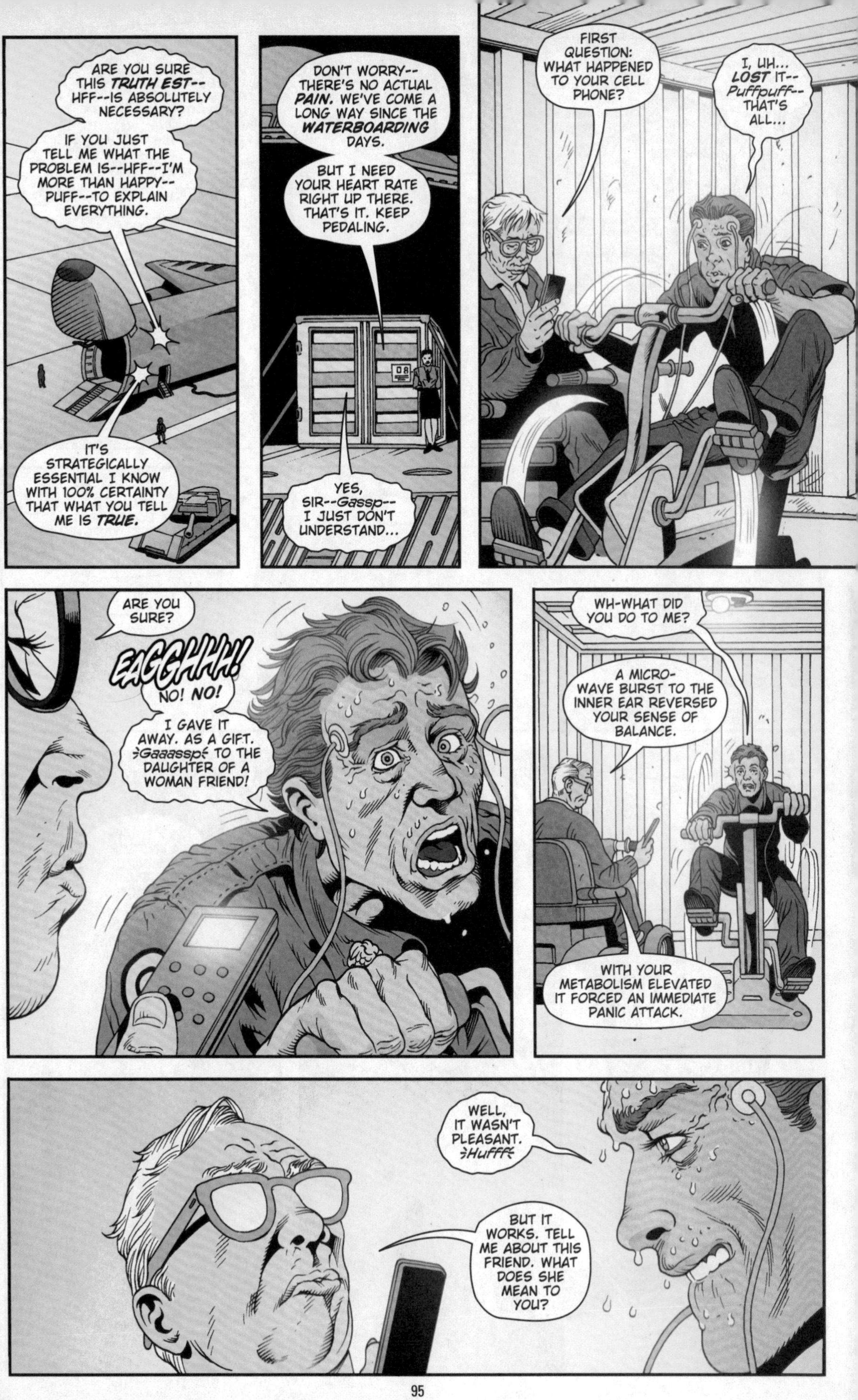

ARE YOU SURE THIS TRUTH EST--HFF--IS ABSOLUTELY NECESSARY?
IF YOU JUST TELL ME WHAT THE PROBLEM IS--HFF--I'M MORE THAN HAPPY--PUFF--TO EXPLAIN EVERYTHING.
IT'S STRATEGICALLY ESSENTIAL I KNOW WITH 100% CERTAINTY THAT WHAT YOU TELL ME IS TRUE.
DON'T WORRY--THERE'S NO ACTUAL PAIN. WE'VE COME A LONG WAY SINCE THE WATERBOARDING DAYS.
BUT I NEED YOUR HEART RATE RIGHT UP THERE. THAT'S IT. KEEP PEDALING.
YES, SIR--Gassp--I JUST DON'T UNDERSTAND...
FIRST QUESTION: WHAT HAPPENED TO YOUR CELL PHONE?
I, UH... LOST IT--Puffpuff--THAT'S ALL...
ARE YOU SURE?
EAGGHHH!
NO! NO!
I GAVE IT AWAY. AS A GIFT. Gaaassp TO THE DAUGHTER OF A WOMAN FRIEND!
WH-WHAT DID YOU DO TO ME?
A MICRO-WAVE BURST TO THE INNER EAR REVERSED YOUR SENSE OF BALANCE.
WITH YOUR METABOLISM ELEVATED IT FORCED AN IMMEDIATE PANIC ATTACK.
WELL, IT WASN'T PLEASANT. Hufff
BUT IT WORKS. TELL ME ABOUT THIS FRIEND. WHAT DOES SHE MEAN TO YOU?

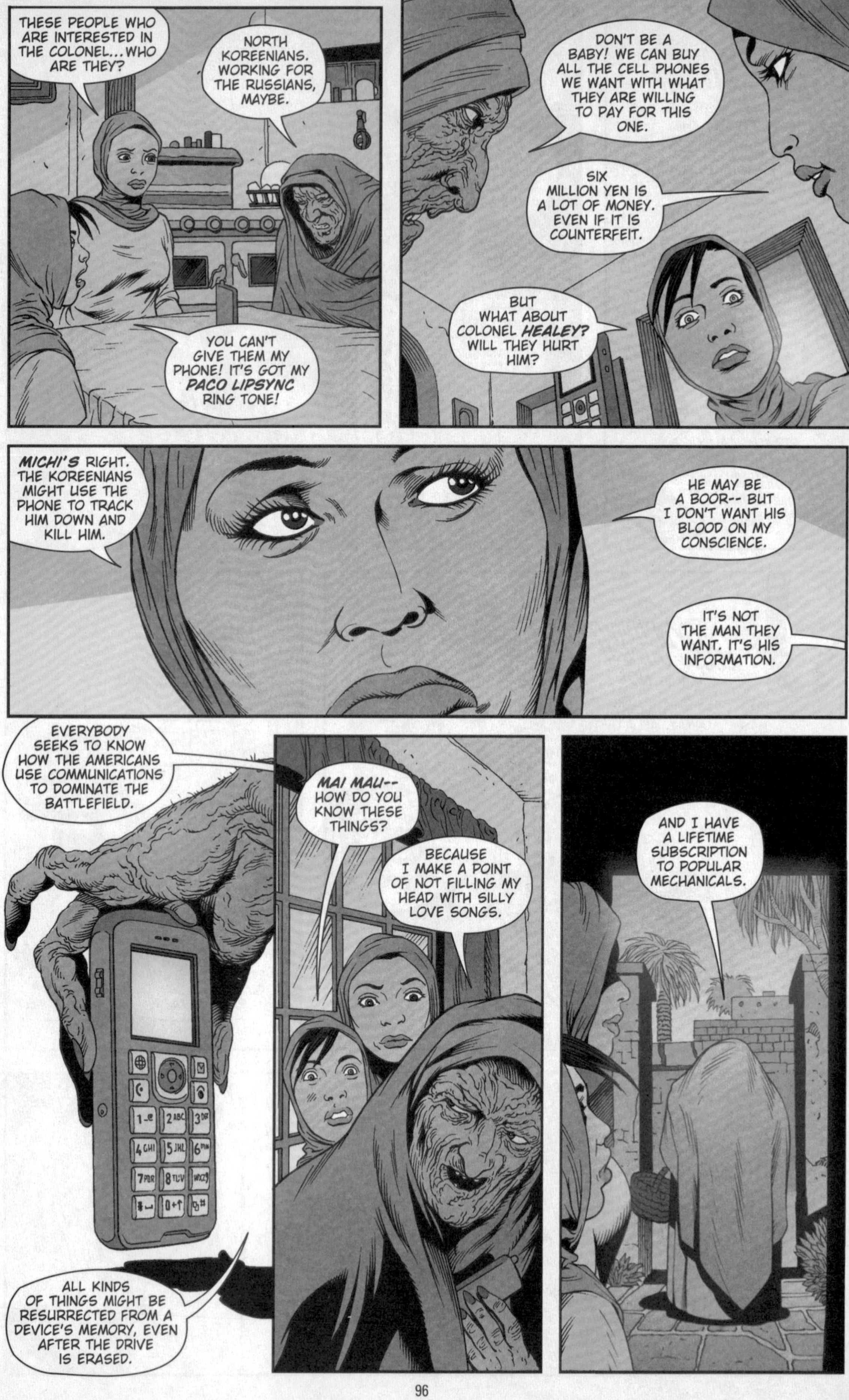

THESE PEOPLE WHO ARE INTERESTED IN THE COLONEL...WHO ARE THEY?
NORTH KOREENIANS. WORKING FOR THE RUSSIANS, MAYBE.
YOU CAN'T GIVE THEM MY PHONE! IT'S GOT MY *PACO LIPSYNC* RING TONE!
DON'T BE A BABY! WE CAN BUY ALL THE CELL PHONES WE WANT WITH WHAT THEY ARE WILLING TO PAY FOR THIS ONE.
SIX MILLION YEN IS A LOT OF MONEY. EVEN IF IT IS COUNTERFEIT.
BUT WHAT ABOUT COLONEL *HEALEY?* WILL THEY HURT HIM?
MICHI'S RIGHT. THE KOREENIANS MIGHT USE THE PHONE TO TRACK HIM DOWN AND KILL HIM.
HE MAY BE A BOOR-- BUT I DON'T WANT HIS BLOOD ON MY CONSCIENCE.
IT'S NOT THE MAN THEY WANT. IT'S HIS INFORMATION.
EVERYBODY SEEKS TO KNOW HOW THE AMERICANS USE COMMUNICATIONS TO DOMINATE THE BATTLEFIELD.
ALL KINDS OF THINGS MIGHT BE RESURRECTED FROM A DEVICE'S MEMORY, EVEN AFTER THE DRIVE IS ERASED.
MAI MAU-- HOW DO YOU KNOW THESE THINGS?
BECAUSE I MAKE A POINT OF NOT FILLING MY HEAD WITH SILLY LOVE SONGS.
AND I HAVE A LIFETIME SUBSCRIPTION TO POPULAR MECHANICALS.

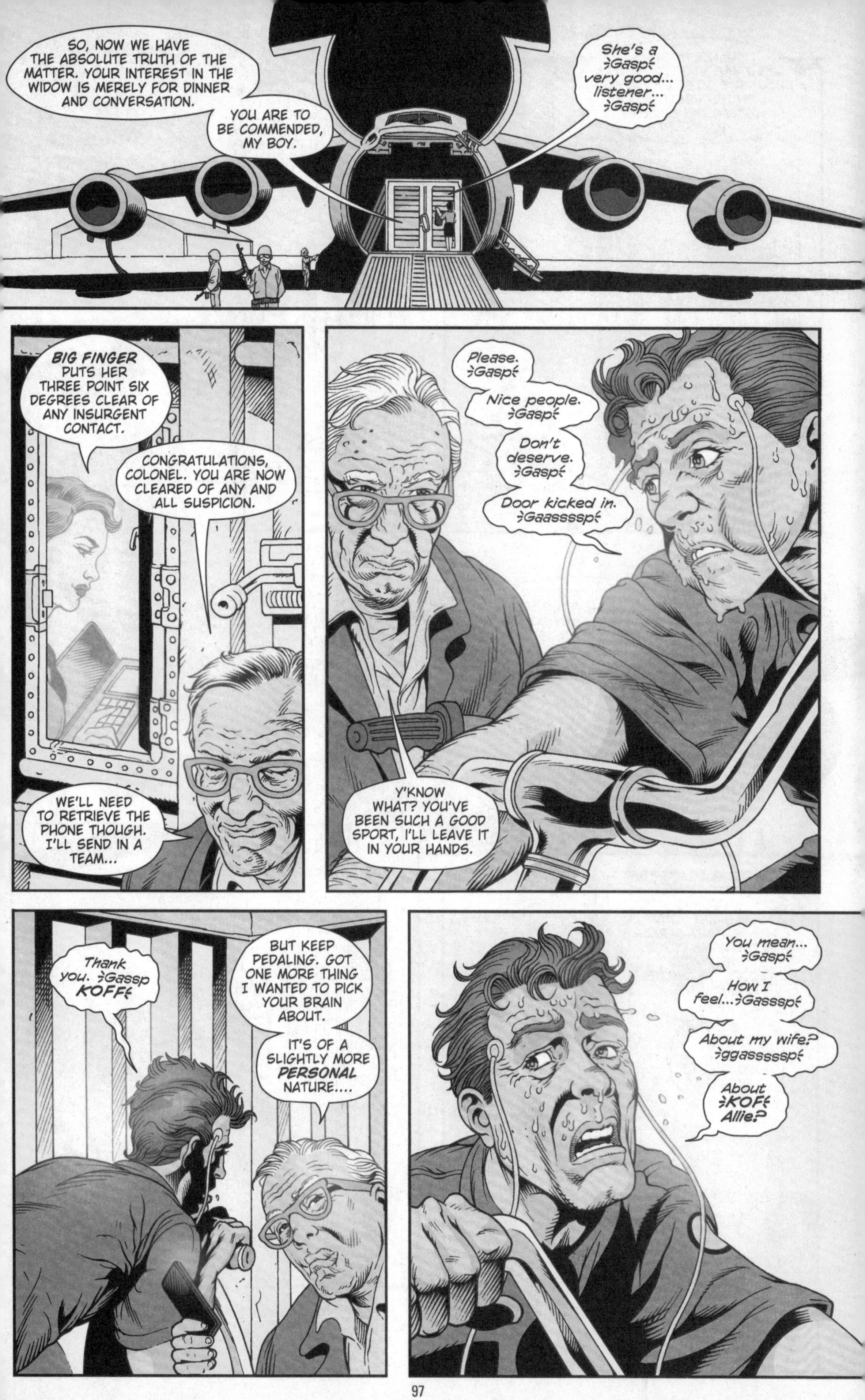
SO, NOW WE HAVE THE ABSOLUTE TRUTH OF THE MATTER. YOUR INTEREST IN THE WIDOW IS MERELY FOR DINNER AND CONVERSATION.
YOU ARE TO BE COMMENDED, MY BOY.
She's a ⪤Gasp⪤ very good... listener... ⪤Gasp⪤
BIG FINGER PUTS HER THREE POINT SIX DEGREES CLEAR OF ANY INSURGENT CONTACT.
CONGRATULATIONS, COLONEL. YOU ARE NOW CLEARED OF ANY AND ALL SUSPICION.
WE'LL NEED TO RETRIEVE THE PHONE THOUGH. I'LL SEND IN A TEAM...
Please. ⪤Gasp⪤
Nice people. ⪤Gasp⪤
Don't deserve. ⪤Gasp⪤
Door kicked in. ⪤Gaassssp⪤
Y'KNOW WHAT? YOU'VE BEEN SUCH A GOOD SPORT, I'LL LEAVE IT IN YOUR HANDS.
Thank you. ⪤Gassp KOFF⪤
BUT KEEP PEDALING. GOT ONE MORE THING I WANTED TO PICK YOUR BRAIN ABOUT.
IT'S OF A SLIGHTLY MORE PERSONAL NATURE....
You mean... ⪤Gasp⪤
How I feel...⪤Gasssp⪤
About my wife? ⪤ggassssssp⪤
About ⪤KOF⪤ Allie?

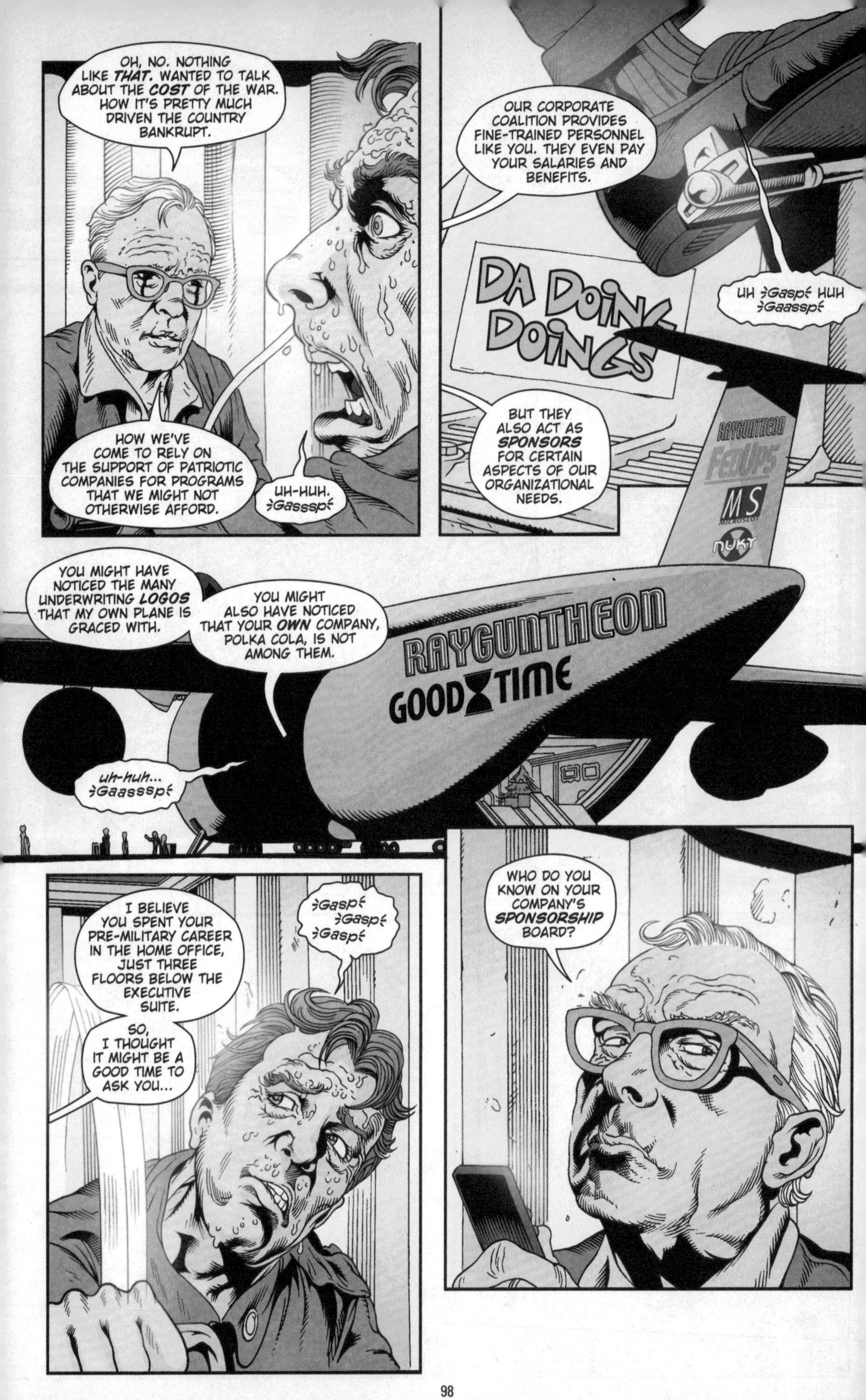

OH, NO. NOTHING LIKE THAT. WANTED TO TALK ABOUT THE COST OF THE WAR. HOW IT'S PRETTY MUCH DRIVEN THE COUNTRY BANKRUPT.
HOW WE'VE COME TO RELY ON THE SUPPORT OF PATRIOTIC COMPANIES FOR PROGRAMS THAT WE MIGHT NOT OTHERWISE AFFORD.
UH-HUH. Gassssp
OUR CORPORATE COALITION PROVIDES FINE-TRAINED PERSONNEL LIKE YOU. THEY EVEN PAY YOUR SALARIES AND BENEFITS.
DA DOING DOINGS
UH Gasp HUH Gaassp
BUT THEY ALSO ACT AS SPONSORS FOR CERTAIN ASPECTS OF OUR ORGANIZATIONAL NEEDS.
RAYGUNTHEON
FEDUPS
MS MICROSLOT
NUKY
YOU MIGHT HAVE NOTICED THE MANY UNDERWRITING LOGOS THAT MY OWN PLANE IS GRACED WITH.
YOU MIGHT ALSO HAVE NOTICED THAT YOUR OWN COMPANY, POLKA COLA, IS NOT AMONG THEM.
RAYGUNTHEON
GOOD TIME
uh-huh... Gaaassp
I BELIEVE YOU SPENT YOUR PRE-MILITARY CAREER IN THE HOME OFFICE, JUST THREE FLOORS BELOW THE EXECUTIVE SUITE.
SO, I THOUGHT IT MIGHT BE A GOOD TIME TO ASK YOU...
Gasp Gasp Gasp
WHO DO YOU KNOW ON YOUR COMPANY'S SPONSORSHIP BOARD?

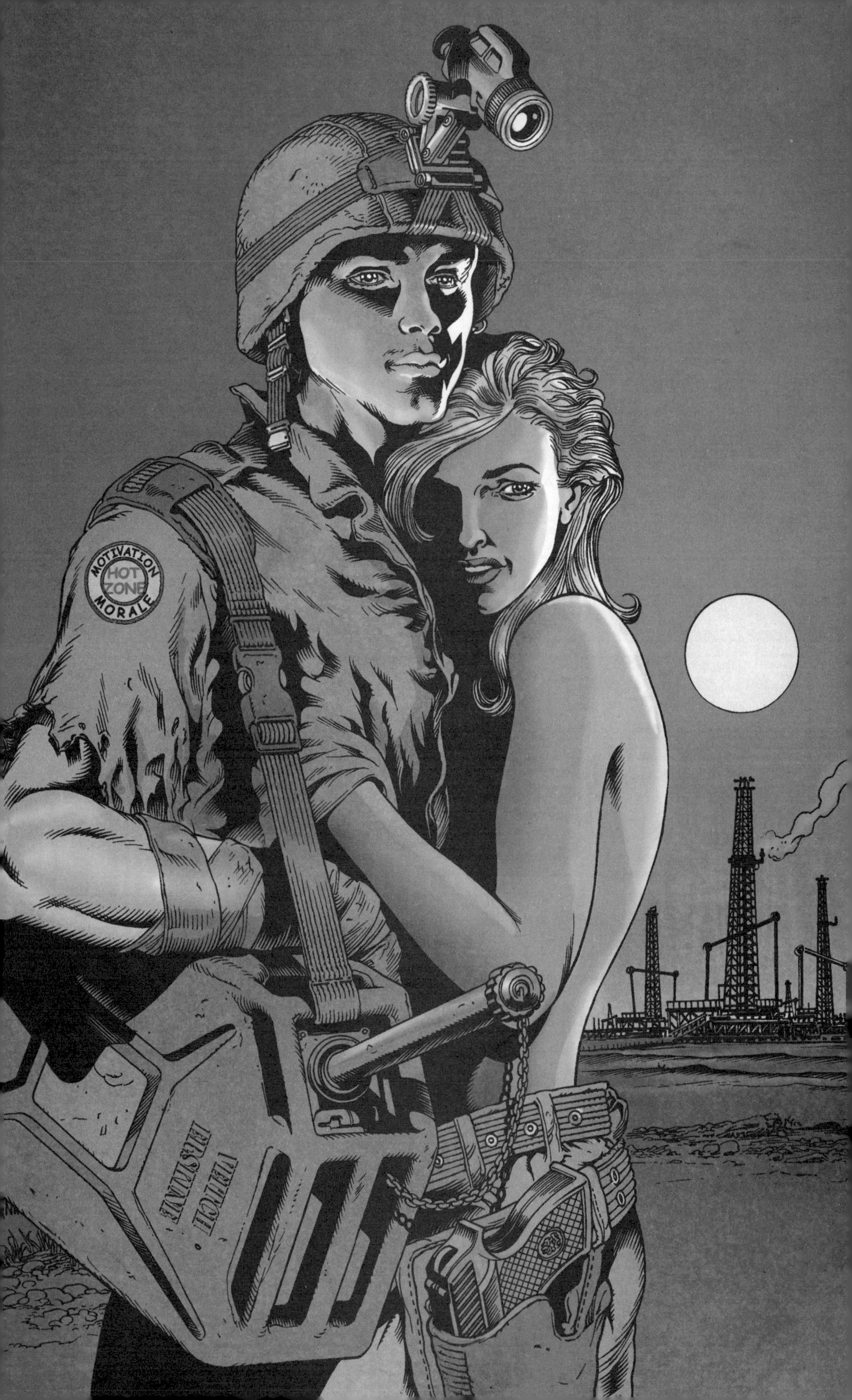
MOTIVATION
HOT ZONE
MORALE

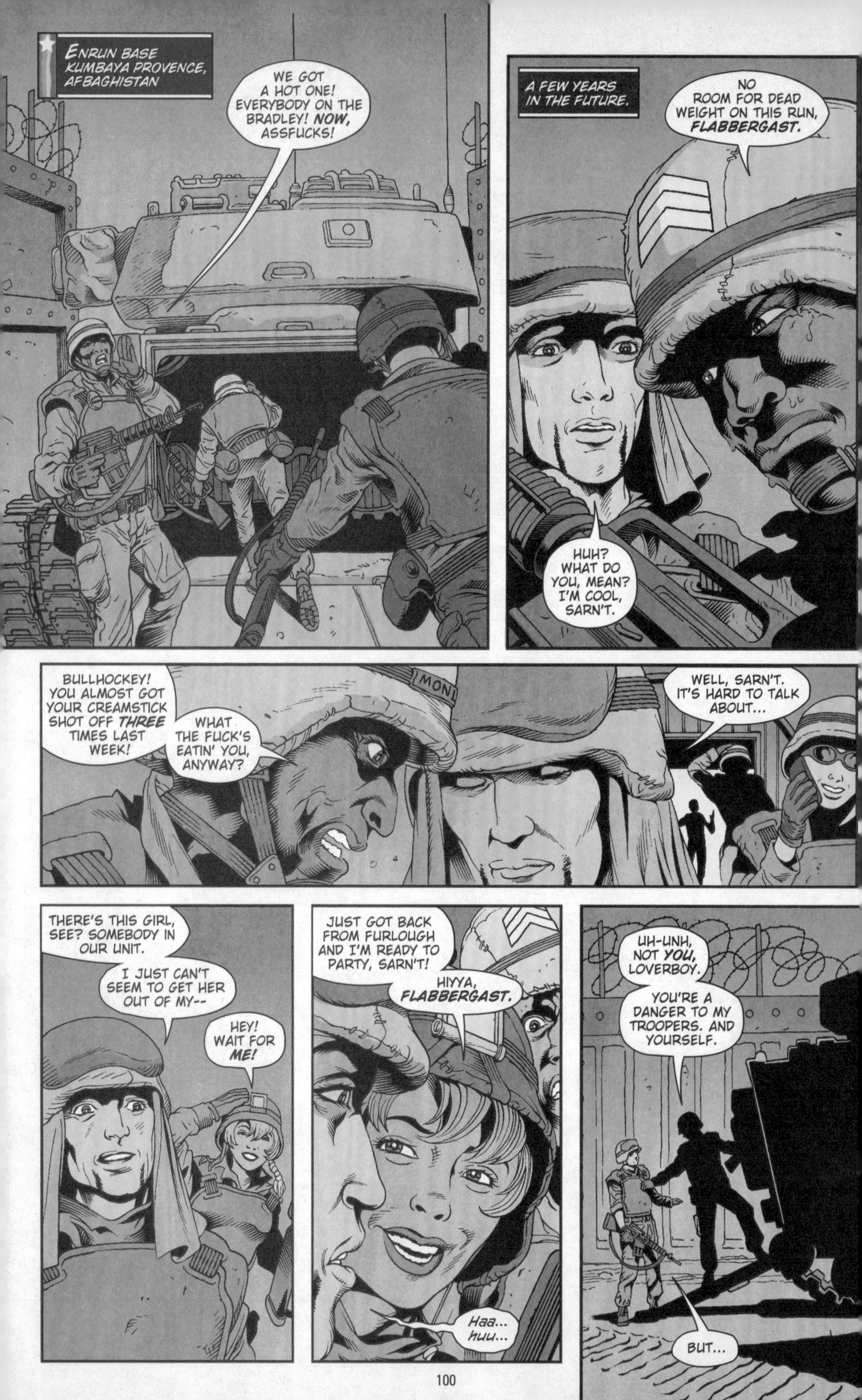

ENRUN BASE
KUMBAYA PROVENCE, AFBAGHISTAN
WE GOT A HOT ONE! EVERYBODY ON THE BRADLEY! NOW, ASSFUCKS!
A FEW YEARS IN THE FUTURE.
NO ROOM FOR DEAD WEIGHT ON THIS RUN, FLABBERGAST.
HUH? WHAT DO YOU, MEAN? I'M COOL, SARN'T.
BULLHOCKEY! YOU ALMOST GOT YOUR CREAMSTICK SHOT OFF THREE TIMES LAST WEEK!
WHAT THE FUCK'S EATIN' YOU, ANYWAY?
WELL, SARN'T. IT'S HARD TO TALK ABOUT...
THERE'S THIS GIRL, SEE? SOMEBODY IN OUR UNIT.
I JUST CAN'T SEEM TO GET HER OUT OF MY--
HEY! WAIT FOR ME!
JUST GOT BACK FROM FURLOUGH AND I'M READY TO PARTY, SARN'T!
HIYYA, FLABBERGAST.
Haa... huu...
UH-UNH, NOT YOU, LOVERBOY.
YOU'RE A DANGER TO MY TROOPERS. AND YOURSELF.
BUT...

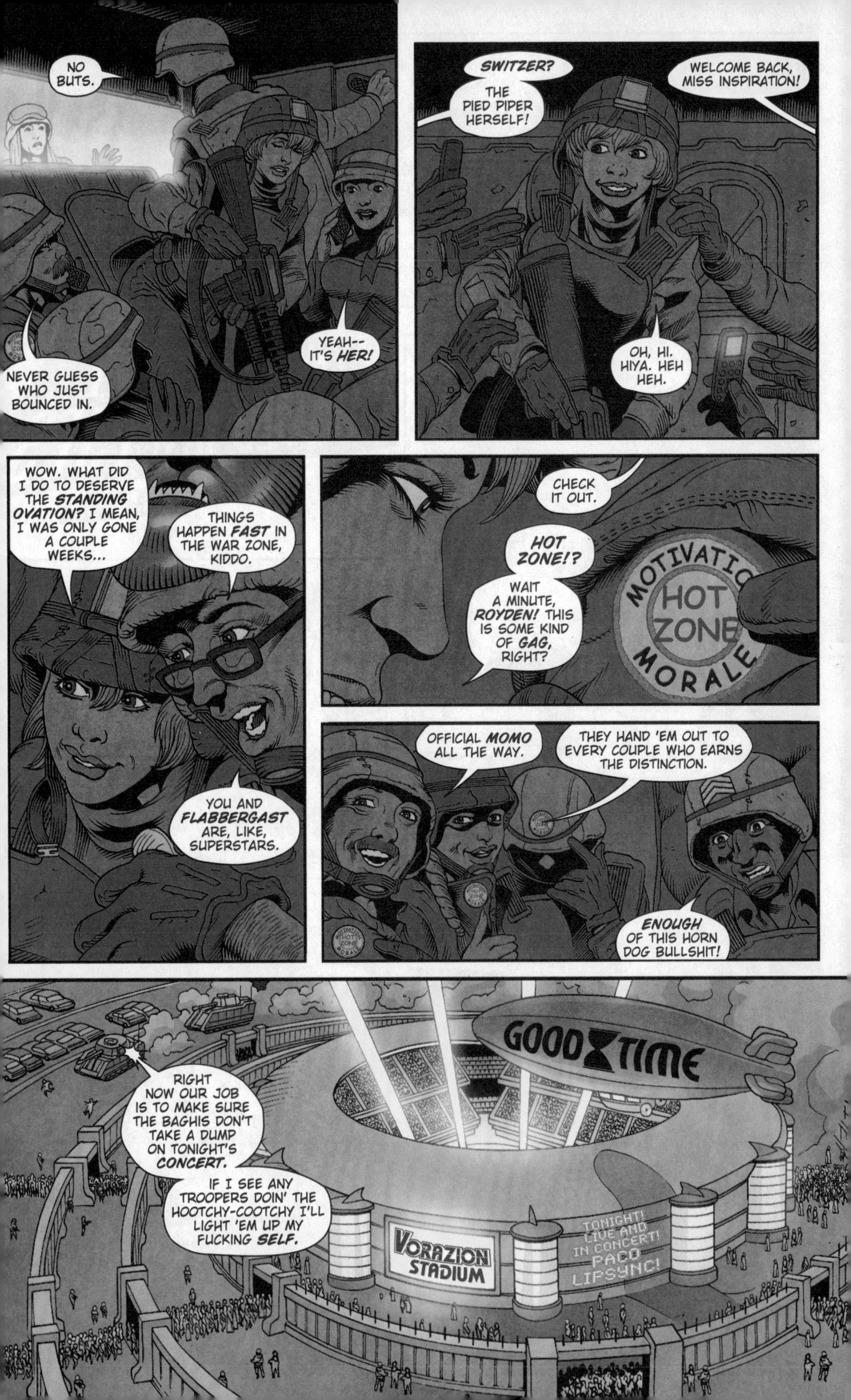
NO BUTS.
NEVER GUESS WHO JUST BOUNCED IN.
YEAH-- IT'S HER!
SWITZER? THE PIED PIPER HERSELF!
WELCOME BACK, MISS INSPIRATION!
OH, HI. HIYA. HEH HEH.
WOW. WHAT DID I DO TO DESERVE THE STANDING OVATION? I MEAN, I WAS ONLY GONE A COUPLE WEEKS...
THINGS HAPPEN FAST IN THE WAR ZONE, KIDDO.
YOU AND FLABBERGAST ARE, LIKE, SUPERSTARS.
CHECK IT OUT.
HOT ZONE!?
WAIT A MINUTE, ROYDEN! THIS IS SOME KIND OF GAG, RIGHT?
MOTIVATIO HOT ZONE MORALE
OFFICIAL MOMO ALL THE WAY.
THEY HAND 'EM OUT TO EVERY COUPLE WHO EARNS THE DISTINCTION.
ENOUGH OF THIS HORN DOG BULLSHIT!
GOOD TIME
RIGHT NOW OUR JOB IS TO MAKE SURE THE BAGHIS DON'T TAKE A DUMP ON TONIGHT'S CONCERT.
IF I SEE ANY TROOPERS DOIN' THE HOOTCHY-COOTCHY I'LL LIGHT 'EM UP MY FUCKING SELF.
VORAZION STADIUM
TONIGHT! LIVE AND IN CONCERT! PACO LIPSYNC!

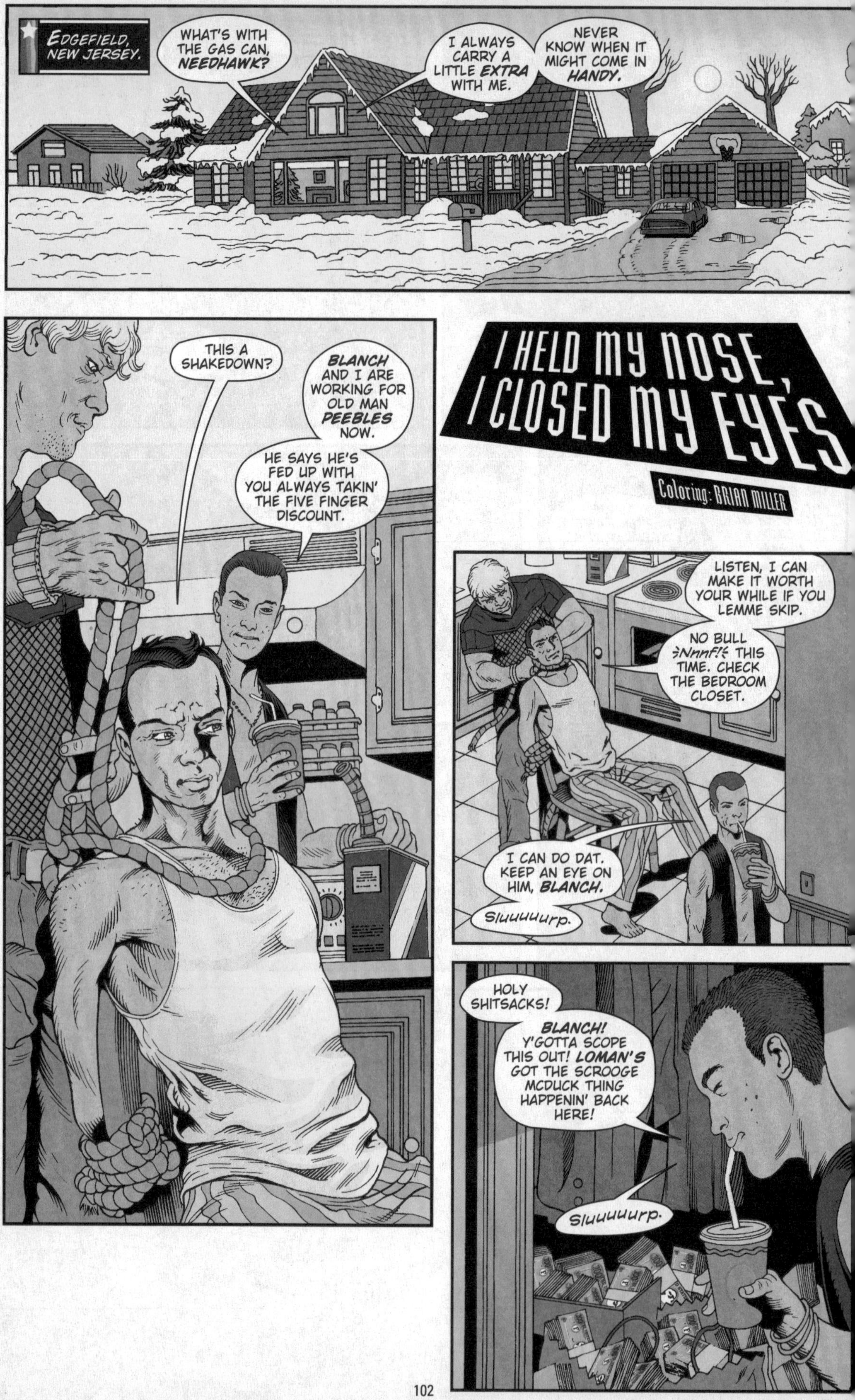
EDGEFIELD, NEW JERSEY.
WHAT'S WITH THE GAS CAN, NEEDHAWK?
I ALWAYS CARRY A LITTLE EXTRA WITH ME.
NEVER KNOW WHEN IT MIGHT COME IN HANDY.
I HELD MY NOSE, I CLOSED MY EYES
Coloring: BRIAN MILLER
THIS A SHAKEDOWN?
BLANCH AND I ARE WORKING FOR OLD MAN PEEBLES NOW.
HE SAYS HE'S FED UP WITH YOU ALWAYS TAKIN' THE FIVE FINGER DISCOUNT.
LISTEN, I CAN MAKE IT WORTH YOUR WHILE IF YOU LEMME SKIP.
NO BULL -Nnnf!- THIS TIME. CHECK THE BEDROOM CLOSET.
I CAN DO DAT. KEEP AN EYE ON HIM, BLANCH.
Sluuuuurp.
HOLY SHITSACKS!
BLANCH! Y'GOTTA SCOPE THIS OUT! LOMAN'S GOT THE SCROOGE MCDUCK THING HAPPENIN' BACK HERE!
Sluuuuurp.

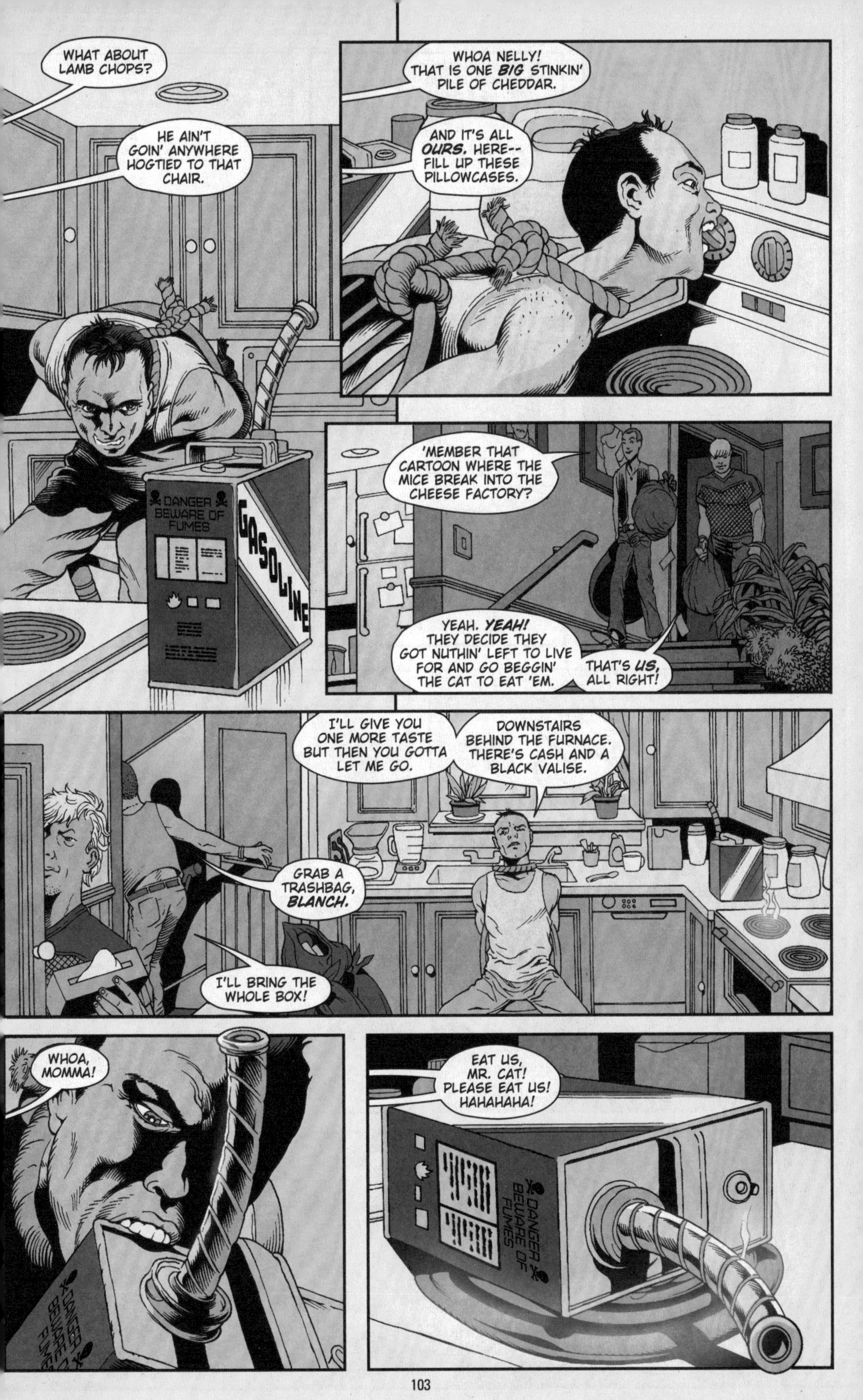
WHAT ABOUT LAMB CHOPS?
WHOA NELLY! THAT IS ONE BIG STINKIN' PILE OF CHEDDAR.
HE AIN'T GOIN' ANYWHERE HOGTIED TO THAT CHAIR.
AND IT'S ALL OURS. HERE-- FILL UP THESE PILLOWCASES.
DANGER BEWARE OF FUMES
GASOLINE
'MEMBER THAT CARTOON WHERE THE MICE BREAK INTO THE CHEESE FACTORY?
YEAH. YEAH! THEY DECIDE THEY GOT NUTHIN' LEFT TO LIVE FOR AND GO BEGGIN' THE CAT TO EAT 'EM.
THAT'S US, ALL RIGHT!
I'LL GIVE YOU ONE MORE TASTE BUT THEN YOU GOTTA LET ME GO.
DOWNSTAIRS BEHIND THE FURNACE. THERE'S CASH AND A BLACK VALISE.
GRAB A TRASHBAG, BLANCH.
I'LL BRING THE WHOLE BOX!
WHOA, MOMMA!
DANGER BEWARE OF FUMES
EAT US, MR. CAT! PLEASE EAT US! HAHAHAHA!
DANGER BEWARE OF FUMES

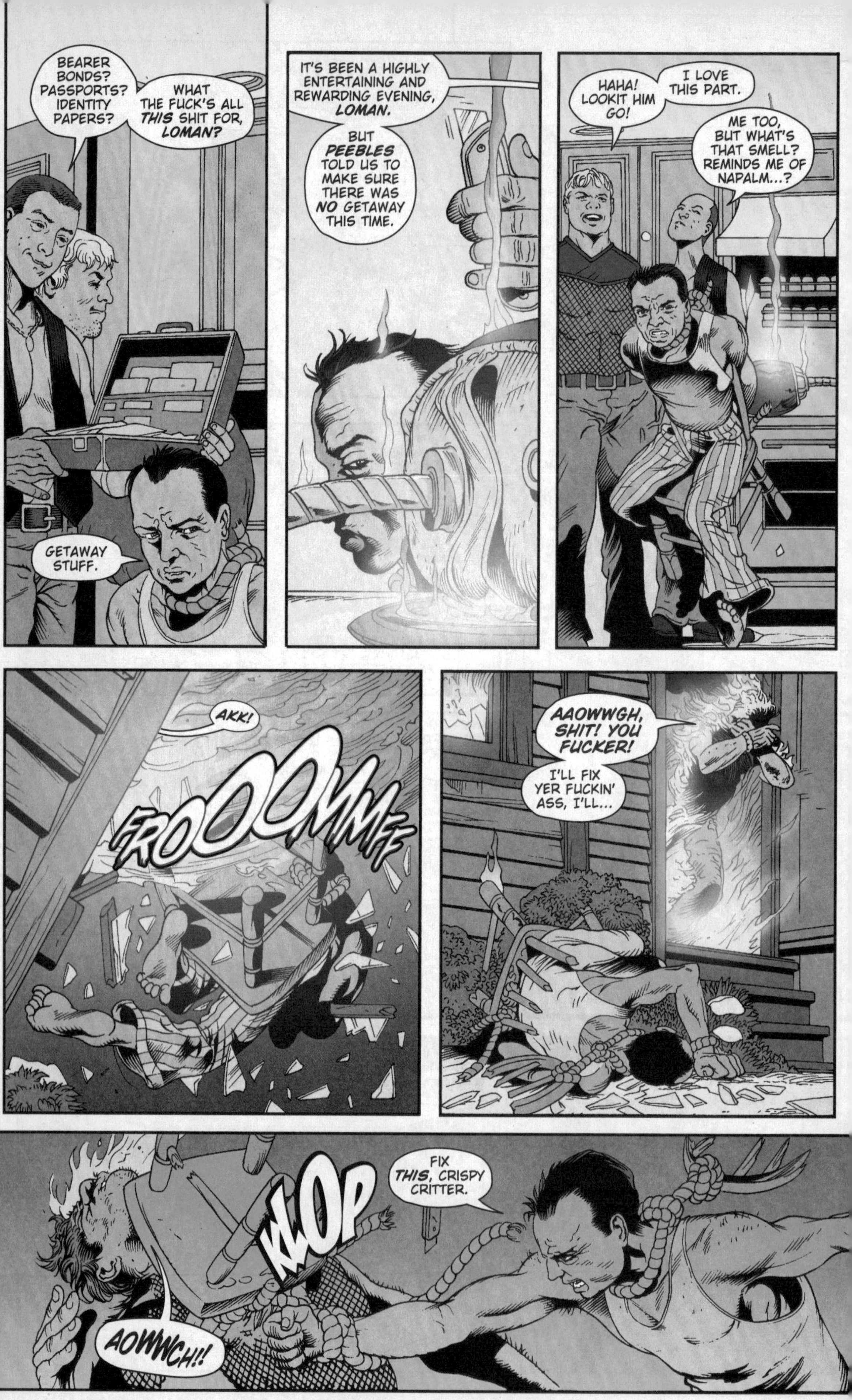
BEARER BONDS? PASSPORTS? IDENTITY PAPERS?
WHAT THE FUCK'S ALL THIS SHIT FOR, LOMAN?
GETAWAY STUFF.
IT'S BEEN A HIGHLY ENTERTAINING AND REWARDING EVENING, LOMAN.
BUT PEEBLES TOLD US TO MAKE SURE THERE WAS NO GETAWAY THIS TIME.
HAHA! LOOKIT HIM GO!
I LOVE THIS PART.
ME TOO, BUT WHAT'S THAT SMELL? REMINDS ME OF NAPALM...?
AKK!
FROOOMMFF
AAOWWGH, SHIT! YOU FUCKER!
I'LL FIX YER FUCKIN' ASS, I'LL...
FIX THIS, CRISPY CRITTER.
KLOP
AOWWCH!!

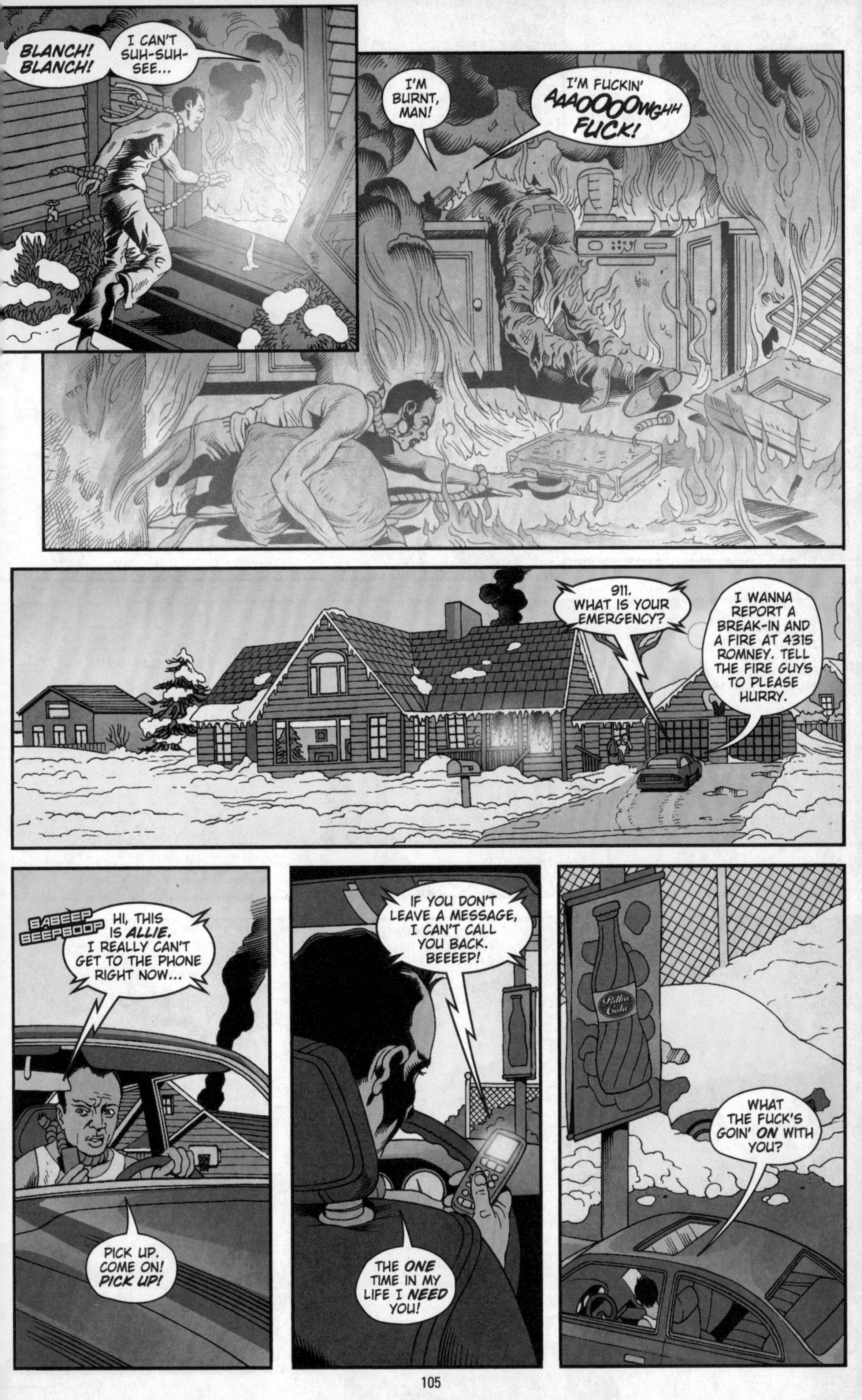
BLANCH! BLANCH!
I CAN'T SUH-SUH-SEE...
I'M BURNT, MAN!
I'M FUCKIN' AAAOOOOOWGHH FUCK!
911. WHAT IS YOUR EMERGENCY?
I WANNA REPORT A BREAK-IN AND A FIRE AT 4315 ROMNEY. TELL THE FIRE GUYS TO PLEASE HURRY.
BABEEP BEEPBOOP
HI, THIS IS ALLIE. I REALLY CAN'T GET TO THE PHONE RIGHT NOW...
PICK UP. COME ON! PICK UP!
IF YOU DON'T LEAVE A MESSAGE, I CAN'T CALL YOU BACK. BEEEEP!
THE ONE TIME IN MY LIFE I NEED YOU!
Polka Cola
WHAT THE FUCK'S GOIN' ON WITH YOU?

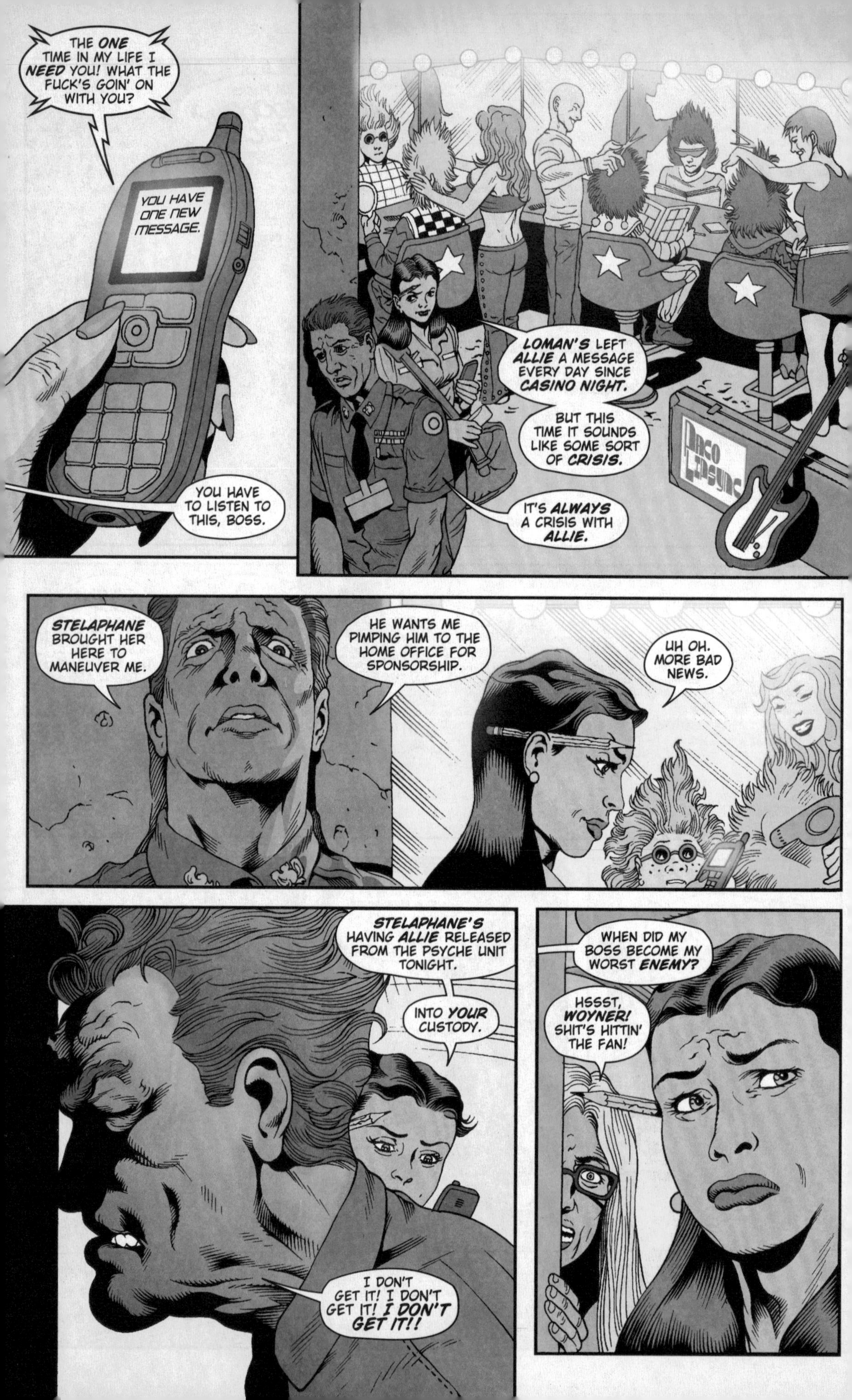

THE ONE TIME IN MY LIFE I NEED YOU! WHAT THE FUCK'S GOIN' ON WITH YOU?
YOU HAVE ONE NEW MESSAGE.
YOU HAVE TO LISTEN TO THIS, BOSS.
LOMAN'S LEFT ALLIE A MESSAGE EVERY DAY SINCE CASINO NIGHT.
BUT THIS TIME IT SOUNDS LIKE SOME SORT OF CRISIS.
IT'S ALWAYS A CRISIS WITH ALLIE.
STELAPHANE BROUGHT HER HERE TO MANEUVER ME.
HE WANTS ME PIMPING HIM TO THE HOME OFFICE FOR SPONSORSHIP.
UH OH. MORE BAD NEWS.
STELAPHANE'S HAVING ALLIE RELEASED FROM THE PSYCHE UNIT TONIGHT.
INTO YOUR CUSTODY.
I DON'T GET IT! I DON'T GET IT! I DON'T GET IT!!
WHEN DID MY BOSS BECOME MY WORST ENEMY?
HSSST, WOYNER! SHIT'S HITTIN' THE FAN!

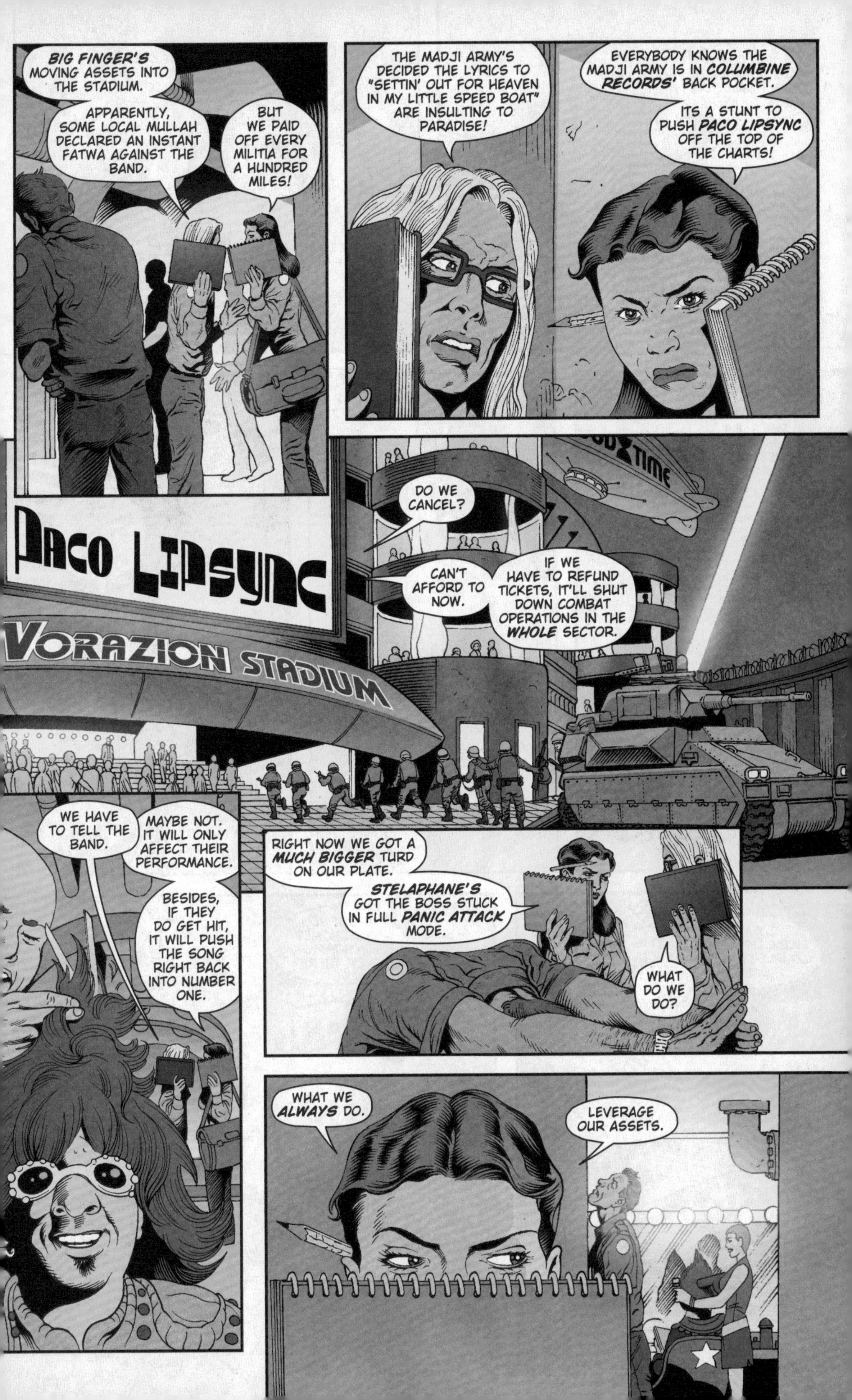
BIG FINGER'S MOVING ASSETS INTO THE STADIUM.
APPARENTLY, SOME LOCAL MULLAH DECLARED AN INSTANT FATWA AGAINST THE BAND.
BUT WE PAID OFF EVERY MILITIA FOR A HUNDRED MILES!
THE MADJI ARMY'S DECIDED THE LYRICS TO "SETTIN' OUT FOR HEAVEN IN MY LITTLE SPEED BOAT" ARE INSULTING TO PARADISE!
EVERYBODY KNOWS THE MADJI ARMY IS IN COLUMBINE RECORDS' BACK POCKET.
ITS A STUNT TO PUSH PACO LIPSYNC OFF THE TOP OF THE CHARTS!
PACO LIPSYNC
VORAZION STADIUM
DO WE CANCEL?
CAN'T AFFORD TO NOW.
IF WE HAVE TO REFUND TICKETS, IT'LL SHUT DOWN COMBAT OPERATIONS IN THE WHOLE SECTOR.
WE HAVE TO TELL THE BAND.
MAYBE NOT. IT WILL ONLY AFFECT THEIR PERFORMANCE.
BESIDES, IF THEY DO GET HIT, IT WILL PUSH THE SONG RIGHT BACK INTO NUMBER ONE.
RIGHT NOW WE GOT A MUCH BIGGER TURD ON OUR PLATE.
STELAPHANE'S GOT THE BOSS STUCK IN FULL PANIC ATTACK MODE.
WHAT DO WE DO?
WHAT WE ALWAYS DO.
LEVERAGE OUR ASSETS.

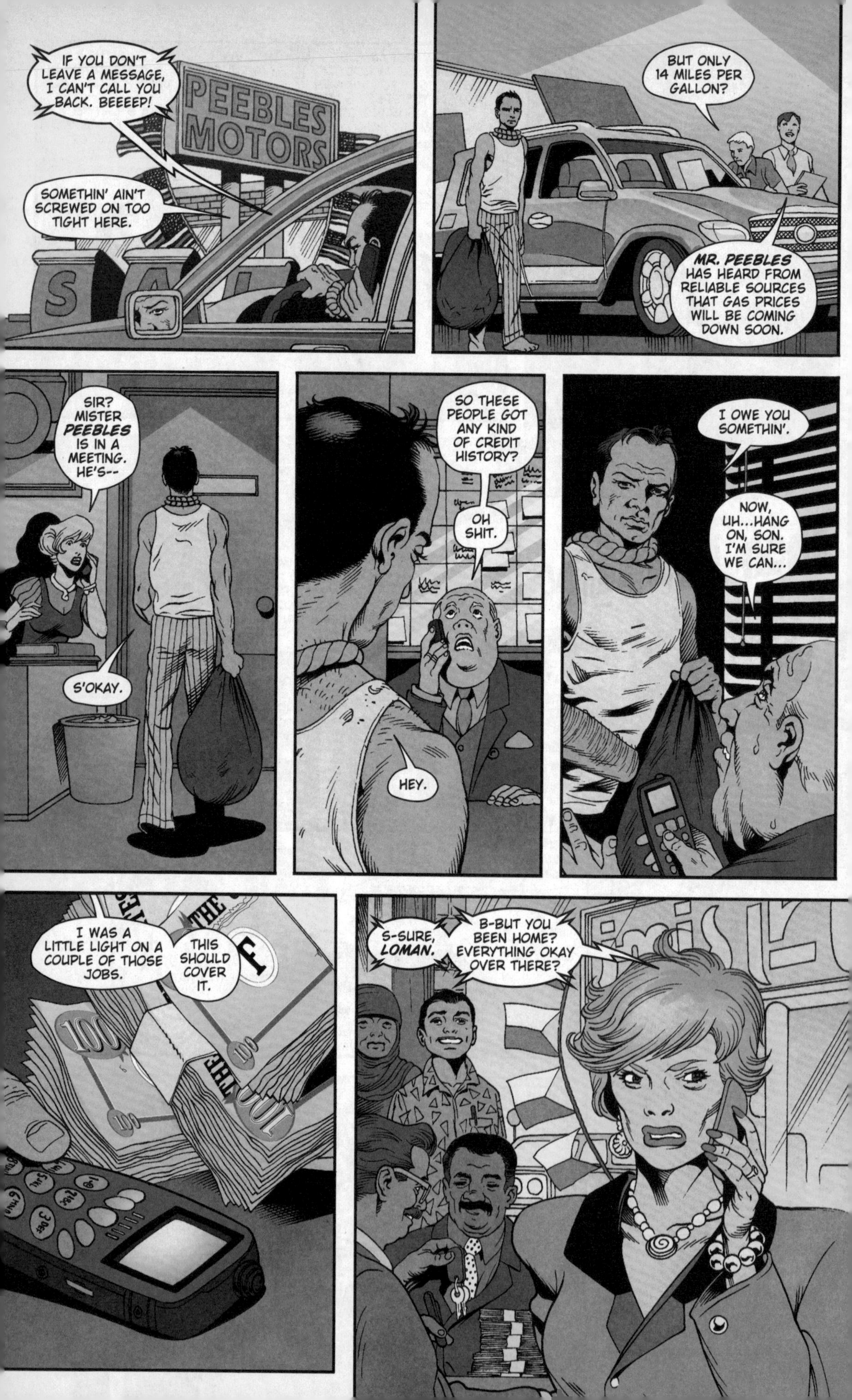
IF YOU DON'T LEAVE A MESSAGE, I CAN'T CALL YOU BACK. BEEEEP!
PEEBLES MOTORS
SOMETHIN' AIN'T SCREWED ON TOO TIGHT HERE.
BUT ONLY 14 MILES PER GALLON?
MR. PEEBLES HAS HEARD FROM RELIABLE SOURCES THAT GAS PRICES WILL BE COMING DOWN SOON.
SIR? MISTER PEEBLES IS IN A MEETING. HE'S--
S'OKAY.
SO THESE PEOPLE GOT ANY KIND OF CREDIT HISTORY?
OH SHIT.
HEY.
I OWE YOU SOMETHIN'.
NOW, UH...HANG ON, SON. I'M SURE WE CAN...
I WAS A LITTLE LIGHT ON A COUPLE OF THOSE JOBS.
THIS SHOULD COVER IT.
S-SURE, LOMAN.
B-BUT YOU BEEN HOME? EVERYTHING OKAY OVER THERE?

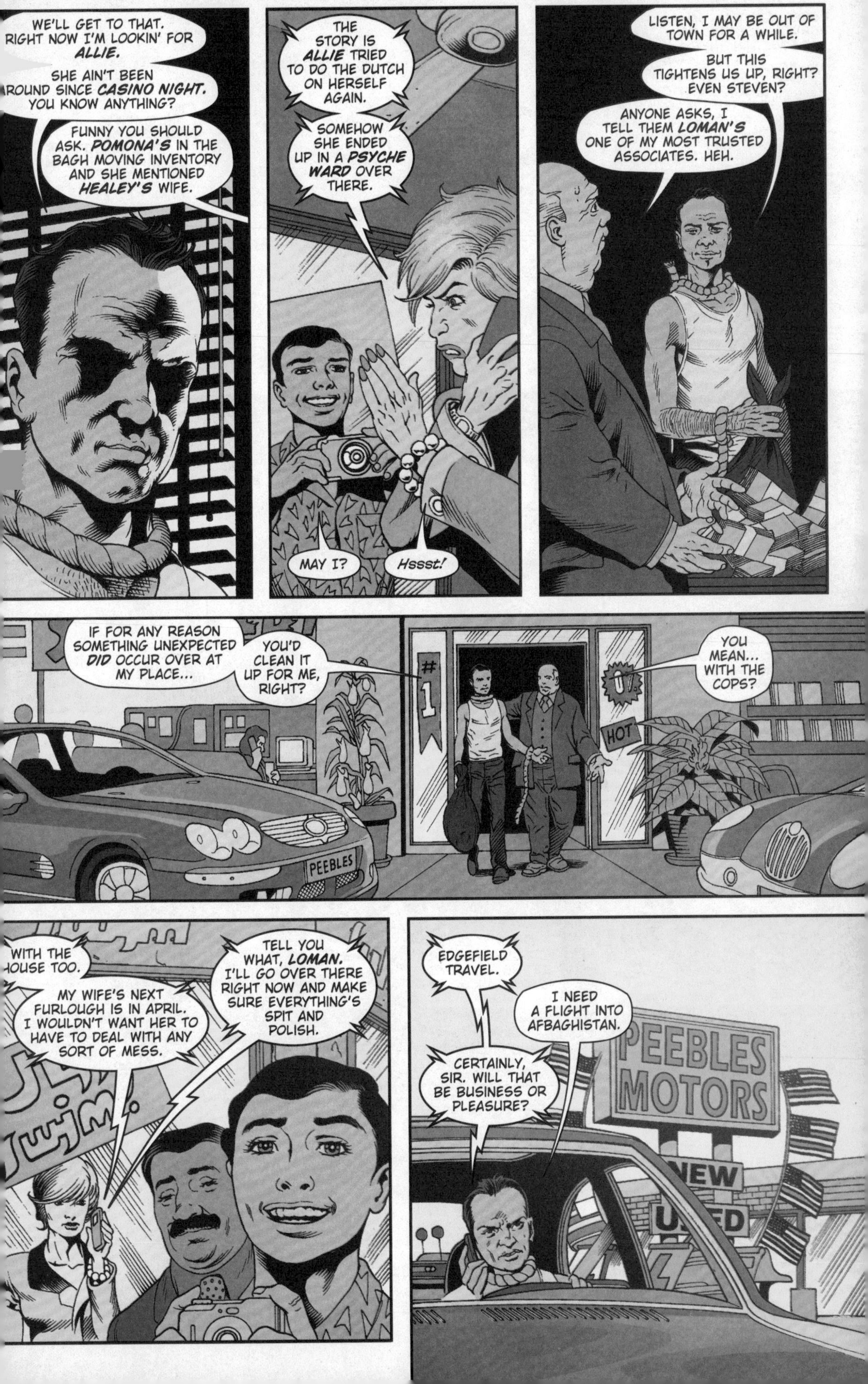
WE'LL GET TO THAT. RIGHT NOW I'M LOOKIN' FOR ALLIE.
SHE AIN'T BEEN ROUND SINCE CASINO NIGHT. YOU KNOW ANYTHING?
FUNNY YOU SHOULD ASK. POMONA'S IN THE BAGH MOVING INVENTORY AND SHE MENTIONED HEALEY'S WIFE.
THE STORY IS ALLIE TRIED TO DO THE DUTCH ON HERSELF AGAIN.
SOMEHOW SHE ENDED UP IN A PSYCHE WARD OVER THERE.
MAY I?
Hssst!
LISTEN, I MAY BE OUT OF TOWN FOR A WHILE.
BUT THIS TIGHTENS US UP, RIGHT? EVEN STEVEN?
ANYONE ASKS, I TELL THEM LOMAN'S ONE OF MY MOST TRUSTED ASSOCIATES. HEH.
IF FOR ANY REASON SOMETHING UNEXPECTED DID OCCUR OVER AT MY PLACE...
YOU'D CLEAN IT UP FOR ME, RIGHT?
#1
YOU MEAN... WITH THE COPS?
HOT
PEEBLES
WITH THE HOUSE TOO.
MY WIFE'S NEXT FURLOUGH IS IN APRIL. I WOULDN'T WANT HER TO HAVE TO DEAL WITH ANY SORT OF MESS.
TELL YOU WHAT, LOMAN. I'LL GO OVER THERE RIGHT NOW AND MAKE SURE EVERYTHING'S SPIT AND POLISH.
EDGEFIELD TRAVEL.
I NEED A FLIGHT INTO AFBAGHISTAN.
CERTAINLY, SIR. WILL THAT BE BUSINESS OR PLEASURE?
PEEBLES MOTORS
NEW
USED

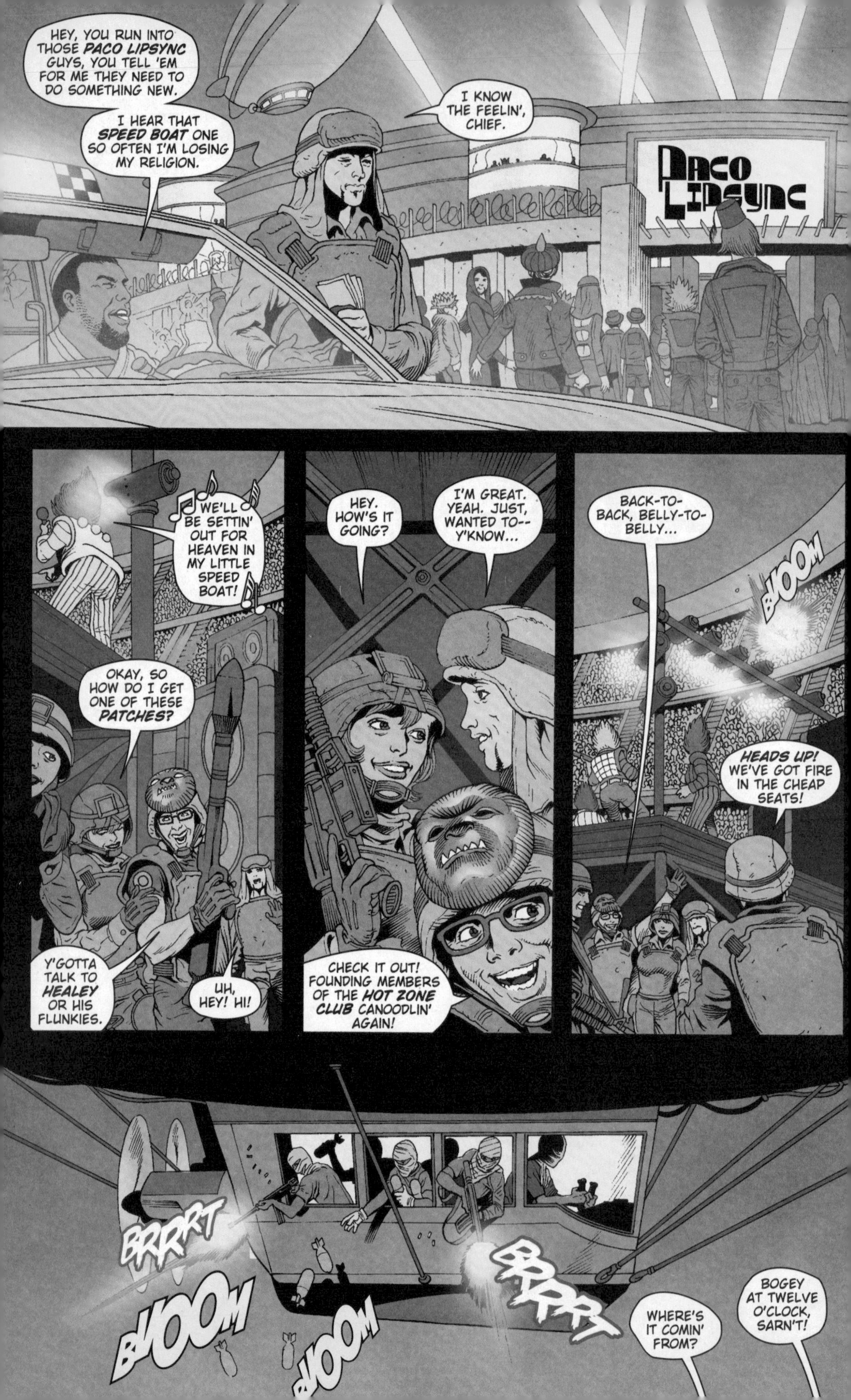
HEY, YOU RUN INTO THOSE PACO LIPSYNC GUYS, YOU TELL 'EM FOR ME THEY NEED TO DO SOMETHING NEW.
I HEAR THAT SPEED BOAT ONE SO OFTEN I'M LOSING MY RELIGION.
I KNOW THE FEELIN', CHIEF.
PACO LIPSYNC
WE'LL BE SETTIN' OUT FOR HEAVEN IN MY LITTLE SPEED BOAT!
OKAY, SO HOW DO I GET ONE OF THESE PATCHES?
Y'GOTTA TALK TO HEALEY OR HIS FLUNKIES.
UH, HEY! HI!
HEY. HOW'S IT GOING?
I'M GREAT. YEAH. JUST, WANTED TO-- Y'KNOW...
CHECK IT OUT! FOUNDING MEMBERS OF THE HOT ZONE CLUB CANOODLIN' AGAIN!
BACK-TO-BACK, BELLY-TO-BELLY...
BWOOM
HEADS UP! WE'VE GOT FIRE IN THE CHEAP SEATS!
BRRRT
BWOOM
BWOOM
BRRRT
WHERE'S IT COMIN' FROM?
BOGEY AT TWELVE O'CLOCK, SARN'T!

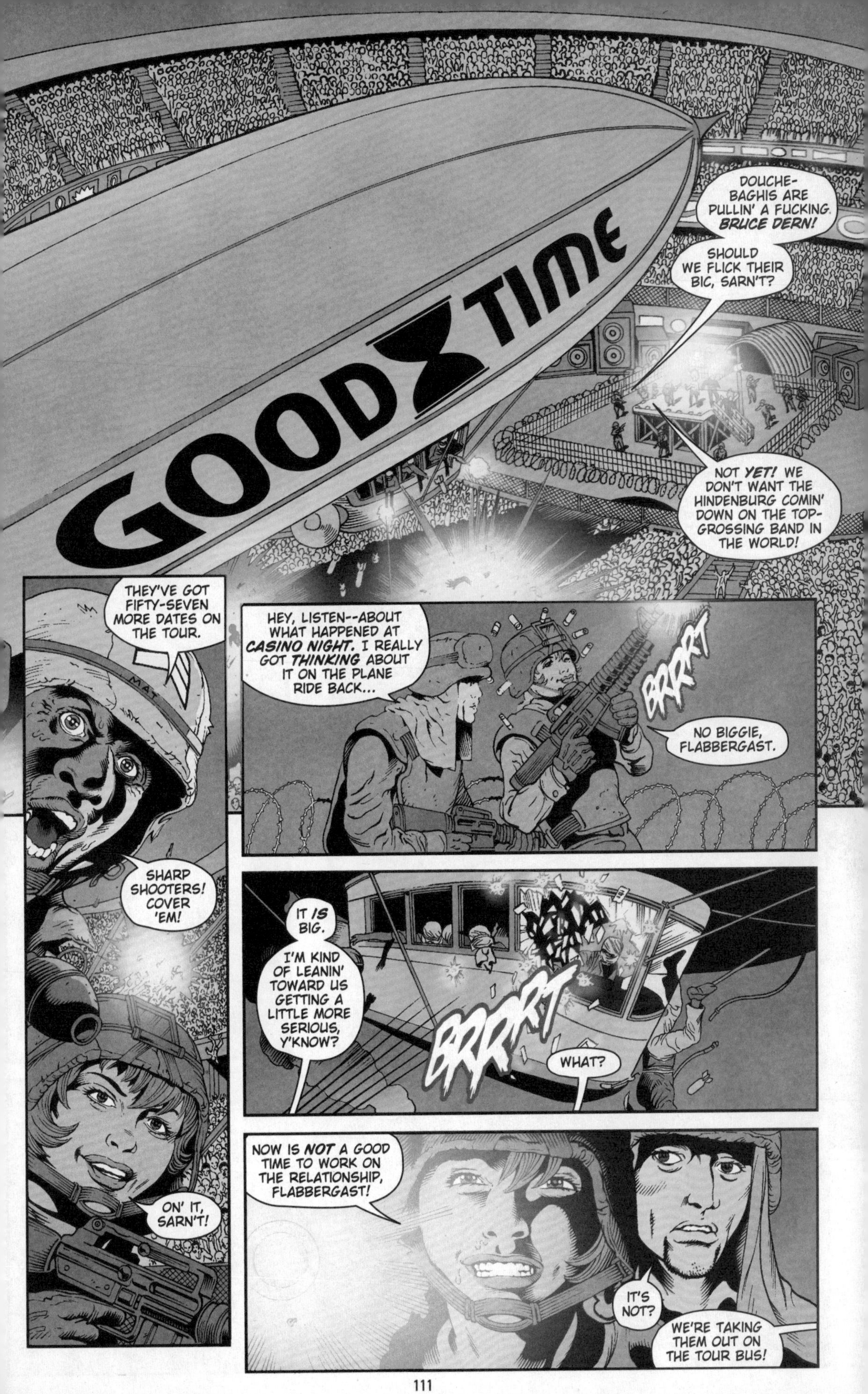
GOOD TIME
DOUCHE-BAGHIS ARE PULLIN' A FUCKING BRUCE DERN!
SHOULD WE FLICK THEIR BIC, SARN'T?
NOT YET! WE DON'T WANT THE HINDENBURG COMIN' DOWN ON THE TOP-GROSSING BAND IN THE WORLD!
THEY'VE GOT FIFTY-SEVEN MORE DATES ON THE TOUR.
MAT
HEY, LISTEN--ABOUT WHAT HAPPENED AT CASINO NIGHT. I REALLY GOT THINKING ABOUT IT ON THE PLANE RIDE BACK...
BRRRT
NO BIGGIE, FLABBERGAST.
SHARP SHOOTERS! COVER 'EM!
IT IS BIG.
I'M KIND OF LEANIN' TOWARD US GETTING A LITTLE MORE SERIOUS, Y'KNOW?
BRRRT
WHAT?
ON' IT, SARN'T!
NOW IS NOT A GOOD TIME TO WORK ON THE RELATIONSHIP, FLABBERGAST!
IT'S NOT?
WE'RE TAKING THEM OUT ON THE TOUR BUS!

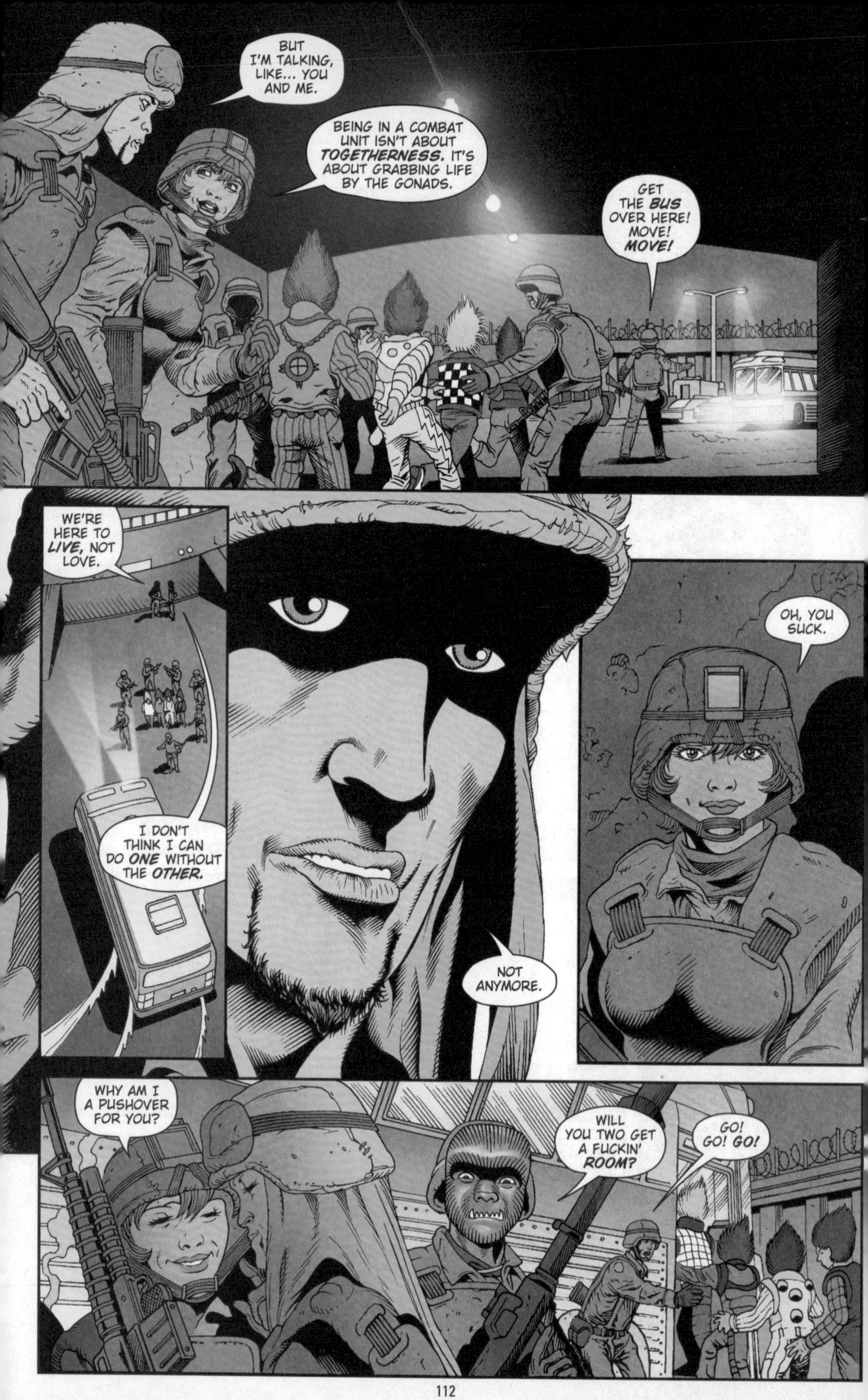
BUT I'M TALKING, LIKE... YOU AND ME.
BEING IN A COMBAT UNIT ISN'T ABOUT TOGETHERNESS. IT'S ABOUT GRABBING LIFE BY THE GONADS.
GET THE BUS OVER HERE! MOVE! MOVE!
WE'RE HERE TO LIVE, NOT LOVE.
I DON'T THINK I CAN DO ONE WITHOUT THE OTHER.
NOT ANYMORE.
OH, YOU SUCK.
WHY AM I A PUSHOVER FOR YOU?
WILL YOU TWO GET A FUCKIN' ROOM?
GO! GO! GO!

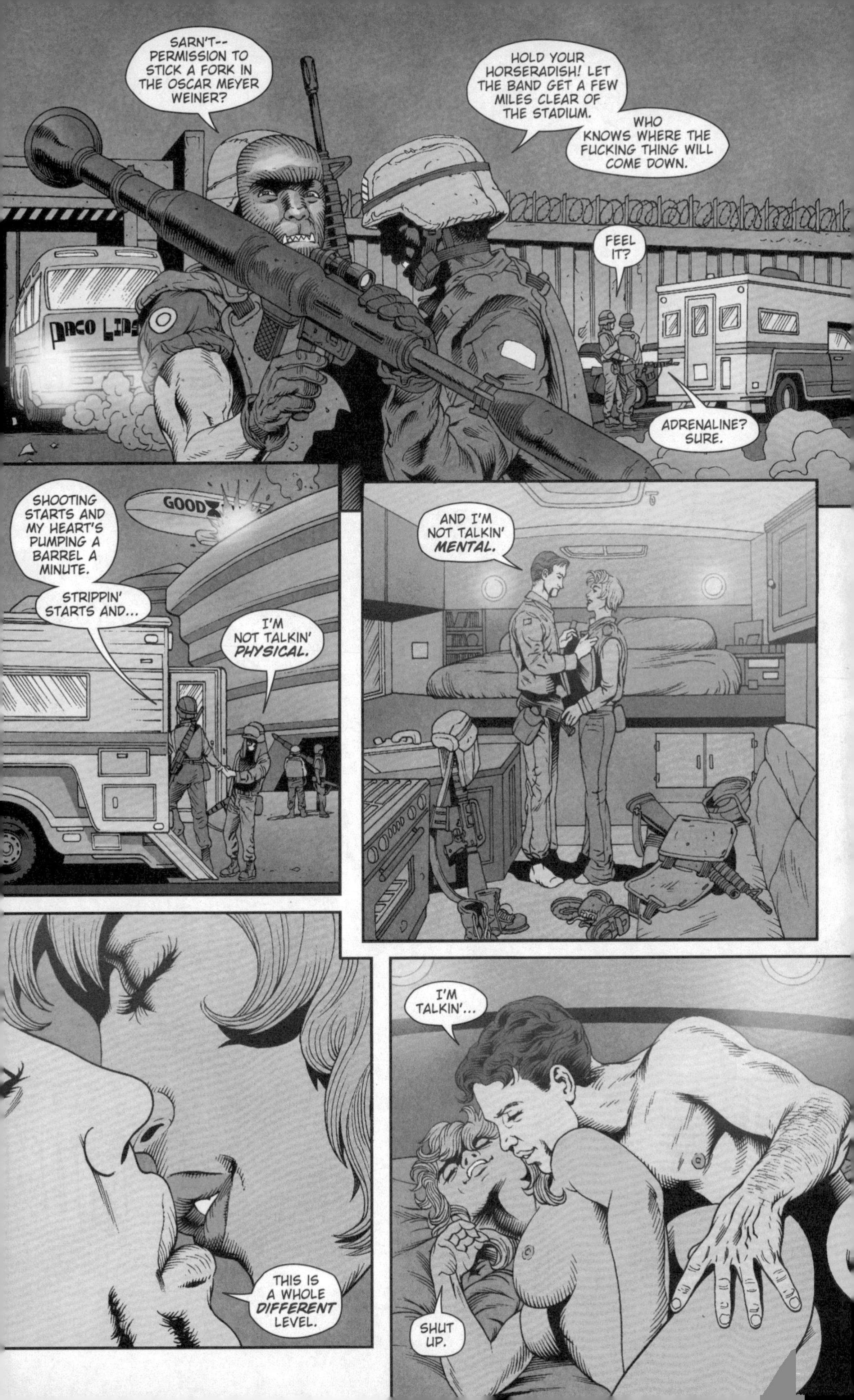
SARN'T-- PERMISSION TO STICK A FORK IN THE OSCAR MEYER WEINER?
HOLD YOUR HORSERADISH! LET THE BAND GET A FEW MILES CLEAR OF THE STADIUM.
WHO KNOWS WHERE THE FUCKING THING WILL COME DOWN.
FEEL IT?
ADRENALINE? SURE.
SHOOTING STARTS AND MY HEART'S PUMPING A BARREL A MINUTE.
GOOD
STRIPPIN' STARTS AND...
I'M NOT TALKIN' PHYSICAL.
AND I'M NOT TALKIN' MENTAL.
THIS IS A WHOLE DIFFERENT LEVEL.
I'M TALKIN'...
SHUT UP.

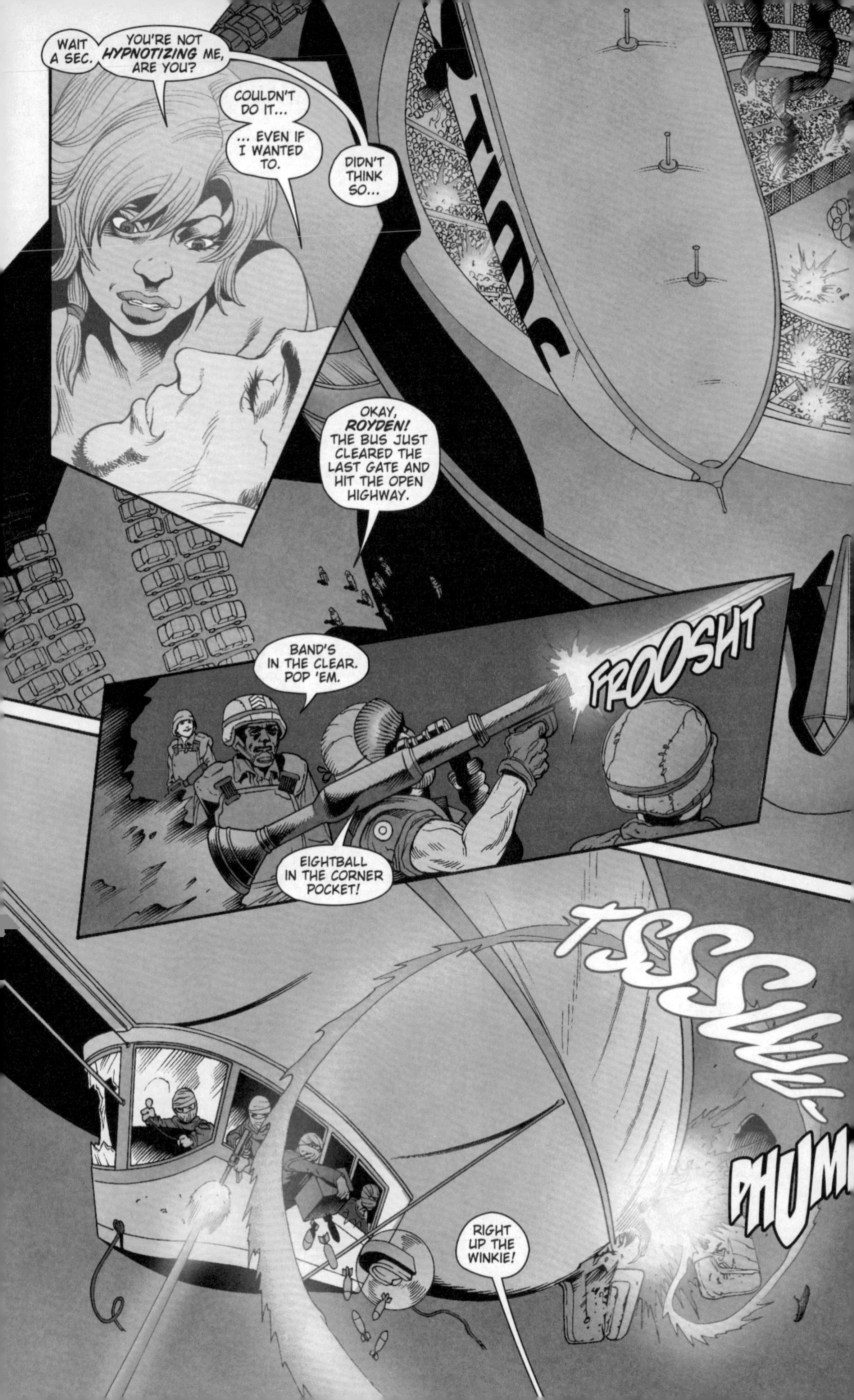
WAIT A SEC.
YOU'RE NOT HYPNOTIZING ME, ARE YOU?
COULDN'T DO IT...
... EVEN IF I WANTED TO.
DIDN'T THINK SO...
OKAY, ROYDEN! THE BUS JUST CLEARED THE LAST GATE AND HIT THE OPEN HIGHWAY.
BAND'S IN THE CLEAR. POP 'EM.
FROOSHT
EIGHTBALL IN THE CORNER POCKET!
TSSSWW
PHUM
RIGHT UP THE WINKIE!

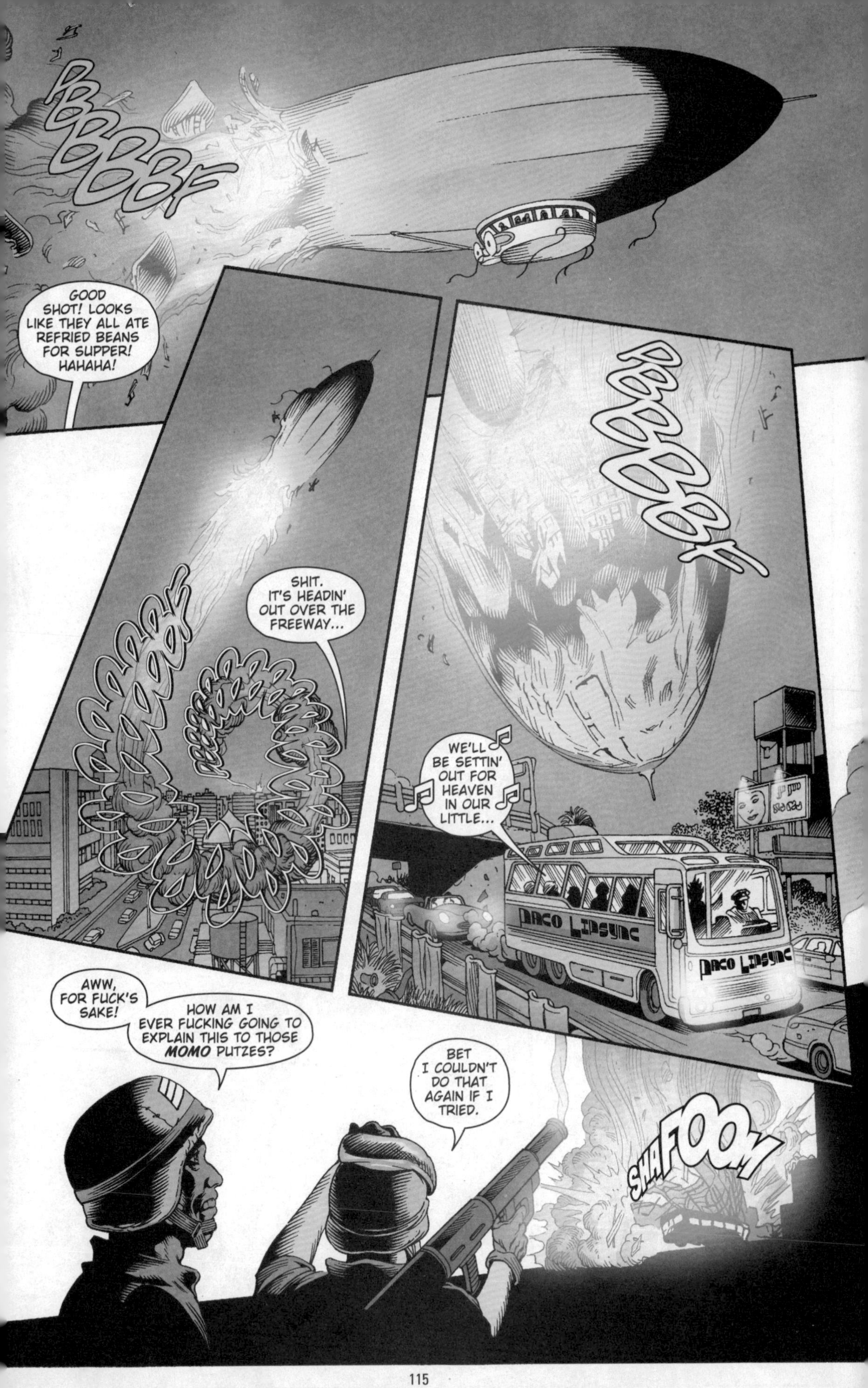
PBBBBF
GOOD SHOT! LOOKS LIKE THEY ALL ATE REFRIED BEANS FOR SUPPER! HAHAHA!
SHIT. IT'S HEADIN' OUT OVER THE FREEWAY...
PBBBBF
WE'LL BE SETTIN' OUT FOR HEAVEN IN OUR LITTLE...
PACO LIPSYNC
AWW, FOR FUCK'S SAKE!
HOW AM I EVER FUCKING GOING TO EXPLAIN THIS TO THOSE MOMO PUTZES?
BET I COULDN'T DO THAT AGAIN IF I TRIED.
SHAFOOM

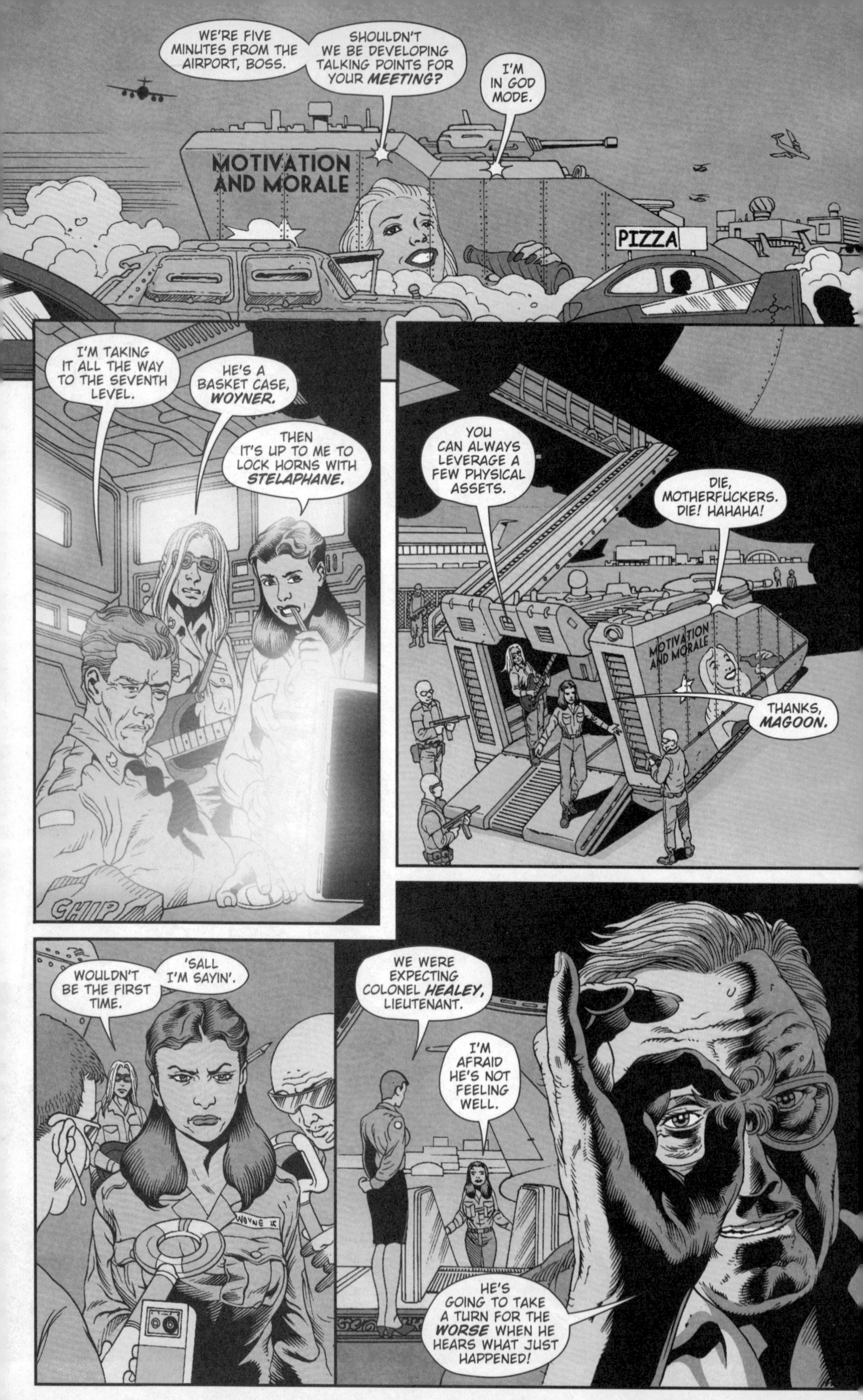
WE'RE FIVE MINUTES FROM THE AIRPORT, BOSS.
SHOULDN'T WE BE DEVELOPING TALKING POINTS FOR YOUR MEETING?
I'M IN GOD MODE.
MOTIVATION AND MORALE
PIZZA
I'M TAKING IT ALL THE WAY TO THE SEVENTH LEVEL.
HE'S A BASKET CASE, WOYNER.
THEN IT'S UP TO ME TO LOCK HORNS WITH STELAPHANE.
YOU CAN ALWAYS LEVERAGE A FEW PHYSICAL ASSETS.
DIE, MOTHERFUCKERS. DIE! HAHAHA!
MOTIVATION AND MORALE
THANKS, MAGOON.
WOULDN'T BE THE FIRST TIME.
'SALL I'M SAYIN'.
WE WERE EXPECTING COLONEL HEALEY, LIEUTENANT.
I'M AFRAID HE'S NOT FEELING WELL.
HE'S GOING TO TAKE A TURN FOR THE WORSE WHEN HE HEARS WHAT JUST HAPPENED!

PACO LIPSYNC'S TOUR BUS WAS ATTACKED.

ALL FOUR OF THE BAND MEMBERS HAVE BEEN KILLED.

MY GOD. THAT'S *HORRIBLE*. AN ABSOLUTE TRAGEDY.

MADE DOUBLY SO AS THEIR BODIES WERE BURNED *COMPLETELY* TO ASH.

NOT A HAIR LEFT ON THEIR HEADS.

YOU WERE HOPING TO ADD THEM TO YOUR COLLECTION, SIR?

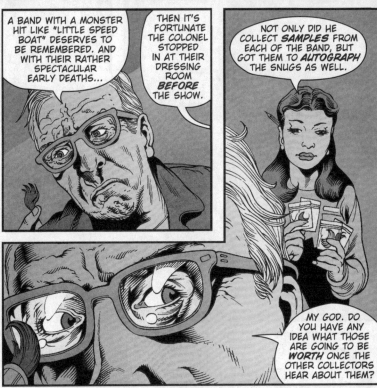

A BAND WITH A MONSTER HIT LIKE "LITTLE SPEED BOAT" DESERVES TO BE REMEMBERED. AND WITH THEIR RATHER SPECTACULAR EARLY DEATHS...

THEN IT'S FORTUNATE THE COLONEL STOPPED IN AT THEIR DRESSING ROOM *BEFORE* THE SHOW.

NOT ONLY DID HE COLLECT *SAMPLES* FROM EACH OF THE BAND, BUT GOT THEM TO *AUTOGRAPH* THE SNUGS AS WELL.

MY GOD. DO YOU HAVE ANY IDEA WHAT THOSE ARE GOING TO BE *WORTH* ONCE THE OTHER COLLECTORS HEAR ABOUT THEM?

I KNOW WHAT THEY ARE WORTH TO COLONEL *HEALEY*.

AH. YES. COME OVER HERE THEN. SIT DOWN.

LET'S TALK A LITTLE TURKEY. WHAT DOES MY GOOD FRIEND THE COLONEL NEED?

WHAT WE'RE IN THE MARKET FOR IS A PERMANENT *SOLUTION*.

TO HIS *ALLIE* PROBLEM.

WOYNER

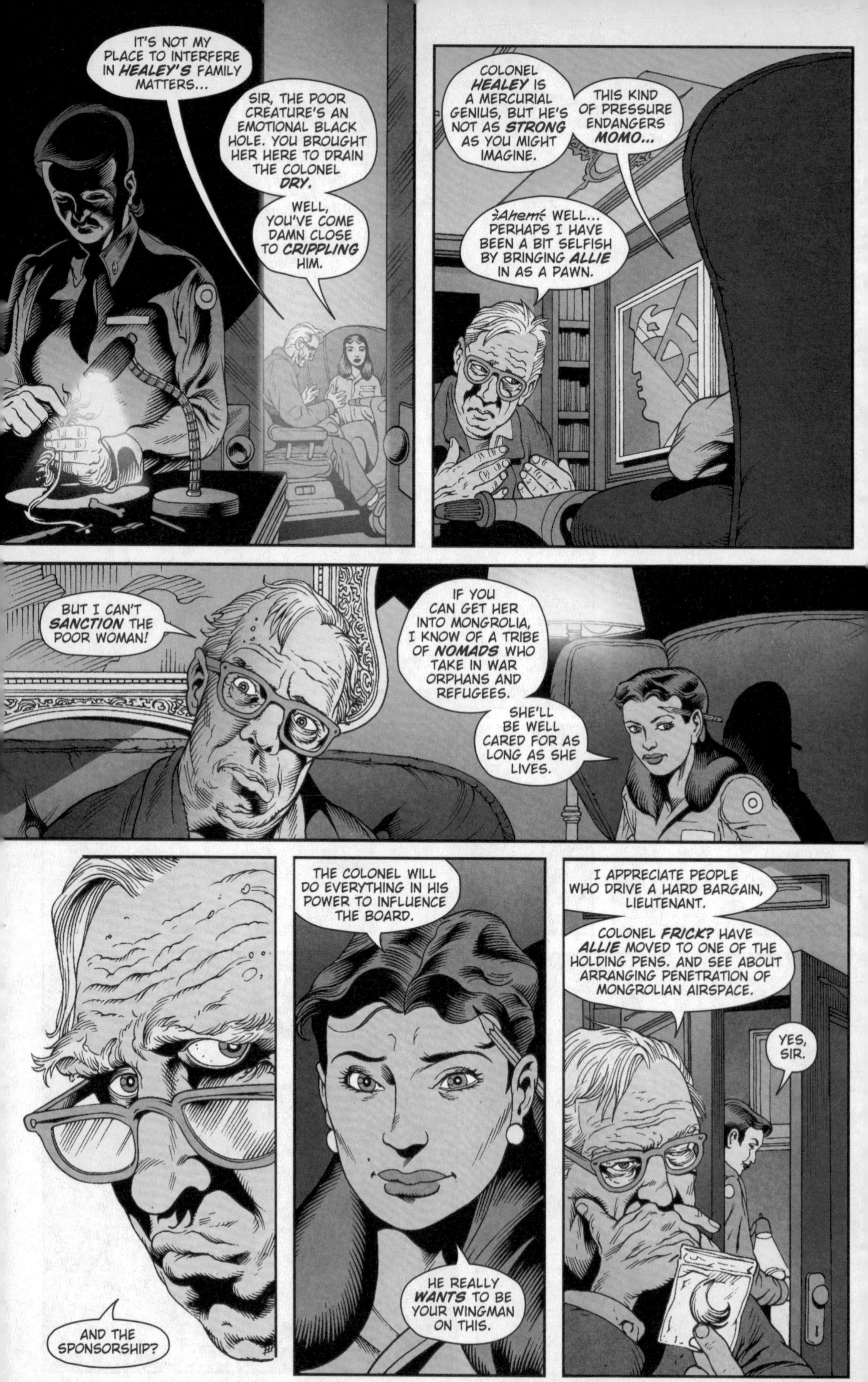
IT'S NOT MY PLACE TO INTERFERE IN HEALEY'S FAMILY MATTERS...
SIR, THE POOR CREATURE'S AN EMOTIONAL BLACK HOLE. YOU BROUGHT HER HERE TO DRAIN THE COLONEL DRY.
WELL, YOU'VE COME DAMN CLOSE TO CRIPPLING HIM.
COLONEL HEALEY IS A MERCURIAL GENIUS, BUT HE'S NOT AS STRONG AS YOU MIGHT IMAGINE.
THIS KIND OF PRESSURE ENDANGERS MOMO...
Ahem WELL... PERHAPS I HAVE BEEN A BIT SELFISH BY BRINGING ALLIE IN AS A PAWN.
BUT I CAN'T SANCTION THE POOR WOMAN!
IF YOU CAN GET HER INTO MONGROLIA, I KNOW OF A TRIBE OF NOMADS WHO TAKE IN WAR ORPHANS AND REFUGEES.
SHE'LL BE WELL CARED FOR AS LONG AS SHE LIVES.
AND THE SPONSORSHIP?
THE COLONEL WILL DO EVERYTHING IN HIS POWER TO INFLUENCE THE BOARD.
HE REALLY WANTS TO BE YOUR WINGMAN ON THIS.
I APPRECIATE PEOPLE WHO DRIVE A HARD BARGAIN, LIEUTENANT.
COLONEL FRICK? HAVE ALLIE MOVED TO ONE OF THE HOLDING PENS. AND SEE ABOUT ARRANGING PENETRATION OF MONGROLIAN AIRSPACE.
YES, SIR.

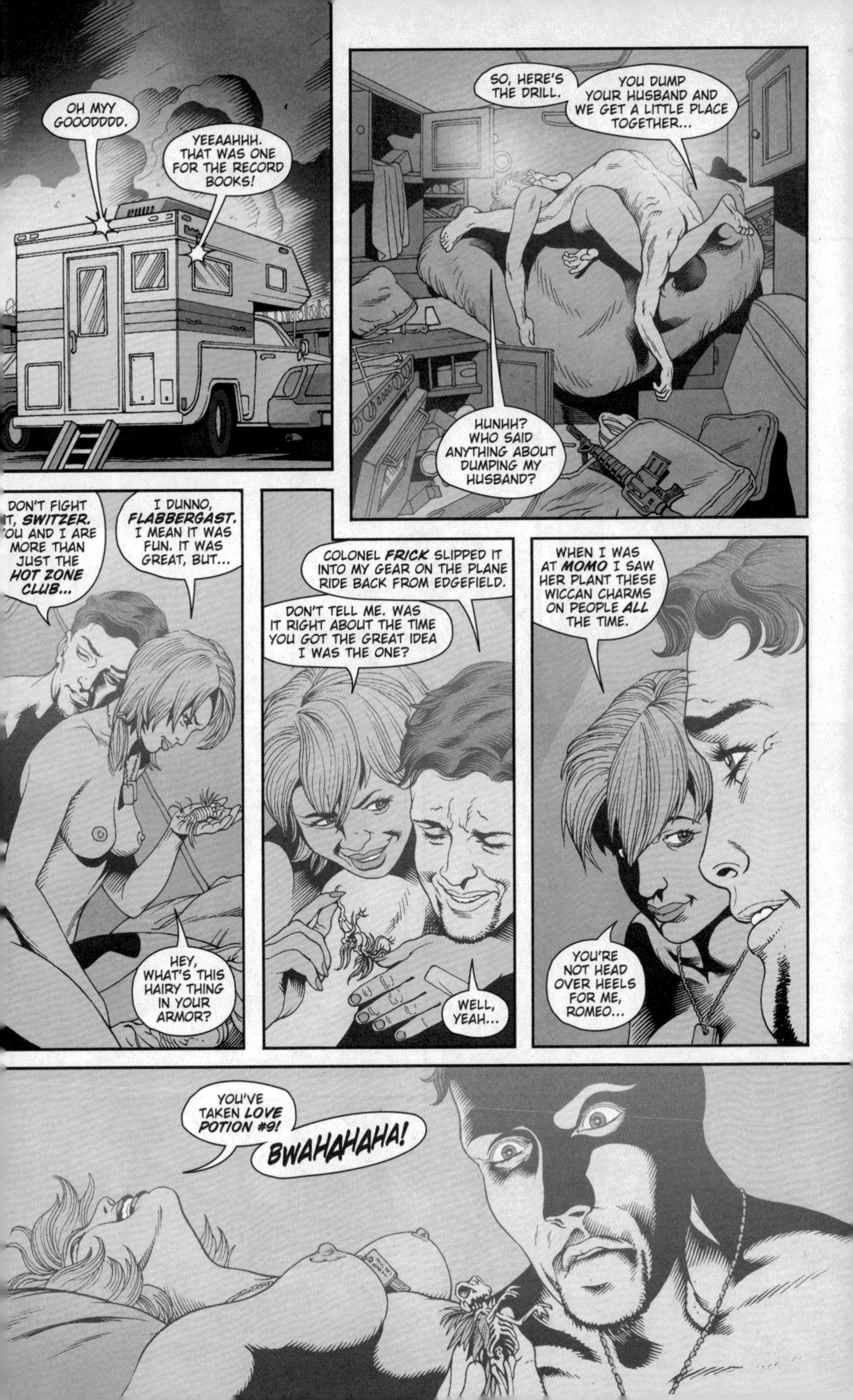
OH MYY GOOODDDD.
YEEAAHHH. THAT WAS ONE FOR THE RECORD BOOKS!
SO, HERE'S THE DRILL.
YOU DUMP YOUR HUSBAND AND WE GET A LITTLE PLACE TOGETHER...
HUNHH? WHO SAID ANYTHING ABOUT DUMPING MY HUSBAND?
DON'T FIGHT IT, SWITZER. YOU AND I ARE MORE THAN JUST THE HOT ZONE CLUB...
I DUNNO, FLABBERGAST. I MEAN IT WAS FUN. IT WAS GREAT, BUT...
HEY, WHAT'S THIS HAIRY THING IN YOUR ARMOR?
COLONEL FRICK SLIPPED IT INTO MY GEAR ON THE PLANE RIDE BACK FROM EDGEFIELD.
DON'T TELL ME. WAS IT RIGHT ABOUT THE TIME YOU GOT THE GREAT IDEA I WAS THE ONE?
WELL, YEAH...
WHEN I WAS AT MOMO I SAW HER PLANT THESE WICCAN CHARMS ON PEOPLE ALL THE TIME.
YOU'RE NOT HEAD OVER HEELS FOR ME, ROMEO...
YOU'VE TAKEN LOVE POTION #9!
BWAHAHAHA!

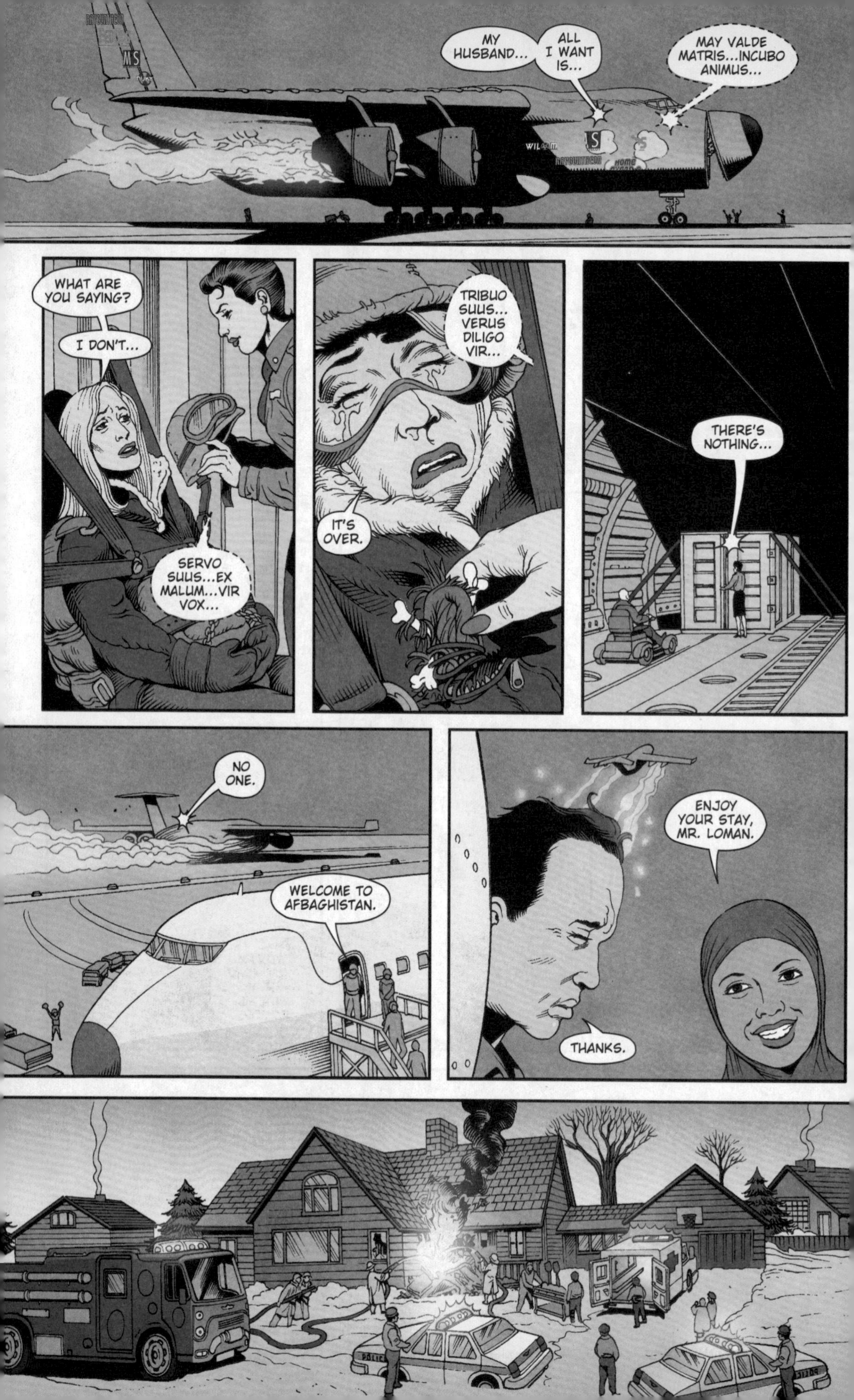
MY HUSBAND...
ALL I WANT IS...
MAY VALDE MATRIS...INCUBO ANIMUS...
WHAT ARE YOU SAYING?
I DON'T...
SERVO SUUS...EX MALUM...VIR VOX...
TRIBUO SUUS... VERUS DILIGO VIR...
IT'S OVER.
THERE'S NOTHING...
NO ONE.
WELCOME TO AFBAGHISTAN.
ENJOY YOUR STAY, MR. LOMAN.
THANKS.

A@L MISSION INTEL [Advance]:

CLASSIFIED
Office of Motivation and Morale

ASSET CONCEPTUALIZATIONS

By Rick Veitch

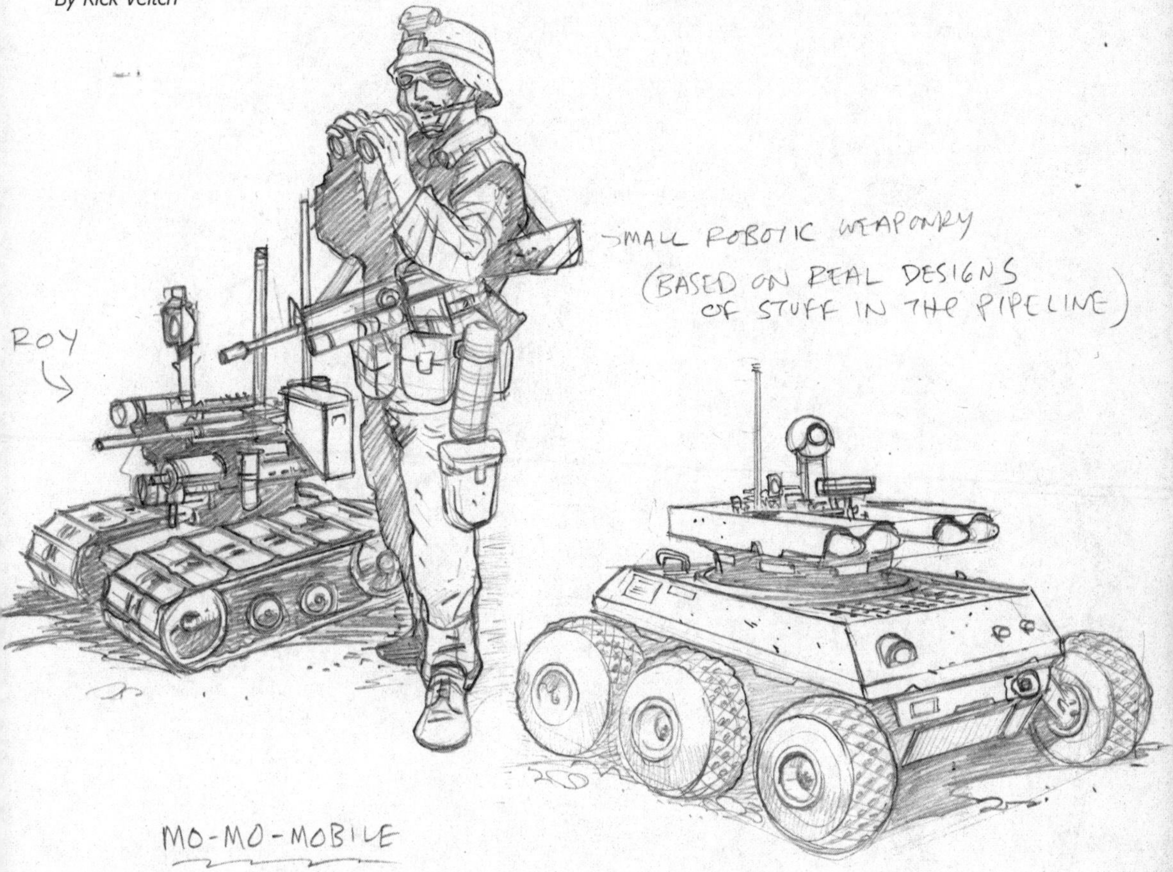

SMALL ROBOTIC WEAPONRY
(BASED ON REAL DESIGNS OF STUFF IN THE PIPELINE)
ROY

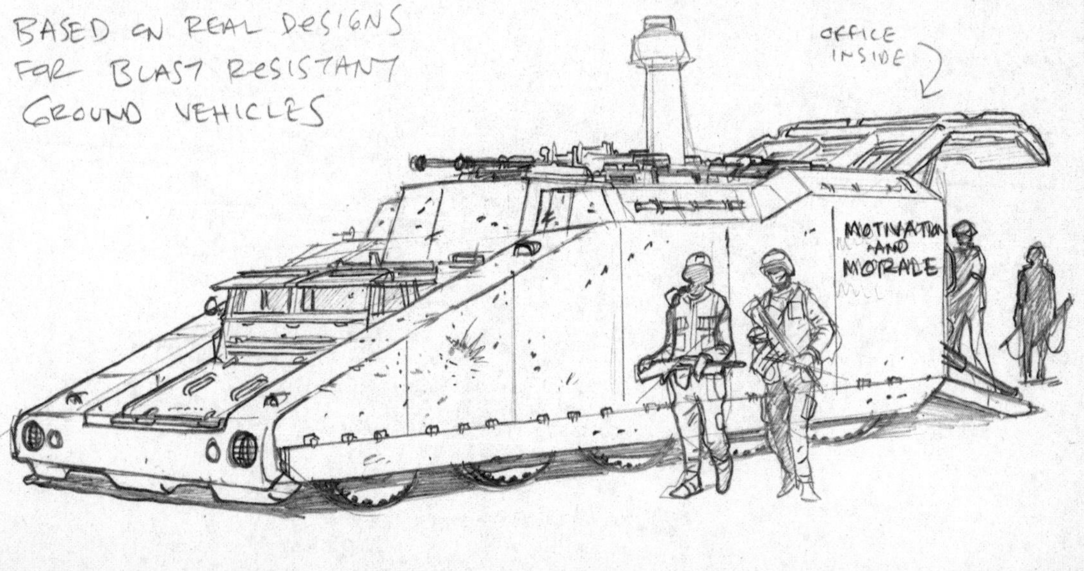

MO-MO-MOBILE
BASED ON REAL DESIGNS FOR BLAST RESISTANT GROUND VEHICLES
OFFICE INSIDE
MOTIVATION AND MORALE

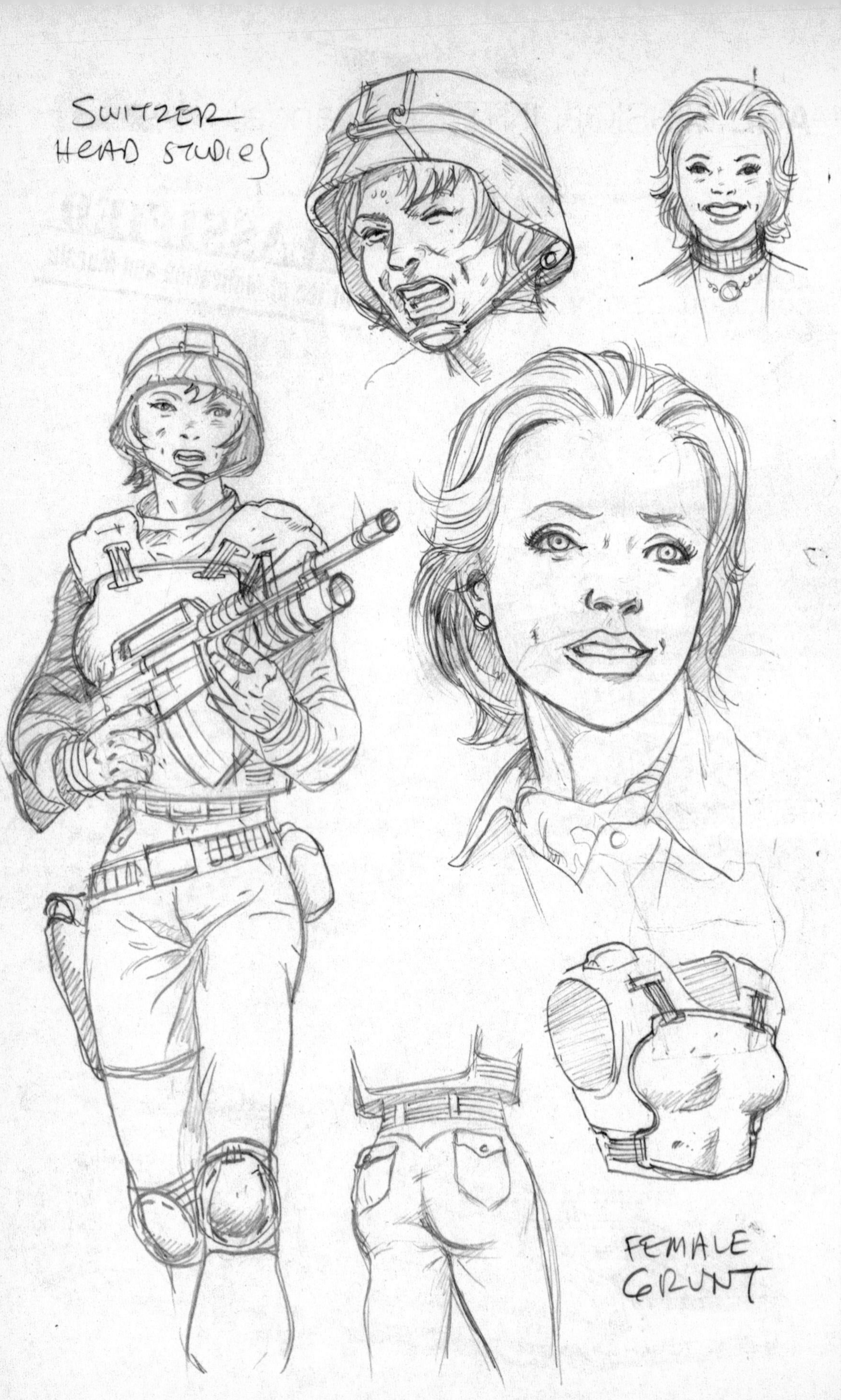
SWITZER
HEAD STUDIES
FEMALE
GRUNT

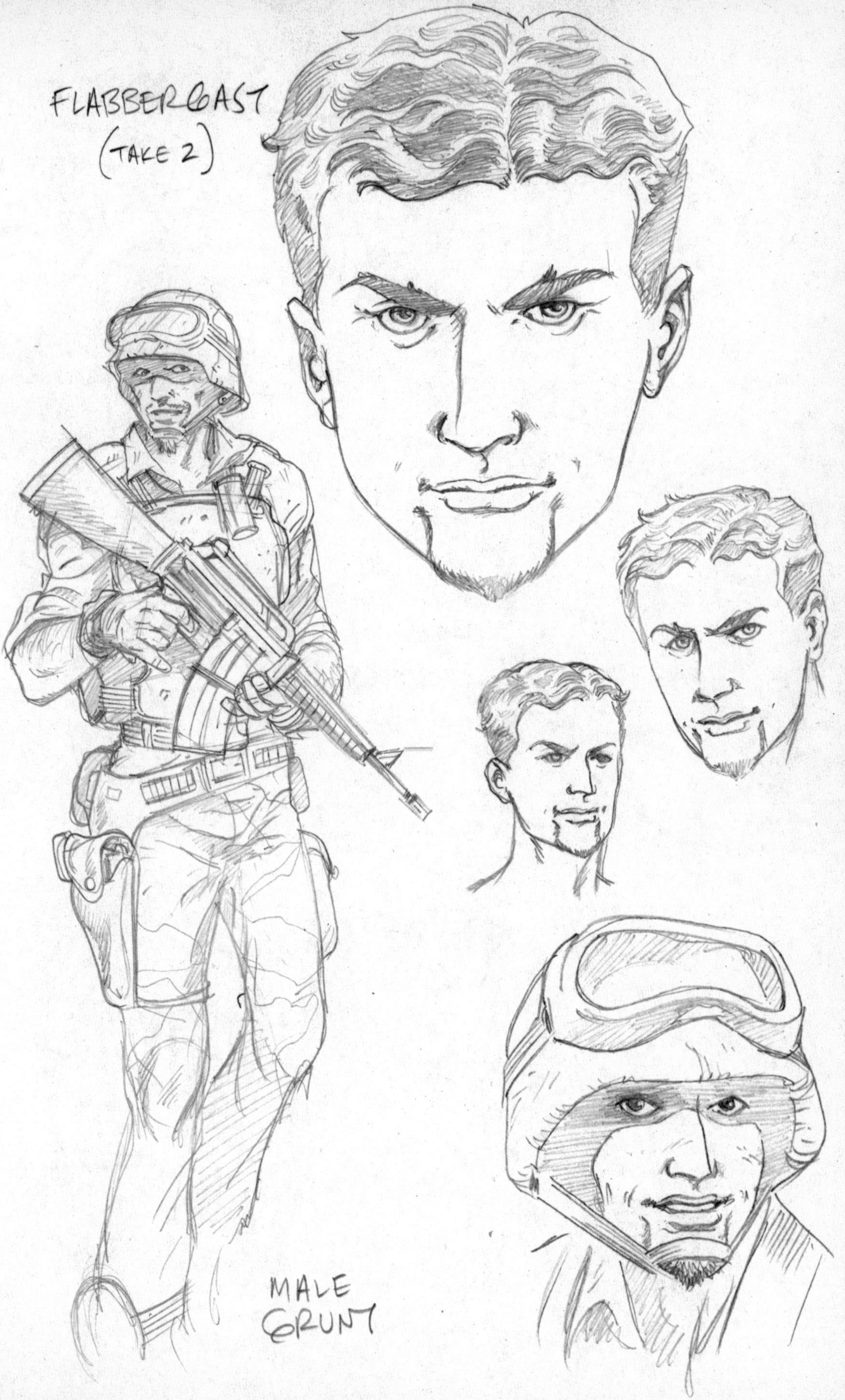
FLABBERGAST
(TAKE 2)
MALE
GRUNT

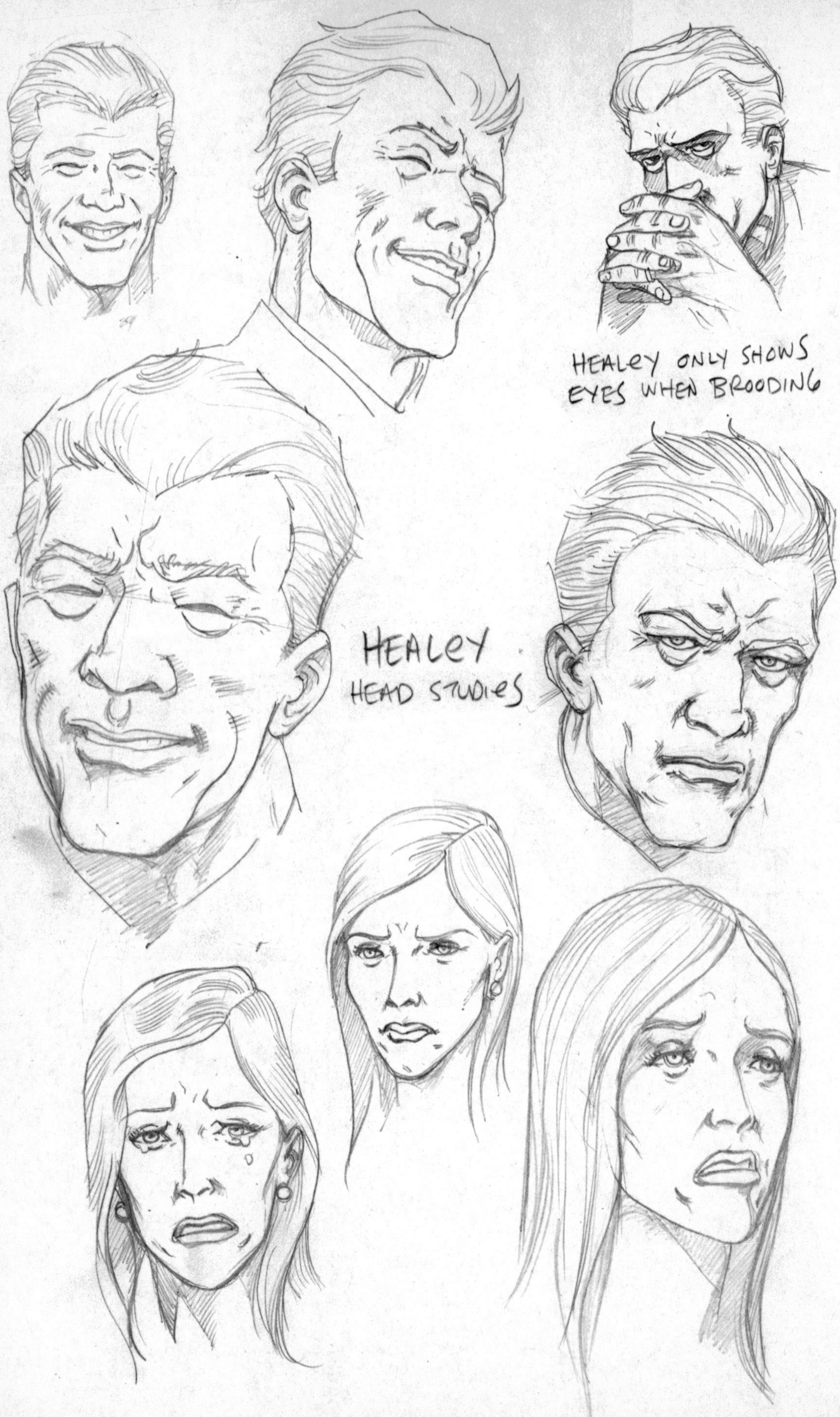
HEALEY ONLY SHOWS
EYES WHEN BROODING
HEALEY
HEAD STUDIES

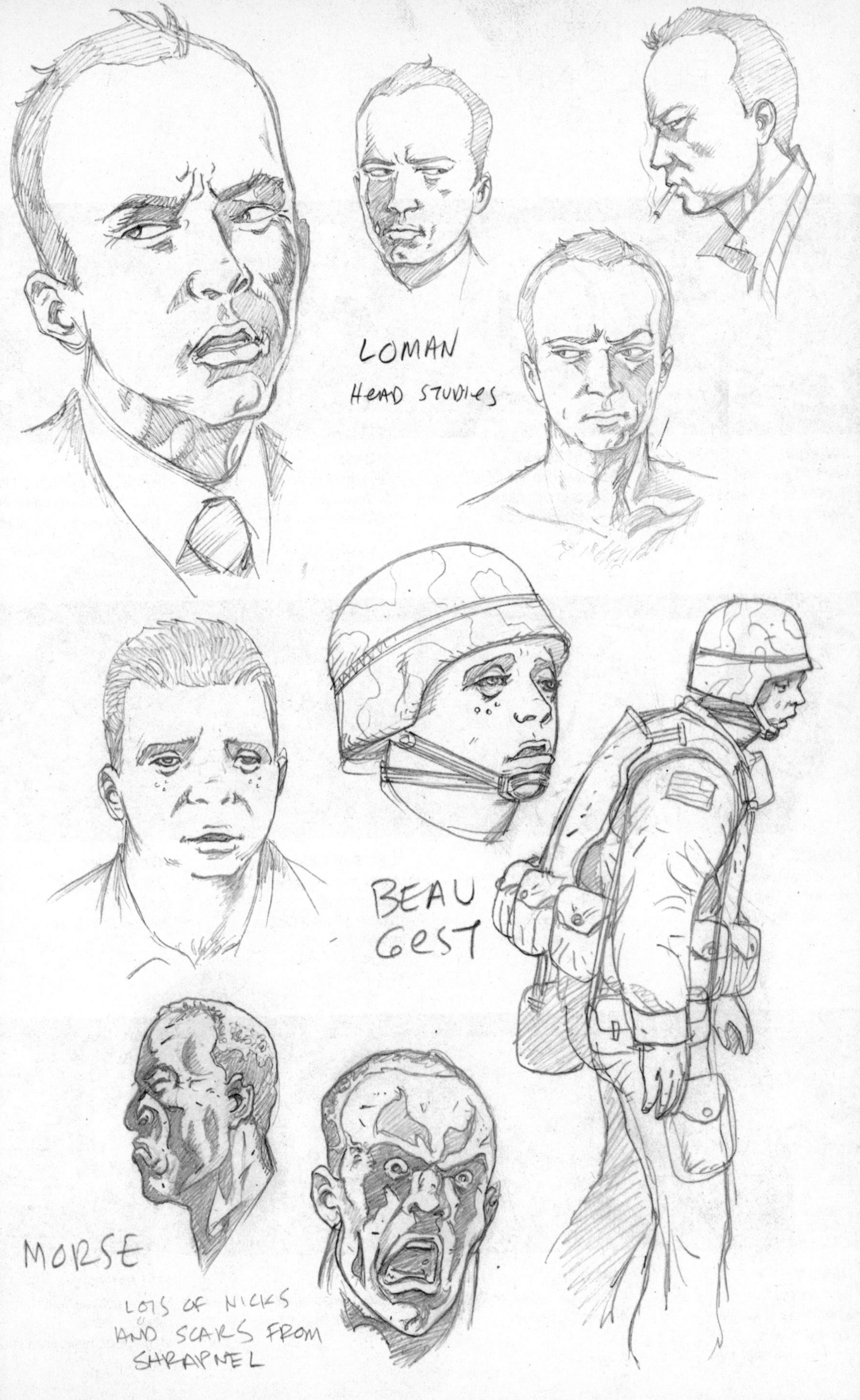
LOMAN
HEAD STUDIES
BEAU GEST
MORSE
LOTS OF NICKS AND SCARS FROM SHRAPNEL

A@L PERSONNEL FILES

THE FRONT LINES

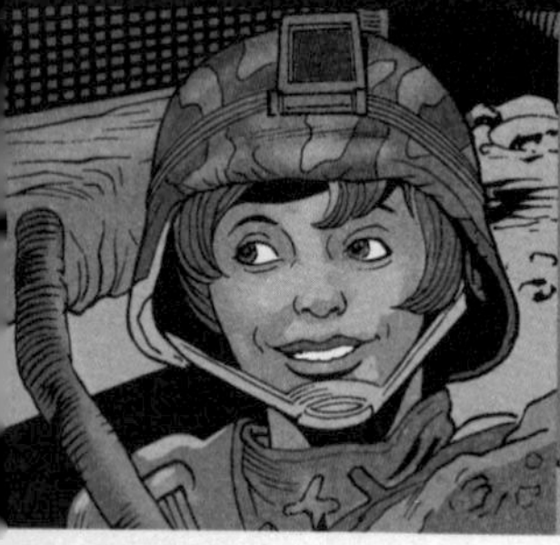

SWITZER
Good girl gone wild.
Answers to: Sgt. Morse
Married to: Loman
Sleeping with: Flabbergast

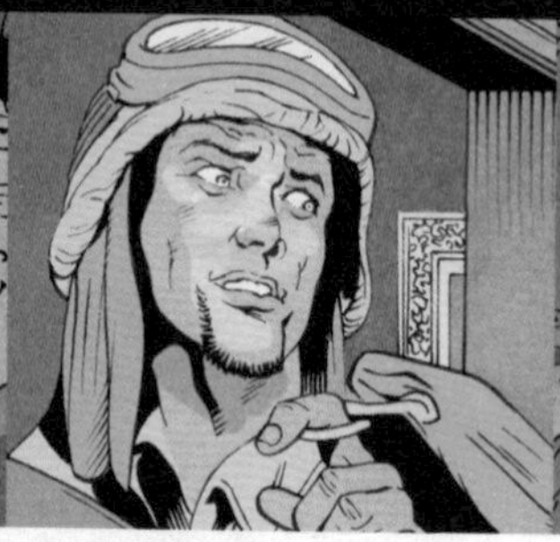

FLABBERGAST
Stage magician and lothario.
Answers to: Sgt. Morse
Sleeping with: Switzer

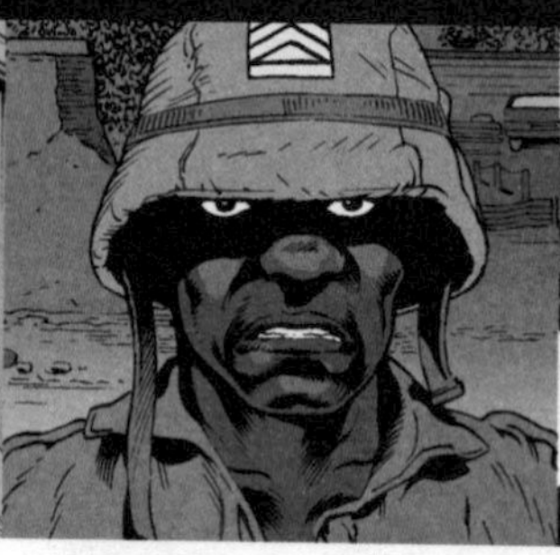

MORSE
Old school non-com.
In charge of: Beau Gest, Flabbergast and Switzer

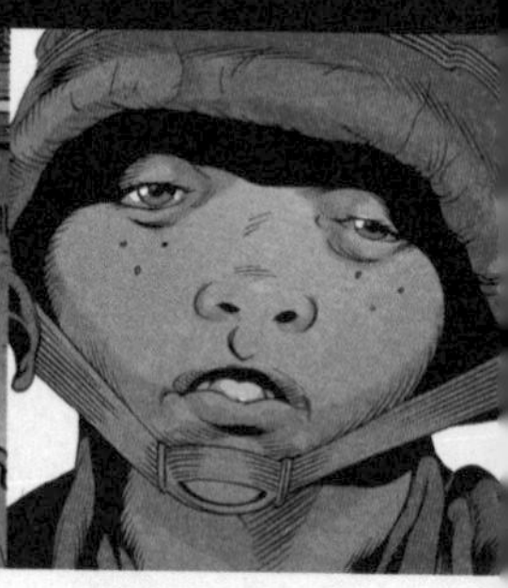

BEAU GEST
Robotic Control specialist first class, with Down's syndrome.
In charge of: Roy the Robot

THE HOME FRONT

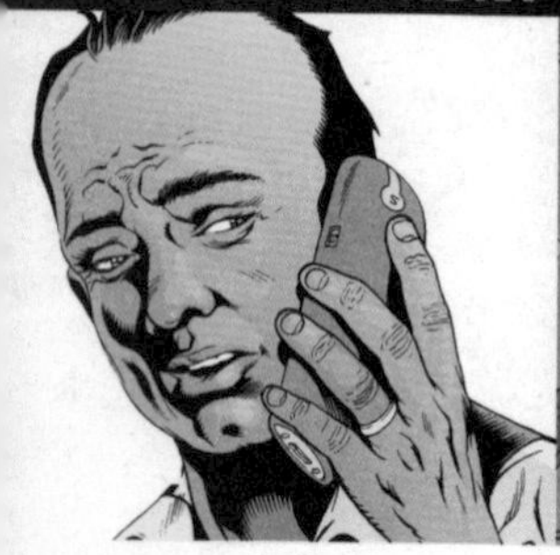

LOMAN
Hometown bagman.
Married to: Switzer
Sleeping with: Allie

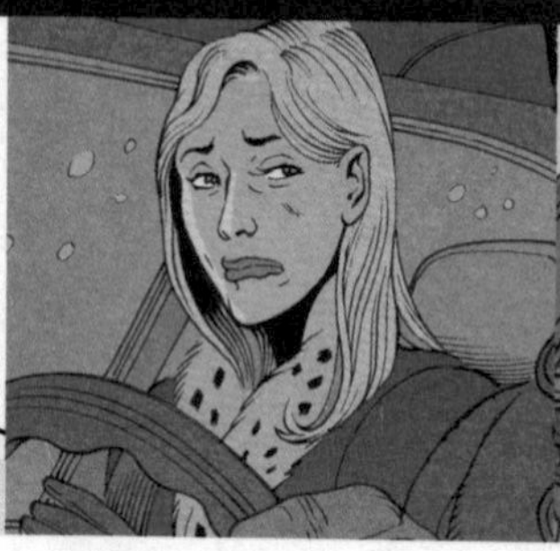

ALLIE
Lost, lonely and left behind by Healey.
Married to: Healey
Sleeping with: Loman

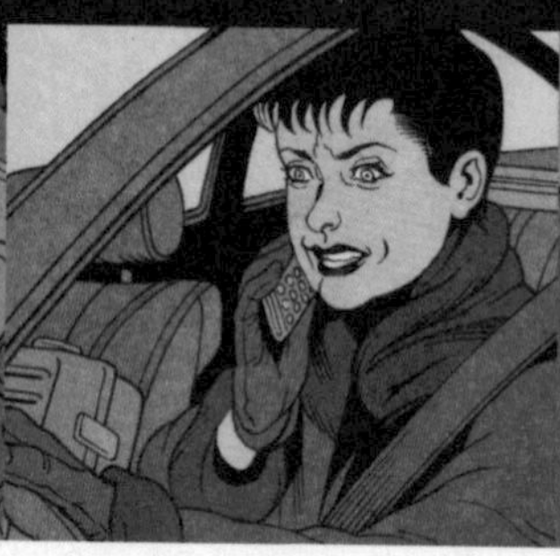

DEE DEE GEST
Never met a system she couldn't work.
Mother of: Beau Gest
Sister of: Loman

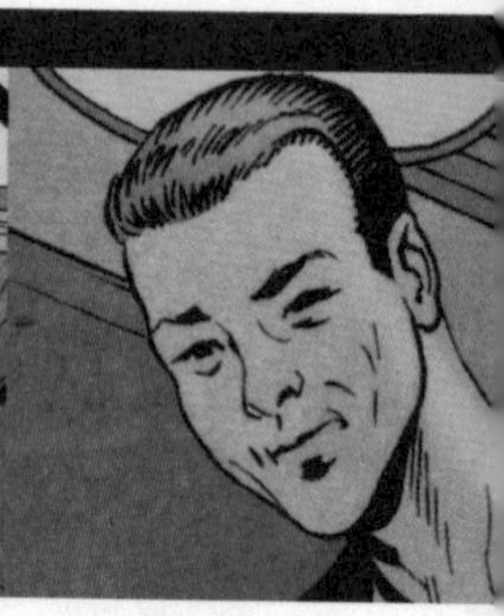

NEEDHAWK
Brains of Edgefield's hot car ring.
Answers to: Peebles

MOTIVATION AND MORALE

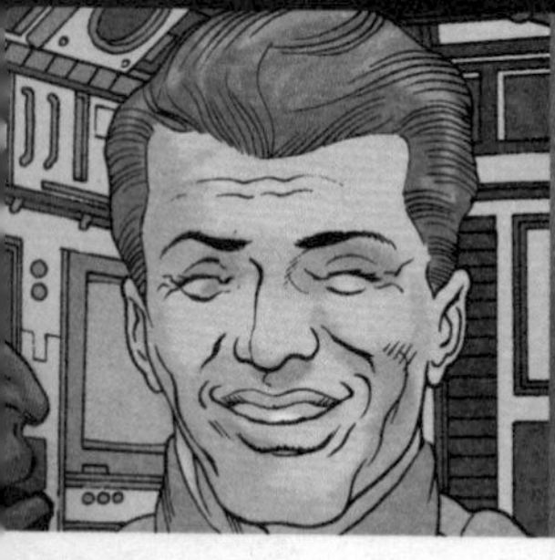

HEALEY
Head honcho of Motivation and Morale.
Married to: Allie
Answers to: Stelaphane

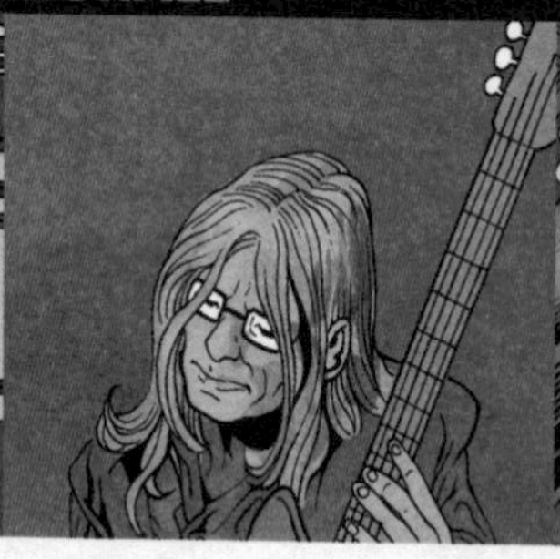

MAGOON
Creative Consultant for MoMo.
Answers to: Healey

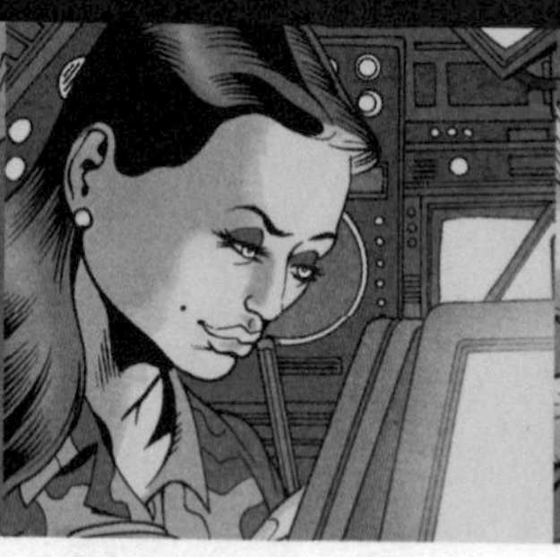

WOYNER
Healey's hyper-efficient secretary.
Answers to: Healey

CABINET

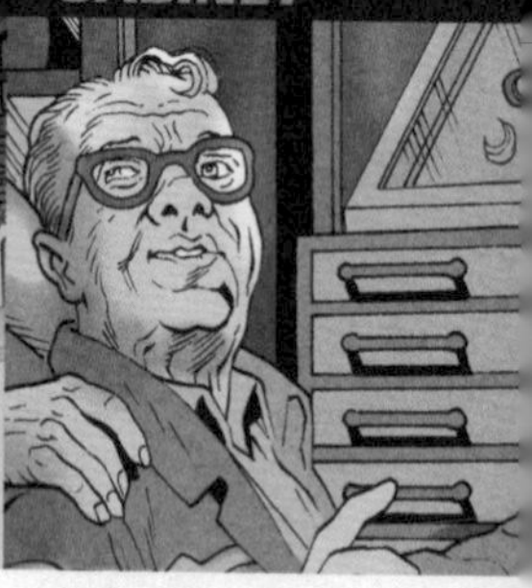

STELAPHANE
Secretary of War with strange collecting habits.
In charge of: Healey and Frick

CLASSIFIED
Office of Motivation and Morale

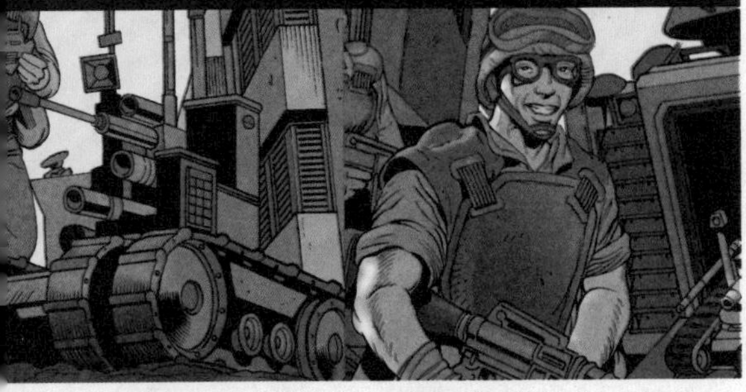

:OY THE ROBOT
.dvanced Attack Mobile Weapons
nd Surveillance Platform.
nswers to: Beau Gest
pying on: Switzer and
labbergast

ROYDEN
In love with monsters since
he saw his first horror movie.
Answers to: Sgt. Morse
Sleeping with: Anyone he can

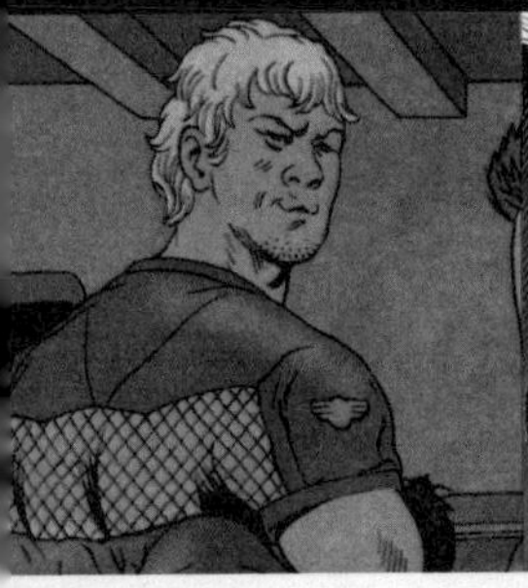

LANCHE
uscle of Edgefield's
t car ring.
swers to: Needhawk

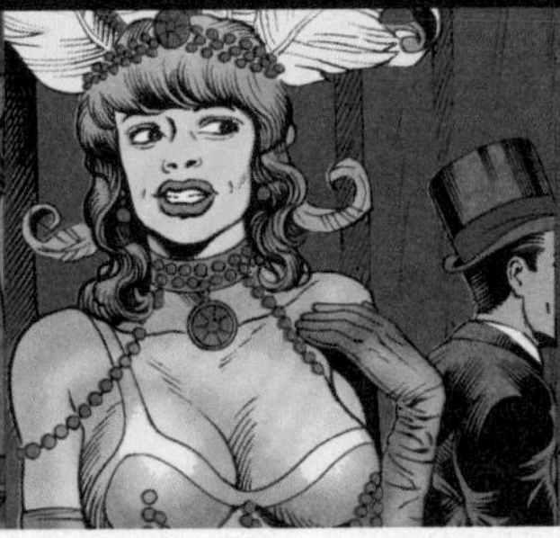

WIGGINS
The best magician's assistant in
the business.
Sleeping with: Text book
Answers to: Quintessence

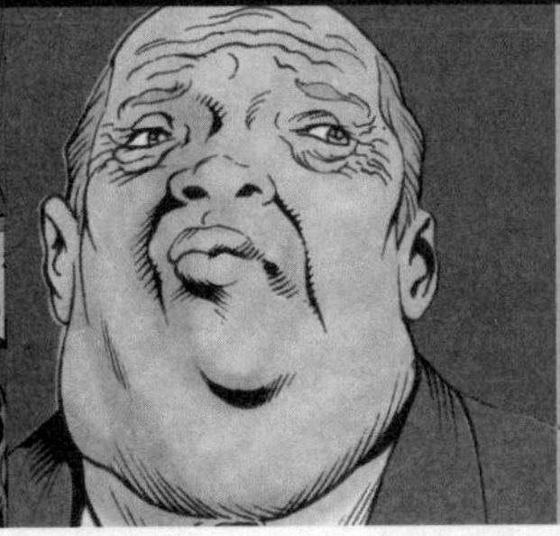

PEEBLES
Wants to put all of Afbaghistan
in the driver's seat.
Answers to: The Almighty Dollar

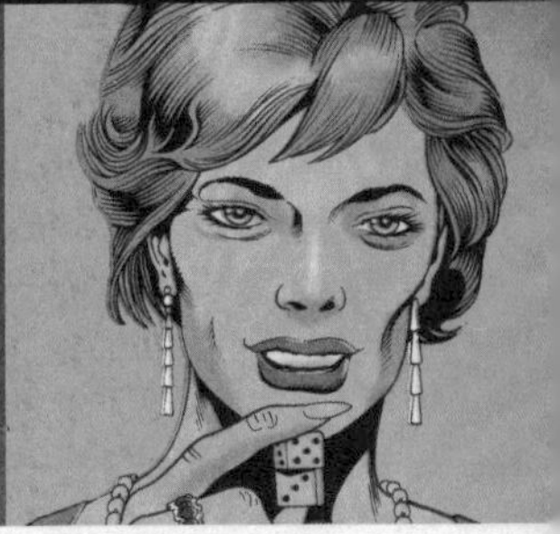

POMONA PEEBLES
Chip off the old block.
Sleeping with: Not picky
Answers to: Her father

WAR ZONE

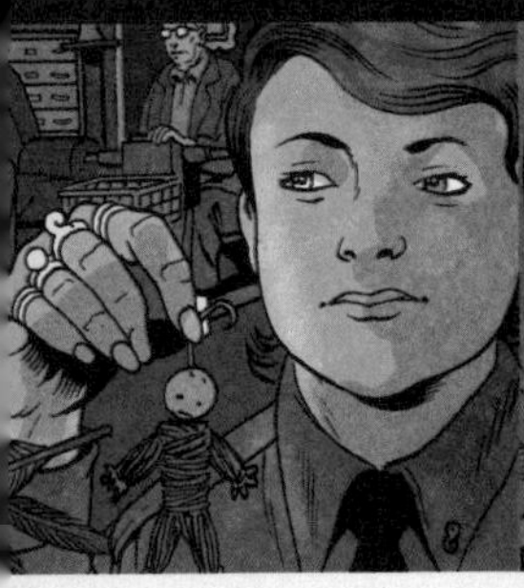

RICK
elaphane's Wiccan
iief of Staff.
swers to: Stelaphane

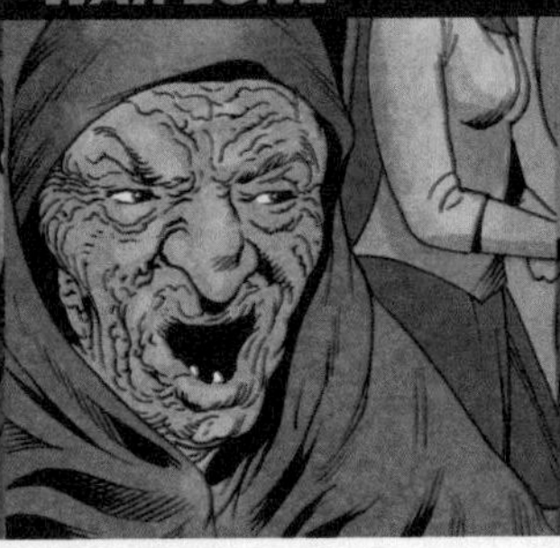

MAI MAU
Reads every issue of
Popular Mechanicals.

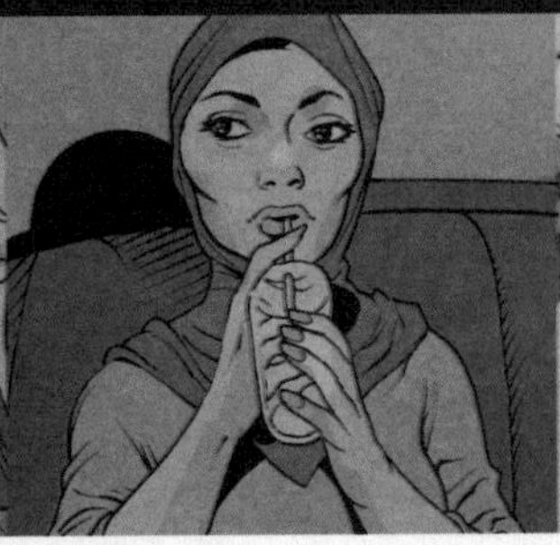

JENAN
War widow with designs on Healey.
Answers to: Mai Mau

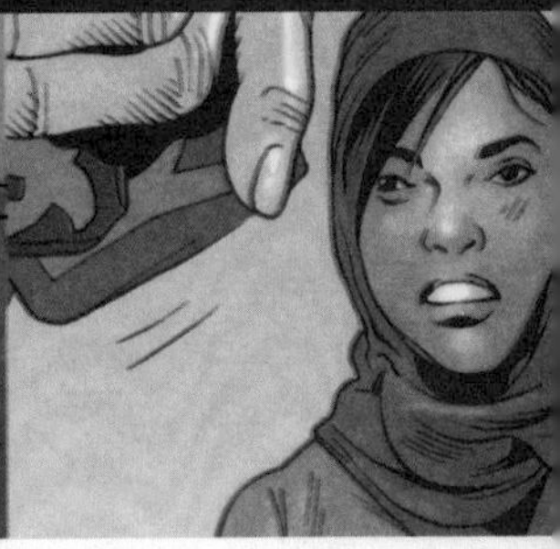

MICHI
Thirteen going on twenty.
Answers to: Mai Mau and
Jenan

A@L COMMAND FILES

EYES ONLY
Office of Motivation and Morale

RICK VEITCH (O-6, CO)

Rick Veitch is a lifelong cartoonist who was an early contributor to *Epic Illustrated* and *Heavy Metal* magazines. After collaborating with writer Alan Moore and inker Alfredo Alcala on the ground-breaking series SWAMP THING, Veitch both wrote and drew a long run on the title which can be found in the Vertigo collections SWAMP THING: REGENESIS, SWAMP THING: SPONTANEOUS GENERATION and SWAMP THING: INFERNAL TRIANGLES. He was also one of the founding artists on Moore's America's Best Comics line, co-creating Greyshirt for TOMORROW STORIES. The character was later spun off into the graphic novel GREYSHIRT: INDIGO SUNSET.

Veitch's most recent graphic novel, CAN'T GET NO, garnered fulsome critical praise and was named by *Publishers Weekly* as one of the best books of 2006. His other graphic novels include *Abraxas and the Earthman, Heartburst, The One, Brat Pack, The Maximortal, Rabid Eye, Pocket Universe* and *Crypto Zoo.*

Veitch is the co-founder, with Steve Conley, of the Internet comic site Comicon.com. He lives in Vermont with his wife Cindy and their two sons, Kirby and Ezra.

GARY ERSKINE (E-9, CSM)

Hailing from just outside Glasgow, Scotland, Gary Erskine began his comics career on *The Knights of Pendragon* and *Warheads* for Marvel UK. He went on to contribute artwork to the British anthology magazines *2000 AD* and *Crisis* (illustrating stories for such writers as Garth Ennis, Dan Abnett, Steve White and Michael Cook), and in 1993 he created the Tundra graphic novel *The Lords of Misrule* with writer John Tomlinson.

After working on various titles for DC, Dark Horse and Malibu through the 1990s (including STARMAN, *The Mask: World Tour, Terminator 2: Nuclear Twilight* and *Codename: Firearm*), in 2000 Erskine co-created the critically acclaimed Image miniseries *City of Silence* with writer Warren Ellis. Since then he has also contributed to two of Garth Ennis's WAR STORIES — JOHANN'S TIGER and ARCHANGEL — as well as inking Chris Weston's pencils on the 13-issue Vertigo maxiseries THE FILTH, written by Grant Morrison.

Erskine is currently inking ARMY@LOVE and GREATEST HITS for Vertigo, as well as drawing covers for the Dark Horse miniseries *X-Wing: Rogue Leader*. He lives with his partner Mhairi in Glasgow and Heidelberg, Germany.